TWAYNE'S WORLD LEADERS SERIES

Louis XI

TWLS 82

Louis XI

LOUIS XI

By JOSEPH M. TYRRELL

Old Dominion University

TWAYNE PUBLISHERS

A DIVISION OF G. K. HALL & CO., BOSTON

Printed on permanent/durable acid-free paper and bound
in the United States of America

First Printing

Frontispiece portrait of Louis XI courtesy of
Photographie Giraudon, Paris, France

Library of Congress Cataloging in Publication Data

Tyrrell, Joseph M
Louis XI.

(Twayne's world leaders series ; TWLS 82)
Bibliography: p. 194 - 97
Includes index.
1.   Louis XI, King of France, 1423 - 1483.
2.   France—Kings and rulers—Biography.
DC106.T9   944'.027'0924 [B]   79-20907
ISBN 0-8057-7728-8

To my mother
Dora Madeleine Tyrrell

Contents

About the Author

Joseph M. Tyrrell is Professor of History at Old Dominion University in Norfolk, Virginia, where he has taught since 1959. Medieval History is his area of specialization with particular emphasis on Medieval France. He received the Bachelor of Arts, and Master of Arts degrees from the University of Toronto, and the Doctor of Philosophy degree from Emory University, Atlanta, Georgia.

Professor Tyrrell's first book, *A History of the Estates of Poitou*, was published by Mouton Publishers, The Hague, in 1968. In addition, he is the author of articles which have appeared in *Mediaeval Studies* and *The Journal of Popular Culture*.

Preface

Louis XI is a highly controversial figure whose character has aroused much interest and has been interpreted in many different ways during the five centuries that have elapsed since his reign. The impression he made on the majority of writers of his own day was not favorable. A king who lived simply, hated pomp and ceremony, increased taxes, and won his greatest triumphs by bribery and diplomacy rather than by arms was not likely to be popular in the fifteenth century. Most of those contemporary writers who helped create the image of Louis as a tyrant were motivated either by personal hatred, as in the case of Thomas Basin, or a partisan attitude, as in the case of the Burgundian historians. The complaints of the deputies to the Estates General in 1484, the year after his death, showed however, widespread resentment against his heavy taxes and indicated his general unpopularity. He was slightly better treated by the historians of the seventeenth and eighteenth centuries. Tristan l'Hermite de Soliers, in 1661, stressed Louis's good qualities as well as his cruelty. Duclos, in the first half of the eighteenth century, in the best history of his reign written up to that time, was fairly impartial and showed great insight into his character. Voltaire, although picturing Louis primarily as a ruthless and superstitious tyrant, recognized that he also had some good qualities and that some of his actions were wise and beneficial. The most famous and most colorful distortion of Louis XI's character came from the vivid imagination of Sir Walter Scott, who, in *Quentin Durward* (1823), described him as a sort of demon who delighted in keeping prisoners in iron cages. Victor Hugo, in *Nôtre Dame de Paris* (1831), depicted Louis in much the same way as Scott. The great historian Michelet took a more impartial view. Scholars of the late nineteenth and twentieth centuries, particularly those of the past two decades, have brought much new light to bear on Louis XI, making possible a more accurate evaluation of his character and importance.

To attempt such an undertaking in a short book such as this is indeed a hazardous task. A biographer who chooses as his subject a medieval ruler or statesman, rather than a modern one, is faced with a special problem. Considerable information is usually available about the character and private lives of famous men and women of modern times. This is seldom the case for even the most important people of the Middle Ages. Therefore, the author is forced to supplement the scanty, reliable accounts of their personalities and daily lives with impersonal documents, such as official decrees, letters, and statistics. As a result, though the writer must try to shed as much light as possible upon the character of his subject, if he is a king, the book will tend to become more a history of his reign, and less a biography, than is intended. More personal documentation has survived for several great men of the fifteenth century, such as Louis XI, than for those of earlier times, but still not enough to free the biographer from this difficulty.

When this book was started, no significant biography of Louis XI had been written for nearly forty years. Then, in 1971, there appeared Paul Kendall's splendidly written *Louis XI: The Universal Spider,* including some new information from previously unused Italian diplomatic documents. Like all previous biographies of Louis XI, it relied heavily on the fifteenth-century French chronicler Commynes. However, Kendall's book, and all preceding biographies of Louis XI, were soon made virtually obsolete by the remarkable work of the German scholar Karl Bittmann. Basing his conclusions upon hundreds of unpublished and largely unused original documents, he proved, to the satisfaction of most specialists in the field, that Commynes was unreliable, not only on points of detail, but also on major descriptions and interpretations of policy that had been accepted by most historians for centuries. More than this, where Bittmann showed Commynes to be in error, he was able to indicate what really happened. He published his findings in three installments between 1964 and 1972, and his work is not yet completed.

Bittmann's study has given a new potential value to this present book. The author believes it to be the first biography of Louis XI to take advantage of his findings and, hopefully, to correct the many false interpretations, based on Commynes, which are found in all previous biographies.

I am indebted to several of my colleagues who gave me their time, knowledge, and advice in reading and criticizing parts of the manuscript. From among them, I would like to express my

Preface

gratitude particularly to Dean Heinz K. Meier who not only read
the entire manuscript and suggested many improvements, but also
translated from the German Karl Bittmann's new account of the
dramatic meeting of Louis XI and Charles the Bold at Péronne.
Finally, I am indebted to my wife for her repeated help in
proofreading and suggesting wording improvements, as well as for
her patient encouragement throughout the long period of research
and writing that this book required.

JOSEPH M. TYRRELL

Old Dominion University

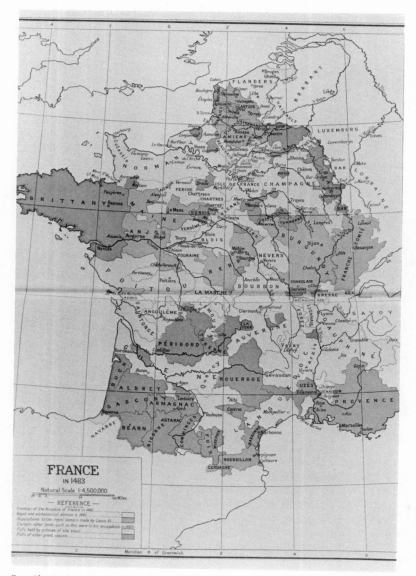

From The Cambridge Medieval History, *ed. C. W. Previté-Orton and Z. N. Brooke (1936; rpt. New York: Cambridge University Press, 1959) VIII.*

Chronology

1467	Death of Philip the Good, Duke of Burgundy. Succeeded by Charles the Bold.
1467 - 1468	Revolts of Liège against Charles the Bold.
1468	Meeting of the Estates General. Marriage of Charles the Bold and Margaret of York. Meeting of Louis XI and Charles the Bold at Péronne.
1469	Grants Guyenne to his brother Charles, and they become allies.
1470	Birth of Louis's son and heir, Charles. Edward IV of England overthrown by Warwick "the King-Maker," with French help, and Henry VI restored to the throne as an ally of France.
1471	Edward IV regains throne of England, with Burgundian help. Henry VI imprisoned and died.
1472	Death of Louis's brother, Charles of France. Louis seizes Guyenne. War with Burgundy and Brittany.
1473	Loss of Cerdagne and Roussillon to John II of Aragon. Meeting between Charles the Bold and the Emperor Maximilian at Trier.
1474	Formation of the League of Constance.
1474 - 1475	Seige of Neuss by Charles the Bold.
1475	Louis recaptures Cerdagne and Roussillon from John II of Aragon. Launches major French offensive against Burgundian lands. English invasion of France, in alliance with Charles the Bold. Treaty of Picqigny between France and England. English army withdraws. Treaty of Soleuvre ends war between Louis XI and Charles the Bold. Charles the Bold captures Lorraine.
1476	Defeat of Charles the Bold at the Battle of Grandson. Defeat of Charles the Bold at Morat.
1477	Defeat and death of Charles the Bold at the Battle of Nancy. Louis begins the seizure, by force, of some of Charles's lands. Marriage of Mary of Burgundy and Maximilian of Habsburg.
1479 or 1480	Louis suffers first attack of apoplexy.
1481 - 1482	Obtains inheritance of René of Anjou; Anjou, Bar, Maine, and Provence. Second attack of apoplexy. Seriously ill.

Death of Mary of Burgundy. Treaty of Arras between Louis XI and Maximilian of Habsburg.

1482 - The ailing Louis XI seldom leaves his fortified manor house
1483   of Plessis-lès-Tours.
1483   Death of Edward IV. Death of Louis XI at Plessis-lès-Tours.

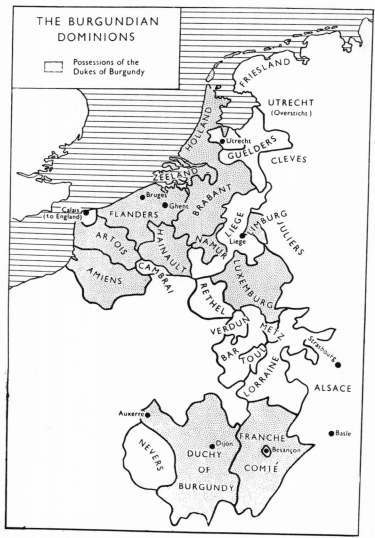

THE BURGUNDIAN DOMINIONS

Possessions of the
Dukes of Burgundy

FRIESLAND

UTRECHT
(Oversticht)

HOLLAND

Utrecht

GUELDERS

CLEVES

ZEELAND

Bruges

Ghent

BRABANT

Calais
(to England)

FLANDERS

LIEGE

LIMBURG

JULIERS

Liege

ARTOIS

HAINAULT

NAMUR

AMIENS

CAMBRAI

LUXEMBURG

RETHEL

VERDUN

METZ

Strasbourg

BAR

TOUL

ALSACE

LORRAINE

Basle

Auxerre

FRANCHE

NEVERS

Dijon

DUCHY

Besançon

OF

COMTÉ

BURGUNDY

From C. W. Previté-Orton, The Shorter Cambridge Medieval History
(Cambridge; At the University Press, 1952), II.

CHAPTER 1

The Early Years

IN the summer of 1423, France was faced with one of the gloomiest situations in her entire history. The Hundred Years' War between France and England had been going on for eighty-six years, with only a few interruptions, and it looked as though the French were on the verge of final defeat. Most of the country north of the Loire River, including Paris, was in the hands of the English or their allies the Burgundians, and recognized King Henry VI of England as lawful monarch. Southwest France was also under English control. The young French King, Charles VII, maintained a shaky authority in the rest of the country. Twenty-one years old, timid, weak, immature, and bothered by doubts about his own legitimacy, Charles seemed to have little hope of improving his position, or even retaining what authority he had. With half the kingdom occupied by his enemies, and the other half in a state of chaos, royal finances were completely disrupted. Normal revenue from royal lands, the salt tax (*gabelle*), and customs duties had been diminished by monetary inflation, brigandage, and reduced consumption of goods. The indirect sales taxes on certain products, known as *aides*, had been abolished in 1418. The Estates General of Languedoil and Languedoc, and local assemblies of provincial estates voted direct taxes almost every year, but collection was difficult and what was raised had to go to pay previous debts. Many nobles defied the king's feudal summons and Charles could not afford to pay many mercenaries. The lethargic young king appeared incapable of any vigorous action and remained inactive in his temporary capital of Bourges.[1]

It is doubtful if the general gloom at the royal court was relieved to any great extent when King Charles proudly announced to the lords, prelates, and good towns of France that the queen, Marie of Anjou, had borne him a son and heir on

17

Saturday, July 3. It was customary on such occasions to decorate
the queen's bedchamber in quite an elaborate manner, but so
poverty-stricken was the royal treasury at the moment that they
had to send to Orleans to borrow some tapestries belonging to
the Duke of Orleans, who had been a prisoner in England ever
since the Battle of Agincourt. The baby was christened Louis
after his maternal grandfather, Louis II of Anjou, and after his
most esteemed ancestor St. Louis.[2] Few kings have been born in
more inauspicious circumstances. Certainly no one could have
predicted that he would live to become the most powerful
monarch in Europe.

While Louis was still a small child, a separate household was
established for him in Bourges. The king was usually away on
military affairs and Louis grew up scarcely knowing his father.
Indeed, his extremely unfilial attitude toward his father in later
years, which was one of scorn and almost hatred, was to become
one of his most striking and disagreeable character traits. The
queen was a gentle and pious woman who might, under other
circumstances, have been an affectionate mother. However, she
often traveled with the king and saw little of her son. Thus Louis
grew up without much maternal tenderness.

During the first six or seven years of his life, Louis was moved
frequently from place to place for safety. Most of the time he
lived in the castle of Loches, a grim, prisonlike structure. It is
very likely that he saw Joan of Arc when she visited there in
1429. He was then moved to the castle of Amboise. He
frequently visited the nearby town of Tours and, on one occasion,
the townsmen presented him with six silver goblets engraved
with his arms and some fine clothing.[3] In view of the continuing
poverty of the royal court, this was undoubtedly a welcome gift.

King Charles arranged carefully for the education of his son
and heir. He selected Jean Majoris, master of arts, licentiate in
law, learned theologian, and friend of the famous scholar Gerson,
as Louis's teacher. Majoris was an excellent Latinist and a skilled
teacher of logic. Louis applied himself diligently to his lessons
and, at the age of ten, was described by Bishop Jouvenel des
Ursins as an intelligent child eager to learn. He was particularly
interested in the lives of saints and in the history of France as
reported in the Chronicles of Saint-Denis. Under Majoris's
guidance, he learned to read Latin easily, speak a very clear
French, and write in a firm hand. Several examples of his

handwriting still exist in the form of annotations written on the dispatches of ambassadors after he became king.

The education of a fifteenth-century monarch inevitably included the use of arms as well as the study of academic subjects. Louis's military training was placed in the hands of Guillaume d'Avaugour, bailiff of Touraine, who taught him to shoot a bow and handle a lance and sword.[4]

Meanwhile, plans were being made for the marriage of the young prince. As early as 1428, a treaty was signed with Scotland calling for the betrothal of Louis to Margaret, daughter of the Scottish King James I. James vacillated for a while, considering a possible English marriage instead. Finally, ambassadors of Charles VII completed the arrangements in 1436, and brought the twelve-year-old Margaret to France. Royal marriages in the Middle Ages were always political. Princesses and noble girls married very young, usually at the age of twelve or fourteen, and sometimes even younger. Margaret landed at La Rochelle on May 5, 1436. The town welcomed her with a colorful procession and a gift of silver vessels. She then proceeded by easy stages to Tours, which she entered on June 24. She was taken to meet the queen, who embraced her tenderly. Louis was presented to her, and they also embraced, although somewhat formally.

The wedding was held the next evening in the chapel of the castle of Tours. Margaret was regally dressed, with a little diadem on her head. Louis was splendidly clad in blue velvet trimmed with gold. He wore a sword that was thought to have belonged to Scotland's hero-king Robert Bruce, which was a wedding gift from his father-in-law. In spite of this attire, he was an unprepossessing youth with a long nose and piercing eyes. The queen was magnificently dressed, but King Charles wore a plain gray traveling costume. The Archbishop of Rheims pronounced the benediction.

The wedding was followed by a banquet at which the guests were entertained by musicians and minstrels. The dinner was followed by dancing, during the course of which one worthy bourgeois performed so vigorously that he split one of his stockings.

In the fifteenth century, royal marriages were always elaborate ceremonies. By comparison with many others, the wedding of Louis and Margaret was rather simple, due to the relative poverty of the French court. It is important to realize the

function of festivals in fifteenth century society. The taste for
unbridled luxury culminated in court festivals. They were the
supreme expression of the culture of the day, the highest mode
of collective solidarity.

Modern man is free to seek his favorite entertainment
individually. At a time when higher pleasures were neither
numerous nor accessible to all, people felt the need of such
collective celebrations as festivals. The more crushing the misery
of daily life, the more necessary was some expression of beauty
and gaiety. As the brilliant Dutch historian Huizinga says, "The
fifteenth century, profoundly pessimistic, a prey to continual
depression, could not forgo the emphatic affirmation of the
beauty of life afforded by these splendid and solemn collective
rejoicings. . . . All literary, musical, and artistic enjoyment was
more or less closely connected with festivals."

What people looked for most was extravagance and huge
dimensions. A good example was the magnificent ceremony at
the marriage of Charles the Bold of Burgundy and Margaret of
York, at Bruges in 1468. The tables were loaded with the most
extravagant decorations. On one table stood the tower of
Gorcum, which was forty-six feet high. On another was a whale
containing more than forty persons. There were also mechanical
marvels, such as living birds flying from the mouth of a dragon
conquered by Hercules. What a contrast to the relatively
unspectacular wedding of the Prince Louis and Margaret of
Scotland! Of course, the great wealth of the court of Burgundy
and the poverty of the French court at the time of the two
respective marriages must be remembered.[5]

As soon as possible after the wedding, the Scottish guests who
had accompanied Margaret were hustled away home. The
French court could not afford to entertain them any longer than
was necessary. Because of the age of the bride and groom there
was no question of consummating the marriage. Margaret lived
henceforth with the gentle and pious queen who treated her as
her own daughter. Louis was given a new household of his own.
Bernard d'Armagnac, Count of La Marche, was appointed as his
governor. The count was a serious man, a model of chivalry,
wisdom, and piety. It is reported that he had the Bible read at
every meal. Jean Majoris, Louis's former teacher, now became
his confessor. The young prince was given a complete household

staff, including a physician, but was granted a rather modest income for its upkeep.[6]

During the next few years Louis was to see very little of his child bride but a great deal of the country he was destined to rule. He and his father left Tours shortly after the wedding. They spent the rest of the summer in other parts of the Loire valley and, in October, began a long tour of those provinces loyal to Charles.

The life of a medieval king was one of continuous travel. A considerable portion of his income and food for the royal court came from the king's domain. The domain consisted of the land held by the monarch directly as opposed to those lands granted out as fiefs to great lords, such as the Duke of Brittany. In the first place, the economic system and poor transportation of the time forced him to consume in place the products of his domain. Also, his authority could only be exercized effectively on the spot in a country that was still quite decentralized and far from accepting unquestioningly the authority of an absolute monarch. The king had the right to have himself and all his retainers fed and housed on such trips. This was a remnant of the feudal *droit de gîte*. Most noble vassals and clergy had purchased an exemption from this onerous duty, but many of the towns still had to bear these expenses. In time of war, it was more important than usual for a king to travel to look to the defenses of his kingdom. By 1436, Charles VII had aroused himself from his youthful lethargy. The chief purposes of his long tour with the dauphin that summer were to see first hand the condition of the lands supporting him and to raise taxes for the continuing struggle with England.

During this trip, Louis saw the usual way in which his father collected taxes for the war. Consent of the taxed was considered necessary in the late Middle Ages. After several rather unsuccessful attempts to obtain this consent from large national assemblies, Charles had turned to provincial assemblies, known as provincial estates, and to the towns. Louis attended an assembly of the estates of Lower Auvergne presided over by his father. In December they entered Lyons, a great commercial center and the second largest city of France. Here the boy received a gift of 500 gold francs. Next they went to Dauphiné. This province was the traditional apanage of the eldest son of

French kings, who therefore always received the title of
"dauphin." Obviously, this region was of particular interest to
Louis. Here he attended an assembly of the estates of Dauphiné
which granted him 10,000 florins. Louis then signed his first
letter that has survived, in January 1437, drawing upon this sum
for expenses for the purchase of equipment for a portable
chapel, travelling clothes, and gifts to his retinue, including his
confessor and his physician. He and his father then went to the
southern province of Languedoc. At Béziers, an assembly of the
clergy voted Louis 100 gold *écus*. They entered Montpellier on
February 27, and spent the next two months there, doubtless
enjoying the semitropical climate. In late April, Charles and
Louis moved north to deal with pillaging soldiers under the
famous Spanish mercenary captain Rodrigue de Villandrando.
They arrived unexpectedly in Saint-Flour in Auvergne. The good
burghers hastened to give them a suitable reception, but were
niggardly with their gifts. In the meantime Rodrigue and his
mercenaries had fled.[7]

During the summer of 1437, King Charles planned an
expedition against small English garrisons in the upper Loire
valley. The Dauphin Louis accompanied him and got his first
taste of war. He participated in the successful siege of Château-
Landon. He and his father then went to Gien in the Loire valley.
Considering himself now a man, the fourteen-year-old Louis
summoned his wife and consummated his marriage.[8]

By this time, the entire course of the Hundred Years' War had
changed, with the tide of battle beginning to turn in favor of the
French. The turning point had been the inspired leadership of
Joan of Arc in 1429 and 1430. A belief that she was sent by God
to save France infused a new spirit into the French armies and
roused the king from his lethargy. Joan's victory at Orleans was
followed by a reckless dash through enemy-held territory to
Rheims where French kings were traditionally crowned.
Charles's coronation there added considerably to his prestige
and confidence. In 1435, the powerful Duke of Burgundy had
been persuaded to switch sides and join the French in return for
many concessions. In April 1436, the French had recaptured
Paris.

King Charles now resolved to visit his newly acquired capital
and, in November 1437, he and the dauphin arrived at Paris. The
city, which had been pro-Burgundian and pro-English, prepared

a magnificent reception. At the gate of Saint-Denis the royal party was greeted by the Provost of Merchants and the town councillors all dressed alike in blue and red robes. The provost presented Charles with the keys to the city. From there all the way to Nôtre-Dame Cathedral the houses were hung with tapestries. Louis, his helmet gleaming with gold, rode a richly ornamented horse in the royal procession a little behind the king. At the Convent of the Filles-Dieu was a fountain whose four mouths sprayed milk, red wine, white wine, and water. At several points along the way mystery plays were acted out on specially erected platforms. The streets were lined with the cheering people of Paris. The procession finally reached Nôtre-Dame, before which were assembled the prelates of Paris and the faculty of the university. The hypocritical Nicolas Midi, judge of Joan of Arc, made a long and pompous speech extolling the virtues of Charles VI and Charles VII and telling of the miseries suffered by the university during the king's long absence. Then Charles and Louis entered the Cathedral to hear the *Te Deum*. That night the streets were illuminated with fires and gay with dancing. The next day, Louis saw the sights of Paris, including the beautiful Sainte-Chapelle. The king and Louis spent three weeks in Paris. They left on December 3 and returned to Tours to join the queen and the dauphiness. The people of Paris were delighted to see them go as the cost of entertaining them was great. For years the surrounding countryside had been ravaged by mercenary soldiers and food was short, cabbages and turnips being the normal diet. The city now settled down to another hard winter of cold and hunger.[9]

Louis spent most of 1438 in and around Bourges where a general assembly of the French clergy was meeting. Early in 1439, he and the king set out for Languedoc. On the way they stopped at Limoges, where Louis stayed in the monastery of Saint-Martial. He had with him a pet lion cub which he kept in the next room. One night it attempted to jump out of the window, became stuck, and choked. Louis, who always loved animals, was much saddened by this incident.

Leaving Limoges, they travelled on through Auvergne to Le Puy, where Louis attended an assembly of the estates of Languedoc presided over by his father. Charles then appointed the fifteen-year-old dauphin lieutenant-governor for Languedoc, gave him some royal councillors to help him, and moved on to Lyons. The task facing Louis was difficult for one so young. Languedoc was suffering from the plague, the depredations of roving bands of mercenaries, and high taxes. The great feudal lords were antagonistic to each other, and there was a constant English threat from the adjoining province of Guyenne.

Louis showed considerable decisiveness and maturity during his six months' administration of Languedoc. Characteristically, he traveled throughout the province examining conditions firsthand. The three *sénéchaussées*[10] of Toulouse, Beaucaire, and Carcassonne, which comprised the province, all granted him money. He took firm measures to deal with the lawless mercenaries, handing out stern punishments to those caught pillaging. He informed the king about English raids from Guyenne. Charles summoned him to come and discuss the problem. Instead Louis acted. He personally supervised the building of fortifications and defenses along the frontier and persuaded the estates of Languedoc to grant the necessary money.

Louis's activity in Languedoc was terminated rather suddenly when he received several urgent letters from the king ordering him to return to the royal court immediately. The reason for the royal action is uncertain, but it is very probable that Charles had learned that the dauphin was in correspondence with several lords who were plotting rebellion, and therefore decided to recall him. Louis left Languedoc reluctantly, feeling that his work had been interrupted.[11]

Louis's actions in 1440 in connection with the feudal uprising, known as the *Praguerie*, in allusion to a recent Hussite revolt in Prague in Bohemia, show his impatience, ambition, and spirit of revolt. This rebellion was one of many such movements of the feudal nobles against the king in French history, and was remarkably similar to that of the League of the Public Weal directed against Louis himself twenty-five years later. The *Praguerie* was touched off by an ordinance of Charles VII in 1439 calling for the creation of a permanent royal army and forbidding the private military actions of the great nobles.[12]

The chief leader of the malcontents was the handsome young Duke of Bourbon. Also involved were the Duke of Brittany, the Duke of Alençon, Dunois, the illegitimate half-brother of the Duke of Orleans and one of the greatest warriors in France, and the mercenary leader Rodrigue de Villandrando, who was married to an illegitimate Bourbon. They were intriguing with the English and with the dauphin.

King Charles, well aware of these plots, appointed Louis as royal lieutenant in Poitou, Saintonge, and Aunis, which were overrun by marauding mercenaries. Perhaps he hoped to win his son over by this grant of authority. At any rate, he hoped to keep him occupied. Louis went to Poitou and firmly restored order. However, his political machinations did not cease. In February 1440 he held a secret meeting with the Duke of Alençon in Niort. Alençon had already signed an agreement with Bourbon, who was in contact with the English. The young, impetuous dauphin perhaps really believed that he could solve France's many problems better than his easygoing, slow-moving father and was easily persuaded to accept the nominal leadership of the conspiracy.

In the meantime, Louis had dismissed his governor, the Count of La Marche, who immediately reported the dauphin's treacherous plans to the king. Contrary to his son's opinion, Charles could act with speed and vigor on occasion. He promptly wrote to the leading towns of the kingdom warning them against the intrigues of the rebels. He sent word to Bourbon to appear before him immediately and explain his actions. Then the king, accompanied by the Constable of France, Richemont, the Count of La Marche, and other loyal commanders, marched against Louis in Poitou.

From his headquarters in Niort, the dauphin sought the support of the local towns by canceling the sales tax known as *aides*. However, Richemont arrived rapidly, and Louis and Alençon were forced to negotiate while awaiting help from Bourbon and possibly the English. As no help arrived, they were forced to withdraw to the mountains of Auvergne, where they joined Bourbon. Louis summoned the estates of upper Auvergne at Clermont to seek money and obtained the support of the local lords against the king. Picturing himself as a liberator who would abolish the *aides* and make peace with England, he sought support in Languedoc and Dauphiné.

Louis was finally besieged in Saint Pourçain by the king. Charles was willing to negotiate and demanded that the rebellious lords dismiss their armies, return to his obedience, and turn over the dauphin to him. The lords agreed to submit. Louis sent a personal message requesting royal pardon for himself and all the rebellious nobles. He asked for the return of all the rebels' goods, lands, and offices, stating that they had acted entirely on his orders and commands. In órder to meet his expenses, he asked that Dauphiné at least be turned over to him, and perhaps more land as well.

The king replied with moderation. He said that if the dauphin would come to him with proper humility he would treat him as his only son and provide for him and the dauphiness in such a way that he would be content. They would discuss the fate of the others mentioned in the dauphin's letter reasonably when Louis appeared before him.

Louis's answer was impertinent. He virtually accused his father of incompetence, and took it upon himself to tell him how to run the kingdom. Suggesting that Charles was not prosecuting the war with sufficient vigor, Louis offered to lead his own men against the English. He also suggested summoning the Estates General and said that he and his followers would submit to its decisions. Charles then broke off the negotiations and the fighting was renewed. The rebels were defeated and Louis was left without support. At this point he thought of seeking refuge in Burgundy. He wrote to Duke Philip the Good, who replied that he would be glad to receive him and help reconcile him with his father but would not give him armed support against the king.[13]

No other course was left but capitulation, so Louis, Bourbon, and three rebel lords set out to meet the king. Charles sent word that he would meet with the dauphin and Bourbon, but not the others. Louis at first refused, but finally gave in, and he and Bourbon entered the town of Cusset to meet the king. They knelt three times in the royal presence and three times requested the king's pardon. Charles said: "Welcome, Louis. You have been away a long time. Go and rest today in your lodgings and tomorrow we shall speak to you." He then affectionately reprimanded Bourbon.

The next day, after Mass, Louis and Bourbon were brought before the king and his council. Louis then requested pardon for the three rebel lords who had been turned back. The king refused. Louis then said, "My lord, I must return, for I have promised them thus." Charles replied gravely:

Louis, the doors are open, and if they are not large enough I will knock down sixteen or twenty panels of the wall to let you pass to anywhere you think better. You are my son and you cannot obligate anyone without my permission. But if you want to go, go, for if it is God's pleasure, we will find someone else of our blood who will help us better to maintain our honor and lordship than you have so far.

Evidently Louis yielded at this point and sought to impose no more conditions for on July 17, 1440, Charles announced by letters patent that the dauphin and the Duke of Bourbon had come to him "in all humility and obedience" and had received his pardon. He then dismissed all Louis's servants and officials except his confessor and his cook. A few days later he granted his son the administration of Dauphiné with a pension of 800 pounds per month.[14]

For the next few years, Louis worked in cooperation with his father, helping him campaign against the English and suppress lawlessness in his own lands. After touring the vanquished province of Auvergne, which had generally supported the *Praguerie*, the king and the dauphin returned to Tours. The pressure of war did not allow them to remain there for long. The English were besieging Harfleur in Normandy and, in September 1440, Charles and Louis went to Orleans to organize an army to march against them. They spent the fall in Chartres organizing the campaign but had to abandon the project to deal with the bands of mercenary soldiers who were ravaging Champagne. In January 1441 the king and Louis were at Bar-sul-l'Aube in Champagne, where they arrested and tried about twenty of the leaders of the mercenary bands, including Alexander, bastard of Bourbon, one of the nobles who had been active with Louis in the *Praguerie*. Alexander was placed in a sack and thrown into the river. His fate must have given Louis some food for thought.[15]

Louis and Charles then traveled through Lorraine to Laon, where they met with Isabelle, Duchess of Burgundy, to discuss plans for peace with the English. The dauphin was then sent to Paris to impose the heaviest tax in fifty years on the impoverished city to raise funds for the proposed siege on Pontoise. It was beginning to seem to the Parisians that Charles and Louis only came when they wanted money. Louis spent June and July 1441 encamped outside Pontoise, which was being besieged by the French. He commanded the final assault on September 19 and was one of the first five or six knights to fight their way into the town.[16]

Louis then accompanied his father to Saumur to help him deal
with several problems in the area that had been aggravated by
the *Praguerie*. In the spring of 1442 they set out for Languedoc.
On the way, while they were spending Easter at Ruffec, Louis
was nearly drowned in a boating accident in the flood-swollen
waters of the Charente River. He prayed to the Virgin Mary and
attributed his survival to her intervention. This seems to have
been the beginning of his special devotion to the Virgin, whom
he regarded as his particular protector for the rest of his life.[17]

In June the king and the dauphin were in Toulouse. They spent
the rest of the year in the south, much of it in Gascony
campaigning against the English. In January and February 1443
they were at Montauban, and on February 26 the king was in
Toulouse to attend an assembly of the estates of Toulouse. A few
days later, Louis made a solemn entry into the town mounted on
a white horse with the queen seated behind him on a pillion.
Over their heads was a canopy carried by the eight *capitouls*
(town officials) of Toulouse.[18]

During the summer of 1443, Louis won one of his most notable
military victories when he relieved the town of Dieppe in
Normandy. The rich and valuable province of Normandy had
been under English rule since 1415. In 1435, a bold corsair,
Charles Desmarets, had seized the port of Dieppe and turned it
over to Charles VII. Early in 1442 a strong English army under
Talbot was sent to take it, and began a long siege. In the summer
of 1443, Charles VII made Louis lieutenant of the lands north of
the Seine and Yonne rivers with orders to relieve Dieppe and
gave him the experienced commander Dunois to help him. Louis
passed through Paris in July and imposed a tax. He then traveled
through northern France raising money and men. He was
magnificently received at Amiens, which welcomed him with
parades and mystery plays. Louis was impressed with the
richness of the town, which had been ceded to the Duke of
Burgundy, along with the other towns of the Somme Valley, by
the Treaty of Arras in 1435. He decided he wanted it back under
French royal control, a decision which he did not forget.

On August 11, Louis and his army arrived before Dieppe.
Desmarets, inside the town, was in desperate straits. The English
had erected a strong fortress, or *bastille*, on a nearby hill, from
which their artillery was bombarding the town. Louis then
besieged the English fortress. A few days later, after giving all

his men wine to fortify their courage, Louis ordered the assault. After three hours of hard fighting, the *bastille* fell. Louis then went barefoot to the church of Saint-Jacques in Dieppe to thank God and St. James, the patron saint of knights, for his victory. He demolished the English *bastille*, spent a few days in Dieppe, and then returned to Paris.[19]

The king summoned Louis to Tours to honor him and his lords for their victory. He then sent the dauphin south to bring the proud and turbulent John IV, Count of Armagnac, into line. Louis besieged the count in his fortress of Ile-Jourdain, and forced him to capitulate in January 1444. Not trusting him, Louis took him and his entire family under close guard to Carcassonne. He then sought to confiscate the county of Rodez from Jean de Lescun, bastard of Armagnac. He besieged the latter in his fortress of Severac and forced him to surrender. Louis then left the bailiff of Lyons to admister Armagnac and Rodez and returned to the royal court at Montils-lez-Tours in late April 1444, well satisfied with the success of his campaign.[20]

In the meantime, Charles VII had decided to renew peace talks with the English. Both sides were weary of the war and, in February 1444, Henry VI appointed ambassadors to go to France. Charles received them in his castle of Montils-lez-Tours on April 17, 1444. After some discussion, a twenty-two-months' truce was signed and a marriage was arranged between Henry VI and Margaret, niece of the King of France and daughter of René, Duke of Anjou, usually known as King René because of his claim to the thrones of Sicily and Naples. The conclusion of the truce was followed by feasting and celebrations. The role of Louis in all these festivities is unknown. As he generally disliked such ceremonies, it is probable that he played very little part.[21]

The dauphin was soon given an opportunity to gain more military experience. The Treaty of Arras in 1435 with Burgundy had left about twenty to thirty thousand soldiers without employment. Most of them became brigands and gained for themselves the picturesque nickname of *écorcheurs* (skinners or fleecers) because of their treatment of their victims. During the next nine years they were occasionally used against the English but, after the truce of April 1444, they were again unemployed and began to plunder various parts of France. A pretext to get rid of them arose when Frederick III, the Holy Roman Emperor, and his son Sigismund, Duke of Austria, requested help against the

Swiss Confederation which was attacking their ally Zurich. Although Zurich was a member of the Swiss Confederation, her expansionist policy had finally led to war with the other members. Zurich had formed an alliance with the Duke of Austria and the Emperor Frederick. Charles and his advisors decided to appoint Louis to lead the *écorcheurs* (called by the Swiss the Armagnacs) to Frederick's help, and thus get them out of France. It is possible that the French also hoped to seize part of Alsace and the rich city of Basel, which was not yet a part of the Swiss Confederation.

During the summer of 1444, the dauphin assembled a well-equipped army of these cutthroats, consisting of about 4,000 men-at-arms and 6,000 archers, plus their wives and followers. They included Lombards, Gascons, Spaniards, Englishmen, Scots, and Bretons. A more ferocious-looking horde would be hard to imagine.

In late July and August Louis and his men marched across Burgundy. That they were following their usual habits is indicated by the complaints of the town council of Dijon about their depredations. They reached the city of Basel late in August. As their vanguard was encamped near the town, they were unexpectedly attacked by a Swiss army of 4,000 men that had rushed to intercept them. The dauphin's men were driven back across the River Birse. The Swiss pursued them, but were met by the main body of Louis's army, strongly supported by German cavalry. Many of the outnumbered Swiss sought refuge in the leper-hospital of Saint-Jacques, where they fought bravely to the last man. The slaughter was terrible. The Swiss were annihilated, but about 8,000 of Louis's *écorcheurs* and their allies also died.[22]

Louis personally had not participated in the battle, but had remained at his headquarters a few miles away. He was delighted to learn that the Swiss, after their heavy losses, had abandoned the seige of Zurich, and it is doubtful if he grieved very much over the casualties suffered by his *écorcheurs*. His men then wanted to capture and sack Basel. Louis refused, as he was unwilling to risk harm to the large number of churchmen from all over Europe assembled there for the Council of Basel. It is possible that the brave resistance of the Swiss at Saint-Jacques also deterred him from besieging the city. He agreed to negotiate, and received a delegation from the town. He finally promised not to sack the town if it would break its alliance with the Swiss Confederation.

Louis saw no point in plundering the poor, mountainous country of Switzerland when the rich imperial lands of Alsace lay nearby. Undisturbed by the fact that these lands belonged to his ally Frederick, the dauphin led his freebooters into Alsace, where they began their usual depredations. In September, Louis received a letter from the burgomaster and council of the imperial town of Colmar protesting about the pillaging of his men. Even the messenger bearing their protest had been seized and robbed of everything, including the letter. The burgomaster and council had been forced to write a second time. This time the messenger was more fortunate and succeeded in delivering his letter. Naturally, Frederick also protested about the pillaging of his lands by his so-called ally. Louis sent ambassadors to the Emperor to discuss the matter but, in the meantime, began discussions at Ensisheim with the Swiss cantons and Basel. He also proceeded to capture one fortified place after another in Alsace. While he was attacking the town of Dambach, on October 7, 1444, an enemy arrow pierced his knee and nailed it to his saddle. While he was recuperating in Ensisheim, he received an embassy from the Emperor. He refused his demands and, instead, signed a treaty with his opponents, the Swiss and Basel at Zofingen. Louis ratified the treaty a week later, in late October, at Ensisheim. It called for cessation of hostilities and perpetual friendship.[23]

By this time, King Charles had become worried about Louis's activities and summoned him to return to court. Louis remained where he was, however, and his men continued to pillage Alsace. Finally, after repeated letters from his father, he set out for the French court leaving the remnants of his freebooters behind. He had removed most of the *écorcheurs* from the kingdom, and had thus performed a great service for France. Most of them had been killed, and the remainder had been left to pillage Alsace. His treaty with the Swiss was the beginning of a long friendship with these valuable allies that was to prove very useful to him in the future.

King Charles had spent the fall of 1444 at the head of a large army helping his brother-in-law, King René, Duke of Anjou, assert his authority over the town of Metz and several other rebellious portions of his duchy of Lorraine. When the cold weather approached, they decided to spend the winter in Nancy, the capital of the province. Louis joined them in early February 1445, after his return from Alsace. Margaret of Anjou was also present, and final arrangments for her marriage to the King of England were being made. The winter was passed in a steady succession of feasts and tournaments in which Louis, as usual, played very little part.[24]

The court left Nancy in late April. The king went on an inspection tour of the towns of the Meuse valley, while the queen, the dauphin, and the dauphiness went to Châlons to meet with Duchess Isabelle of Burgundy. Louis had been instructed by his father to begin negotiations with the duchess to try and settle several points of dispute between France and Burgundy. The meetings did not prove to be very friendly. Louis evidently harbored considerable resentment toward Duke Philip of Burgundy for not having helped him during the *Praguerie* and treated the duchess coldly. The Burgundians, for their part, were seeking indemnification for the damage done by Louis's *écorcheurs* in Burgundy. Negotiations were going badly until King Charles arrived in May and was able to conclude an agreement. The dauphin was forced to ratify the Treaty of Arras of 1435, with its wide concessions to the Duke of Burgundy, which he had always refused to accept and to give up the town of Montbéliard, which his freebooters had seized. This agreement was followed by more tournaments and dances, much to Louis's disgust.[25]

During that summer occurred the death of Louis's first wife, Margaret of Scotland. She had charmed the king and queen with her vivacity, and they loved her like a daughter. The king heaped presents upon her, gratifying her taste for expensive things.[26] Louis had never loved her, however. He disliked her expensive tastes, her love of luxury, her failure to bear him an heir and, according to some, her bad breath. Perhaps, too, he was prejudiced against her because she had been chosen by his father.

During the years of their marriage, Louis was usually away and Margaret lived at the court of the queen. The life of a noble lady in fifteenth-century France was sheltered and dull. At the queen's court one religious service followed another and, in between, the ladies occupied themselves chiefly with sewing and embroidery. Margaret, a gay and imaginative young girl, found this life extremely monotonous. Her health was not robust, and was certainly not improved by her excessive dieting to preserve her figure. As a form of escape she lost herself in fantasy and in writing poetry. She often sat up all night composing elegant *rondeaux*. Unfortunately, all of them were destroyed by her prosaic husband. She was admired by several young courtiers, some of whom also wrote courtly love poetry. This was probably harmless enough, but Louis became suspicious and had her spied on by a young Breton nobleman, Jamet de Tillay. One night during the winter of 1444–45, while the court was at Nancy, Jamet entered her room and found Margaret in the company of two young courtiers, with the room lit only by firelight. During the tournaments at Châlons in the summer of 1445 the dauphiness, like the other ladies of the court, gave lavish gifts to one or other of the various competing knights. Louis was, of course, informed of all these things, and his displeasure and jealousy increased.[27]

Before leaving Châlons to return to Tours, Margaret accompanied the king one hot August day to pray at a well-known shrine at Nôtre-Dame de l'Épine. She returned, hot and weary, to the episcopal palace where she was staying and removed her outer garments. The building was cool and damp, and she caught a chill. The next day she was seriously ill. Jamet de Tillay spread rumors to the effect that her illness was due to love, late nights, and frivolous living. Margaret protested her innocence, and certainly does not seem to have been guilty of any but the most minor indiscretions. The noble Pierre de Brézé, Seneschal of Normandy, left her room saying, "The sorrow and anger that that lady is suffering moves one to pity." Then, referring to Jamet, he burst out, "Ah, false and miserable rascal, she is dying because of you." Louis did not even come to visit her. The last words of this young woman, only twenty-one years old but weary of life, were, "Away with the life of this world. Speak to me no more of it, for it wearies me more than anything else." She died on August 16, 1445.[28]

By this time, Louis was already involved again in political intrigue. He attempted to win the favor of several influential people at court, such as the Duke of Orleans and Pierre de Brézé, to whom he sent a gift of Rhine wine in January 1445. He even gave presents to the royal mistress, Agnès Sorel, of whom he disapproved highly. He was still unable to get along with her very well, however. On one occasion he is reported to have threatened her with his sword and slapped her. Louis never in his life allowed any woman to have much influence over his actions and regarded his father's infatuation with the beautiful Agnès as yet another example of his weakness of character.

To further his plans, the dauphin sought the support of the adventurer Antoine de Chabannes. In the spring of 1446, he even tried to draw Chabannes into an armed conspiracy to overthrow the king's Scottish guard and seize control of the royal person. Chabannes was unwilling to risk this reckless gamble. In May, Louis attempted to persuade the towns of Agenais to desert the king's obedience and place themselves under his authority. His opposition to his father and his impatience to reign were emerging more and more clearly as the chief motivating forces behind his actions.

By September 1446, the king and Pierre de Brézé had learned of Louis's plotting. The king summoned him to explain his actions and accused him of planning the assassination of Brézé. Louis said he had acted on the advice of Chabannes. Chabannes was summoned and denied the charge. Louis called him a liar. Chabannes replied that if Louis were not the king's son he would avenge this insult with arms. At this point King Charles intervened and said, "Louis, I banish you for four months from my kingdom. Go to Dauphiné." Louis left bareheaded swearing. "By this head, which is now uncovered, I will avenge myself on those who have driven me from my home."[29]

CHAPTER 2

The Years of Exile

L OUIS left for Dauphiné in early January 1447, just a few days after the birth of his brother, Charles, who was to become his virtual enemy. His banishment was intended by his father to be a temporary disciplinary measure. In fact, Louis was destined to nearly fifteen years of exile, ending only with the death of his father and his own accession to the throne. The first nine and a half years of this period he spent in Dauphiné, where he accomplished a remarkable task of administration, which is of particular interest as it might be regarded as a sort of prelude to his reign.

Dauphiné, in southeastern France, had been sold to the French crown in 1349 by Humbert II, its last independent count. Since the reign of Charles V (1364-80), the eldest sons of the French kings had born the title of dauphin and held the province as an apanage—a situation somewhat analogous to that of the Prince of Wales in England. More often than not their actual suzerainty over the province was nominal. Much of the land was poor, and the region was sparsely populated and anarchic. Only the bishops had any real authority. The land had some potential value, however, based principally upon the production of wheat and wine and the raising of livestock. There were two sizable towns, Grenoble and Valence.

Louis had taken formal possession of Dauphiné in August 1440. For the next six years he had never entirely neglected his apanage, although he did not go there in person. During this time, he had frequently issued instructions aimed at improving the administration of the province. For example, in August 1445, he had written letters regulating the value of money in Dauphiné, and had issued an important edict regulating justice and finance.[1]

After his banishment from the royal court, Louis arrived in

Dauphiné to begin his personal administration of the province on January 15, 1447. His first act was to order all nobles holding fiefs to do homage to him within a month. He then traveled throughout Dauphiné confirming the privileges of the chief towns, cathedral chapters, and monasteries and receiving the homage of nobles. He made his official entry into his capital city of Grenoble on August 12.

Louis generally centralized and reformed the adminstration of Dauphiné. He reorganized the administrative districts of the province, reducing them to two *bailliages* and *sénéchaussée*. He established a central law court and a central bureau of revenue in Grenoble. He created a Grand Council consisting of high officials of the province and a certain number of prelates, abbots, and great lords. He chose most of his more intimate advisors from the lesser nobility. Many of them remained high in his service after he became king. Future royal favorites, such as Jean de Lescun, bastard of Armagnac, Regnier de Bouligny, Louis, seigneur de Crussol, Jean de Daillon, Amaury, seigneur d'Estissac, Charles de Melun, and Jean, seigneur de Montauban all entered Louis's service during his years of exile in Dauphiné.

One of the dauphin's chief objectives was to force the powerful ecclesiastical lords in the province to recognize his authority. Between June and October 1450 he succeeded in forcing the Bishop of Gap, the Bishop of Valence and Die, the Archbishop of Vienne, and the Bishop of Grenoble to acknowl- edge his sovereignty and do homage to him. No previous dauphin had accomplished this. This marked the end of the temporal power of the great churchmen in Dauphiné. In 1452, when the archbishopric of Vienne became vacant, Louis succeeded in demonstrating further his authority over the church in his province. He opposed the candidate selected by the king, seized possession of the archiepiscopal lands, and, in spite of royal remonstrances, had his own protégé named archbishop by the cathedral chapter.[2]

Louis took several steps to make the collection of taxes more efficient and more just. In December 1449 he had the three estates of Dauphiné declare that, henceforth, all allodial land would contribute to taxes levied on the province. These allods were prefeudal free tenures, where the holder held his land directly from the king without any intermediate lords. They were becoming increasingly rare in France by this time, but quite a few still existed in Dauphiné. As they had previously been exempt from most taxes, this step increased the dauphin's revenues significantly. To make the burden of taxes fall more fairly, he frequently lightened taxes in areas struck by natural or military disasters. For example, in September 1447 he authorized an exemption for ten years from all subsidies or gifts granted by the estates of Dauphiné for all inhabitants of the town of La Mure because of a recent fire which had destroyed more than one-third of the houses. Louis also turned his attention to revising the local units of tax assessment in Dauphiné known as *feux*. These *feux* had originally corresponded to one household, but had been modified to take into account differences in wealth. By this time, they were merely assessment units for fixing the share of taxes for each individual in each locality. Louis found that changes in population and wealth since the last time these units had been fixed rendered the system inequitable. Therefore, in January 1453, he ordered a general revision of *feux* in all of Dauphiné.[3]

Brief mention of some of the other steps taken by Louis to enrich, strengthen, or improve his apanage will indicate the wide range of his activity during the nine and a half years he spent there. He carried out sweeping military reforms, modelled in part on those which his father had initiated in France beginning in 1439. He organized a regular army of five companies of men-at-arms supplemented by several companies of crossbowmen. He issued an edict in October 1452 declaring that all nobles in his lands owed him military service and had to arm and equip themselves at their own expense whenever summoned. He looked to the repair of roads and bridges. To stimulate the economy of the province, he established several fairs; for example, at Gap in May 1444 and at Montélimar in May 1449. To encourage immigration, he issued a decree in November 1451 promising any foreigners who would settle in Dauphiné exemption from all taxes for ten years. In July 1452 he founded the University of Valence.[4]

The years in Dauphiné seem to have been happy ones for Louis. For the first time he was able to gratify his passion to rule. The woods and mountains of the region abounded with game, and he was able to devote considerable time to hunting, which was always his favorite recreation. He evidently did not lack feminine companionship. He is known to have had two mistresses in Dauphiné, Guyette Durand, daughter of a notary of Grenoble, and Félise Reynard, a widow of a noble family of Die. Félise bore him two daughters whom he later legitimized. He gave them both splendid dowries and arranged for them to marry men of wealth and prominence. One of them, Jeanne, married Louis, bastard of Bourbon, Admiral of France. The other, Marie, married Aimar de Poitiers, one of the king's chamberlains.[5]

All the time he was in Dauphiné Louis kept in close touch with affairs in France. He had spies at the royal court who kept him well informed. His hostility to his father remained unabated and was extended to the king's chief advisors and friends. He repeatedly said that his father misgoverned the country and that Agnès Sorel and Pierre de Brézé should be banished, inasmuch as they exerted an evil influence upon him. Agnès died in 1450, but Brézé, a man of honor and of great ability, remained one of Charles's chief advisors.

Louis was also intriguing to gain the suzerainty of Normandy, just recaptured from the English in 1449. He tried to win the support of one of the most influential men in Normandy, Thomas Basin, Bishop of Lisieux. Basin refused to help and informed the king of the dauphin's machinations. Louis never forgave him and secured his banishment, after he became king. The bishop had the last word, however. He wrote a biased history of the reign of Louis XI that did much to blacken Louis's character for all posterity.[6]

During his years in Dauphiné, Louis conducted his own foreign policy. The complicated intrigues and diplomacy of the various Italian states appealed to his subtle mind. His proximity to Italy placed him in a good position to intervene in the affairs of that peninsula. To strengthen his hand, he sought an alliance with the neighboring Duchy of Savoy which controlled the gateway to Italy. In August 1449 he signed a treaty with Louis, Duke of Savoy. Commerce was to be free between their respective subjects. Each agreed not to allow the other's enemies to pass through his lands, and each promised to send armed assistance to the other if needed.

To strengthen this alliance, Louis wanted to marry Charlotte, the eleven-year-old daughter of the Duke of Savoy. Preliminary negotiations indicated the duke's approval of the plan and his willingness to provide a large dowry. Louis then informed his father of his intentions. Charles indicated his disapproval but postponed making any definite decision until he could finish the war with England. In November 1450 two delegates from the dauphin conferred with the king and presented Louis's arguments in favor of the marriage. He said that he had waited long enough to remarry and that he needed heirs. He pointed out that his father had chosen his first wife and argued that he was now old enough to select his own. He also mentioned the large dowry, which would alleviate his present financial distress. While on the subject of his poverty, he suggested that he be given an additional seigneury, such as Guyenne, part of which was still occupied by the English. He denied all accusations that he was plotting against the king.

As usual, Charles took his time answering. He finally sent a royal councillor to tell Louis that he would like to see him suitably married, but did not approve of his choice. He suggested either Eleanor of Portugal or the sister of the King of Hungary. He turned down Louis's request for Guyenne.

In the meantime, in spite of his father's opposition, Louis was proceeding with the marriage arrangements. The final marriage contract was signed in Geneva on February 14, 1451. The dowry was fixed at 200,000 *écus* and the Duke of Savoy agreed to pay Charlotte an annual pension until she was old enough for the marriage to be consummated. The wedding was planned for March 8, in Chambéry. Shortly before the ceremony was to begin, a royal herald arrived with letters from the king to the Duke of Savoy calling upon him to stop the wedding. The herald was deliberately delayed by a welcoming committee long enough for the marriage to take place. The Duke of Savoy then wrote the king expressing his regret that he had not received his letter in time. Charles was furious when he learned of his son's defiance of his will. The new dauphiness joined Louis in Grenoble in April, and the towns of the province voted her a handsome gift.

Louis was now prepared to intervene directly in Italian politics. In the summer of 1453, he offered to help Venice make war against Duke Francesco Sforza of Milan. The Venetian town council debated his offer on August 31. After some delay, they finally sent an ambassador, in December, to the Duke of Savoy asking him to invite Louis to come to their help against Milan. Negotiations continued for several months, but Venice, Milan, and Florence concluded their wars by the Peace of Lodi in 1454 before Louis could intervene. By 1455, Louis had reversed his policy and was seeking the friendship of the Duke of Milan. Francesco Sforza had risen from a humble background by a combination of force and intelligence. He was the illegitimate son of a *condottiere* (leader of a band of mercenary soldiers). He had followed the same profession with great success, and had married the illegitimate daughter of the Duke of Milan, Filippo—Maria Visconti, who died without a male heir in 1447. Powerful aspirants to the duchy included the French magnate Charles, Duke of Orleans, claiming from his Visconti mother. Sforza, however, gained control of Milan and proclaimed himself duke in 1450. For the next nine years, he was a secret but determined foe of French intervention in Italy. René, Duke of Anjou, had a claim to Naples after King Alfonso V of Naples and Aragon died, in 1458, leaving Naples to his illegitimate son Ferrante. A triumph for the Duke of Anjou in Naples might lead Charles VII to lend military support to the claims of the Duke of Orleans to Milan. Louis admired Sforza as a master politician and soldier. He wrote Sforza in February 1455, proposing a marriage between the duke's eldest son Galeazzo-Maria and his own sister-in-law, Marie of Savoy. The King of France, however, was aware of these negotiations and sent an envoy to Milan in March 1455 with instructions to tell the duke that he would be very displeased if he signed any agreement or treaty with the dauphin, or gave him any support or aid. Sforza replied in April saying that he would under no circumstances make any such alliance with the dauphin. Thus Louis's first negotiations with Francesco Sforza led to no immediate result. They did, however, mark the beginning of a long and useful friendship with the powerful Milanese duke.[7]

Meanwhile, King Charles resolved to threaten his disobedient son with force. In August 1455 he sent a mission to Geneva seeking to settle his differences with the Duke of Savoy. Also, Antoine de Chabannes was sent at the head of an army to Lyons to conduct military operations in Dauphiné, if necessary, while the king himself followed with more troops to Bourbonnais. Louis sent several embassies to his father, trying to calm his anger. He promised to serve the king, not cross the Rhône without royal permission, and renounce his alliances if the king would give him a free hand in Dauphiné. Charles was unwilling to bargain with his rebellious son. At this point, Louis panicked and decided to flee, fearing that his father might not only seize his apanage, but actually imprison him.

On August 30, 1456, the dauphin and a few of his closest followers rode to a shrine at Saint-Claude as if on a pilgrimage. From there he wrote his father telling him that he was going to the court of Duke Philip the Good of Burgundy to join him in a projected crusade against the Turks. He said that he would also ask the duke to help reconcile him with the king. He then fled as rapidly as possible to the lands of the Prince of Orange, a small principate just south of Dauphiné, and one of the few remnants of the old Kingdom of Burgundy which had not been swallowed up by larger powers. There he rested briefly. He had left his young bride, Charlotte, behind in Dauphiné. The Prince of Orange arranged for Jean de Neufchâtel, Marshal of Burgundy, to conduct him safely to the duke, avoiding French territory. The marshal took him through Lorraine, but wrote to the Duke of Burgundy, who was besieging Deventer in Holland, telling him what he was doing. The duke was extremely surprised and wrote to King Charles to inform him of the dauphin's actions. Louis then reached Louvain in the lands of Burgundy, where he rested for a short time in security. Finally, in October, he entered Brussels, where he was welcomed by the Duchess of Burgundy and her daughter-in-law, the Countess of Charolais. Louis offered his arm to the duchess and tried to place her in the position of honor on his right. She refused. The polite discussion over this point of etiquette lasted for fifteen minutes, a rather common characteristic of fifteenth-century manners. Finally she entered on his left, but he insisted on taking her arm.[8]

The Duke of Burgundy was somewhat embarrassed by the presence of the disobedient royal son at his court. He returned from his campaign in mid-October to Brussels to greet the dauphin, however. Louis advanced to the middle of the courtyard to meet him instead of remaining in his place as his position entitled him to do. Philip knelt, but Louis promptly raised him up and they walked up the steps together.

The sixty-year old Philip was a proud and vain man. He undoubtedly saw the possibility of exerting great influence in France by acting as arbiter in the long-standing quarrel between Louis and King Charles. He greeted the dauphin with affection and respect. Kneeling again before him, he said: "You are come as the Angel Gabriel to the Virgin Mary, for I have never felt such joy, nor such an honor as to have been able to see you once in my life and receive you in my lands, which are yours and at your service." Louis tried to raise Philip to his feet and replied:

By my faith, fair uncle, if you do not get up I will leave. You are the one whom I have long wished to see more than anyone else in the world. . . . I praise God that I find you in good health, and the sight of your person is the greatest joy that I have ever had. Good uncle, if it pleases God, we shall make good cheer together, and I shall tell you my adventures and you shall tell me yours.

Philip got up. Both he and Louis had tears in their eyes. Such displays of emotion were common in the fifteenth century. Philip tried to install Louis in his own bedroom. Louis refused and, after a long, polite argument, the duke agreed to let him sleep in the room above. Philip accorded the dauphin every possible honor. When they walked together Philip followed bareheaded and refused to wear a hat in Louis's presence, in spite of the latter's remonstrances. During the next few months, Louis and the duke were constantly in each other's company, hunting and jousting.[9]

Philip then assigned to Louis the castle of Genappe and a sizable pension of 36,000 *francs.* Louis spent the next five years in this pleasant chateau in good hunting country not far from Brussels. As mentioned before, Louis was an avid hunter. He preferred hunting with dogs rather than with falcons. He would often start out at daybreak, with his companions, in any weather, hunt all day, and then spend the night in any village where he happened to find himself. He was frequently accompanied by the young and fiery Charles, Count of Charolais, son of Duke Philip, whom he got to know well, and who was destined to become his greatest enemy.

Louis appears to have read and studied quite a bit during these years at Genappe, sometimes with the professors of the University of Louvain. He acted as godfather for Charolais's daughter, Mary of Burgundy. "Lord, what a godfather," wrote the chronicler of the Hague in the margin of his manuscript. The future was to prove the truth of this comment, when, in later years, Louis attempted to despoil his goddaughter of all her father's lands. He sometimes acted as mediator in the many quarrels between Charolais and Duke Philip. In view of his relationship with his own father, this was a rather ironic role. He

was greatly concerned about these quarrels, however, fearing
that people in France would say that everywhere he went
trouble broke out. On one occasion, Louis was asked by the
duchess herself to intervene. He succeeded in calming Philip's
violent anger against Charolais.

During his stay in Burgundy, Louis travelled widely throughout Flanders with Duke Philip. He was greatly impressed with its
riches, particularly those of the large and flourishing city of
Bruges. One of their projected trips is of particular interest as it
shows clearly the widespread superstition still prevalent in the
fifteenth century. Duke Philip and the dauphin had been invited
to visit the town of Ghent. Then a severe earthquake occurred at
that town. Also Saint Bertulf was heard moving around in his
tomb in the monastery of Saint-Pierre in Ghent. The good saint
was apparently in the habit of performing such gymnastics from
time to time and, when he did, it was always thought to indicate
the approach of some great event. When Louis heard of these
developments, he became very fearful that the townsmen of
Ghent were planning to assassinate both the duke and himself.
He urged Philip not to go. The duke, evidently less superstitious,
was not particularly worried. He did agree to postpone his trip
for a few days while he investigated the situation in Ghent. He
then carried out his visit as planned. Louis, however, refused to
go under any circumstances.

All this time the dauphiness, Charlotte of Savoy, had remained
in Dauphiné and Louis had shown no haste in summoning her.
She is described by contemporary writers as a gentle and
insignificant girl, in no way beautiful. The dauphin finally sent
for her and she arrived in Namur in January 1458. The marriage
was consummated and Charlotte gave birth to a son in July of the
following year. Duke Philip and the Countess of Charolais acted
as godparents. Sumptuous gifts were given by Philip and his
courtiers. Louis knelt before the duke and said, "My dear uncle, I
thank you for the goodness and the honor you do me. I will never
be able to repay you except by offering you my body, that of my
wife, and that of my child." The young prince, whom they
christened Joachim, died in November 1459. About two years
later, the dauphiness gave birth to a daughter, Anne.

Naturally, King Charles was very displeased about the
sanctuary offered his disobedient son by the Duke of Burgundy.
As early as September 1456 he wrote to Philip asking him to

return the dauphin to France. The duke politely refused saying that Louis was weary from his long voyage, which he had made of his own free will. He added that he was merely treating him with the honor and respect due to the son and heir of the King of France. A Milanese agent reported to the Duke of Milan, in November 1456, that the Duke of Burgundy would neither counsel nor aid the dauphin to oppose the king, but that if anyone should attempt to harm Louis, while he was in Burgundian lands, the duke would protect him. Several years later, when ambassadors from Charles asked Philip to send Louis back, Philip again refused, saying that Louis had come of his own free will and was free to go at any time. In the meantime, Philip was honoring him in a manner suitable to his rank. Naturally, relations between France and Burgundy were not improved by this state of affairs.

Louis wrote frequently to his father during his stay in Burgundy. His tone was always humble — that of the patient and obedient, but wronged, son. As early as October 26, 1456, he wrote to the king announcing his arrival at the court of Burgundy and telling of the warm reception he had received. He protested, however, against the occupation of Dauphiné by royal officials. On July 27, 1459, he wrote to King Charles, the Duke of Berry, the Bishop of Paris, and the town of Paris announcing the birth of his son that day. In December 1459 he wrote to his father telling him of the second pregnancy of his wife. He also wrote humble and polite letters in December 1460 and March 1461.

Louis's five years in Burgundy seem to have been enjoyable. The pleasant castle of Genappe stood in the middle of the river Dyle, and was surrounded by gardens and fruit trees. The surrounding countryside was rich, and there was a dense forest nearby which abounded in game. Moreover, he got to know the Count of Charolais very well and became familiar with the weaknesses in his character. This was to stand Louis in good stead later when he engaged in a series of bitter wars with Charolais.[10]

While at Genappe, Louis renewed the diplomatic relations which he had begun in Dauphiné with Duke Francesco Sforza of Milan. During the year 1459, the dauphin and the duke exchanged messages with a view to establishing some sort of formal tie. In December Louis accredited to Sforza Gaston du Lyon, his councillor and chief equerry. Gaston arrived in Milan in

February 1460, supposedly to take part in an annual tournament, but his real mission was to present the dauphin's proposals for an alliance. In March, the Duke of Milan wrote, replying favorably to several specific proposals made by Louis.

The dauphin also sent several other envoys to Milan in the first six months of 1460 seeking to conclude an alliance. Sforza hesitated, as he was trying to keep secret his anti-French activities in Italy so as to avoid a rupture with Charles VII. The French king was well informed, however, not only about the Duke of Milan's policy in Italy, but also about his negotiations with Louis. He sent Sforza several warnings not to intrigue with the dauphin and not to oppose the Angevins (the House of Anjou) in Italy.

By May 1460 Charles's patience was exhausted and a rupture appeared imminent. In a last effort to conciliate him, Sforza sent an envoy to the King of France. He was instructed to tell the king that Sforza had heard that someone had reported to Charles that he was intriguing with the dauphin and the Duke of Burgundy through Gaston du Lyon. He denied it categorically. He repeated the story that Gaston had come merely for the annual joust in February. Due to bad weather, it was postponed until late April. During the interval, Gaston had gone to Savoy, but had returned for the jousting in April. He had said nothing at all to Sforza either time regarding an alliance with the Duke of Burgundy or the dauphin. Sforza claimed that he had told Gaston to urge the dauphin to behave properly to his father and submit himself to the royal will.

In July 1460 events took place which led the Duke of Milan to change his tactics and cease trying to placate Charles VII. John, Duke of Calabria, son of King René of Anjou, routed the army of Sforza's ally Ferrante, King of Naples. An Angevin conquest of Naples seemed imminent. Quickly, Sforza sent military aid to Ferrante and sent an envoy to Genappe to try and conclude a treaty with the dauphin. This began a long and complicated series of negotiations between August 1460 and July 1461 which ended with the signing of the Treaty of Genappe between the dauphin and the Duke of Milan.

The envoy selected by Francesco Sforza in August 1460 to negotiate this treaty was an experienced diplomat, Prospero da Camogli. He took with him a treaty based on the discussions that had taken place that month in Milan between Louis's envoys and the duke. Prospero was instructed to request the dauphin to conclude and seal the agreement. Sforza foresaw no difficulties, and told his envoy to try and finish the matter quickly and return. After spending less than a month at Genappe (September-October 1460), Prospero returned to Milan with the treaty duly signed by the dauphin.

The matter was by no means concluded, however, because Louis had insisted on including one additional point in the treaty. It called for the Duke of Milan to help one of Louis's adherents in Savoy, a certain Giacoma di Valperga, to get back his lands. Valperga, with Louis's support, had become chancellor of Savoy. The Duke of Savoy had ousted him from his position and seized his estates. Valperga had fled to Genappe. Prospero had tried to persuade Louis to leave him out of the treaty, but Louis had insisted that he would not abandon his supporter. Prospero had finally agreed to add the clause that would require Sforza to aid Valperga, subject to Sforza's approval.

The Duke of Milan ratified the treaty, but sent Prospero back to Genappe, in February 1461, with instructions to request the dauphin to remove the clause concerning Valperga.

Prospero's dispatches during these discussions with the dauphin give the first detailed picture of Louis in the role of negotiator. As diplomacy became his forte in later years, it is interesting to see something of this aspect of his activities while he was still dauphin. He drove the Milanese envoy to despair with his subtlety and determination over the relatively minor issue of the Valperga clause. Prospero's letters show a combination of admiration and dislike for the dauphin. Louis had clearly won his respect for the astuteness with which he argued his viewpoint. Yet, his growing distaste for the dauphin is evident, too. In one letter he complains of the bad manners with which Louis had treated him. He added, "Indeed I keep thinking that there are in the dauphin certain qualities that can justify his father ['s treatment of him]. . . ." He complained that he had to be very careful what he told Louis because "the dauphin no more keeps a secret than a wicker basket holds water."

After months of arguing with the Milanese envoy, Louis opened direct negotiations with Sforza, and the Valperga issue was finally resolved. Louis said that he would accept a loan of 18,000 florins for removal of the clause. The Duke of Milan accepted this solution and confirmed and ratified the Treaty of Genappe in July 1461.

The treaty was a pact of mutual assistance. Each agreed to provide several thousand troops if the other was attacked. Both parties swore to keep the treaty secret. No mention was made of the Duke of Burgundy. Although both Louis and the Duke of Milan were negotiating with Burgundy and England, Louis wanted a personal pact, not an Anglo-Burgundian-Milanese alliance that would threaten France when he became king.

By this time, his relations with Duke Philip the Good of Burgundy were steadily deteriorating. This was made clear in a letter of June 1461 from Prospero da Camogli to the Duke of Milan in which he informed the duke about conditions in England and Burgundy. He said that there was "little love. . .lost between the dauphin and the Duke of Burgundy." Every day there was greater danger that this bad feeling would come into the open as "on the dauphin's part, only his necessity keeps it concealed; on the duke's, the advantage of having the dauphin should war come [with France]."

Louis had promised to repay the 18,000 florins lent to him by the Duke of Milan, as part of the Treaty of Genappe, within six months of his reconciliation with his father, or his becoming king, whichever occurred first. By this time the latter possibility appeared imminent.[11]

The King of France had prematurely aged. He was seriously ill in 1457. He was constantly preoccupied with Louis's stay in Burgundy. In fact, an agent of Sforza reported to his master in July 1459 that the king actually was planning war against Burgundy. Charles became ill again in the summer of 1460 and was expected to die. Once again, however, he recovered. Louis kept himself closely informed regarding the state of the king's health through one of Charles's former mistresses, Mlle. de Villequier. He wrote to her on August 30, 1460, asking her to destroy the letter, and to write and let him know if she thought he would remain for long in his present situation. He was referring of course, to the fact that his own position would be completely changed if the king should die.

What is rather strange to the modern reader is Louis's complete lack of filial affection for his father, which had been evident for years. His anxiety to learn of the king's health had nothing to do with pity or solicitude. It merely reflected the dauphin's burning desire to reign.

His father's death would mean to him nothing more or less than an end to his misfortunes and exile, and he looked forward to it eagerly as, at last, it would make him king of France.

As Charles approached death, the prudent royal council wrote Louis a polite letter describing the king's condition and asking what was his pleasure. On receiving the letter, the dauphin set out for Avesnes, still in Burgundian territory, but on the way to the coronation city of Rheims. He wrote to the Duke of Burgundy asking him to come with all his retainers to Rheims as soon as he heard of King Charles's death.

Charles grew steadily weaker. For about eight days he refused to eat, fearing poison, and even suspecting that Louis had poisoned him. His suspicions were completely unfounded. He finally died on July 22, 1461. He was buried at Saint-Denis, traditional burial ground of French kings. As his coffin was being covered the herald cried out, "Pray for the soul of the very excellent, very powerful, and very victorious prince, King Charles, seventh of that name." Then, after a moment of silence, he shouted, "Long live the King." The royal secretaries there responded, "Long live King Louis.".

On Charles's death, many dignitaries rushed to Avesnes, where Louis had been waiting for five days, to pledge their obedience to him. They hoped, of course, that he would retain them in their positions. A few of the chief servants of Charles VII, knowing Louis's hatred of them, feared to go to meet him. When the Archbishop of Rheims came to Avesnes to bid him official welcome on behalf of the town of Rheims Louis, who hated long-winded speeches, urged him three times to be brief.

On August 3, funeral services were held in Avesnes for Charles VII. Louis wore mourning for the first time. (The Duke of Burgundy and all his court had been dressed in mourning ever since the death of the king.) Louis then hastened to Rheims for the coronation. He entered the town to the sound of trumpets. His horse was covered with cloth of gold. He and his men were all dressed in red and white satin. Four men carried a canopy over his head. He was followed by the Duke of Burgundy and his pages and surrounded by many archers on foot. After dismounting briefly at Notre-Dame to pray, Louis went to his lodgings for the night. At midnight he returned to the church and remained there until 5:00 A.M. confessing, taking communion, and praying. He then returned to his room and rested for about three hours. Louis then returned to Notre-Dame and the elaborate coronation ceremony began. The Holy Ampulla, a flask filled with consecrated oil with which French kings were always anointed at their coronation, was placed on the high altar. Louis was invested with spurs and the "Sword of Charlemagne" and then the Bishop of Laon led him to the altar for his consecretion. He was stripped to the waist in order to expose his shoulders and breast for anointment. He knelt in front of the altar while the Archbishop of Rheims anointed him with the Holy Oil from the Ampulla. The archbishop, peers, and prelates then dressed him in his coronation robes. Next, he was invested with the royal scepter, the verge called the *main de justice* (hand of justice), and the royal ring. The archbishop then crowned him with the "crown of Charlemagne" and the Peers of France led him to, and seated him upon, a raised royal throne. The Archbishop of Rheims gave Louis the kiss of homage and cried, "Long live the King!" Then each of the other peers, including the Duke of Burgundy, also gave him the kiss of homage and shouted the same acclamation. The crowd repeated this cry. Bells rang, trumpets sounded, and the noise was almost deafening. The heavy "crown of Charlemagne" was then replaced on the king's head with a lighter one and a procession took place back to the archbishop's palace.

After returning to his room to rest awhile, Louis went down to dinner in his full robes with the lighter crown on his head. The "crown of Charlemagne" was then placed on the table beside him. Magnificent gifts were brought to Louis by Duke Philip the Good, who had already provided all of the table silver for the dinner and paid virtually all the costs for the entire coronation.

Louis left Rheims for Paris on August 17, 1461. The years of exile, impatient waiting, and relative poverty were over. Louis's lifelong ambition was realized. At last, at the age of thirty-eight, he was king of one of the most powerful nations in Europe.[12]

CHAPTER 3

A King at Last: The Early Years of His Reign, 1461–1464

THE new king arrived at Paris on August 31, 1461. The royal entry was colorful and the reception tumultuous. He was met outside the city by the provost of merchants and other officials who presented him with the keys to the gate of Saint-Denis. Next, a herald presented five girls, richly dressed, each of whom wore one of the five letters spelling out Paris. As Louis entered the gate of Saint-Denis, two angels came down from a silver ship and placed a crown upon his head. Soon after entering the gate, he came to a fountain where three beautiful nude girls, representing sirens, sang and danced. The fountain sprayed milk, wine, and hippocras for anyone to drink.

Paris was jammed with people to see the entry of Louis XI. Many were on the rooftops and places at windows were rented. And indeed the sight was well worth seeing. Philip the Good of Burgundy was dressed in black and mounted on a white charger with magnificent trappings. He was followed by the Burgundian nobles, all richly clad. Then came various French nobles and the royal guard, followed by trumpets and heralds and the marshals of France and Burgundy. Next came the king, dressed in a white damask robe and riding a white horse caparisoned with his personal colors—red and white. Six bourgeois of Paris, clad in purple, held a canopy of blue satin sewn with gold fleurs-de-lis over his head. Then followed the Duke of Bourbon, Charles, Count of Charolais, and many other French and Burgundian lords. As they passed through the streets of Paris, various religious scenes were acted out on stages specially built for the occasion. Also, the capture of the Bastille of Dieppe, which Louis had led as dauphin, was enacted. When they reached the Pont aux Changes, the birdkeepers of Paris released hundreds of birds.

The procession finally arrived at Nôtre-Dame Cathedral. The Bishop of Paris, along with many of the clergy, met the king outside the door. Louis then entered the cathedral to the strains of the *Te Deum*. The nave was brilliantly lit and the organ played. The king said a brief prayer and then left to go to the royal palace.

At the palace a sumptuous dinner was served. Magnificent cups, goblets, and silver belonging to the Duke of Burgundy, were used. The festivities continued until the king withdrew to his lodgings about midnight.

Louis remained in Paris for nearly four weeks. During that time, according to the contemporary writer Thomas Basin, he was constantly approached by those hoping to secure offices or favors from him. These people heaped gifts upon those thought to have influence with the king.

Meanwhile, the Duke of Burgundy dazzled Paris with tournaments, gifts, pomp, and ceremony. He had hoped, of course, that after all he had done for Louis, the king would grant some high offices to his followers. Louis refused to do so, however, and left Paris for Touraine later in September, impatient to reign. The disappointed Duke of Burgundy returned to his own lands soon after.[1]

Passing through the countryside, on his way from Paris to Touraine, Louis became increasingly aware of the terrible devastation that France had suffered from the Hundred Years' War. He must have realized that he was confronted with a formidable task if he were to rebuild his shattered nation. He saw poverty and misery on all sides. Already he had been struck by the contrast between the rich plains of Flanders and the deplorable condition of northern France when he had traveled from Burgundy to Paris. According to the contemporary chronicler, Thomas Basin, he had said that he had seen along the route nothing but ruins, uncultivated fields, in fact, a sort of desert. The people were so emaciated that they looked as though they had just come out of prison.

Indeed, most of France had been cruelly ravaged by the Hundred Years' War, which had ended eight years before. All of the fighting had taken place on French soil. During the intervals of peace the mercenary soldiers of both sides, temporarily unemployed, had lived off the country, robbing, killing, and raping at will. All reports agree on the ruined condition of the French countryside. Three or four years after Louis's coronation,

the English traveler Sir John Fortescue crossed northern France
on his way to Paris and his account of the journey shows that
there had still been very little improvement. Speaking of the
country peasants, he said:

They are thus forced by necessity to be so much on their guard [against
brigands], to work, to clear the land for their subsistence, that their
strength is exhausted and their money reduced to nothing. They live in
the most extreme wretchedness.

As much as eight or ten years after the end of the war, a great
deal of rural France was deserted, devastated, and uncultivated.
  Some recovery in the country districts may have begun during
the last years of the reign of Charles VII, but very little. The
countryside lacked workers to recultivate it and was overrun by
bandits and beggars. In Orleanais, only ruins were to be seen.
Even in Dauphiné, removed from the main areas of French-
English combat, many regions were almost uninhabited and
deserted due to the frequent raids of bands of *écorcheurs.* The
rural population of France was greatly reduced in numbers. For
example, in 1459, the estates of Languedoc claimed that, in spite
of the restoration of peace, one third of the population of the
province had perished during the last ten years. Huddled around
castles and fortified towns, the French peasants had completely
abandoned much farm land, which had become a tangle of weeds
and underbrush.
  Of course, some of the peasants derived some benefit from this
situation. Those left were able to demand much higher salaries
or better terms than ever before. Those who contracted to clear
overgrown land received specially favorable terms. Any peasants
who were still serfs were often able to gain their freedom.
However, the damage to the country districts caused by the
Hundred Years' War, was so great that it took many years for
them to recover.
  The Hundred Years' War also left a legacy of violence to
plague the new king. Vagabonds and bandits roamed through
France almost at will. They included peasants whose crops had
been ruined, clerics whose prebends were gone and, most of all,
former mercenary soldiers. The latter group were used to
plunder and pillage and unused to work, so they became bandits
after the war. Some of them were well organized into large

bands, some of which even specialized in particular crimes. The beggars were also well organized and even had their own king. Many lawless students swelled the ranks of the robbers. The life and works of the great poet François Villon reflect this turbulent life. As a student, he frequented almost all the taverns and bawdy houses in Paris. During his brief career he committed nearly every kind of crime from robbery to murder. His lusty poetry describes vividly the type of life that he and his companions led:

> By pillage, thieving, fill the pot:
> Whose is the purchase, whose the pay?
> Taverns and wenches take the lot.

The rudimentary local police forces of the day were completely inadequate to deal with all of this lawlessness.

Finally, the Hundred Years' War had depopulated and ruined France. It had destroyed for years the centers of population, ruined the roads, and demolished buildings and monuments. It had permanently lessened the riches of the great land-holding proprietors of the Middle Ages, the nobles and the clergy. It led to a profound demoralization, indicated by the high rate of crime described above, a decline in the Christian faith, and the decadence of the Church. The war had ruined the Church. Its buildings were demolished and its lands devastated. The monastic rules had broken down. Priests, monks, and nuns were corrupted by the general moral degradation of the day. With their revenues so diminished, many higher prelates sought to hold several benefices at once. This led to absenteeism.[2]

The new king also faced the problem of gaining some authority over the towns and stimulating the country's stagnant industries. Before Louis XI, no consistent, reasoned, royal policy had checked the control of town officials or nobles over industry. The role of Charles VII in the slight industrial recovery during the closing years of his reign was not very active. It was limited chiefly to supervising corporations a bit and deriving some financial profit from them.

In spite of all of these problems confronting the new king, the picture was not entirely black. In many ways, the situation in France in 1461 was highly favorable for a man of ability to establish himself as a strong monarch. Charles VII had created a

permanent army, checked, to some limited extent, the plundering mercenaries, and started a slight revival in trade and
commerce. He and his ministers had also reorganized royal
justice and finance. One of the most important results was that
Charles had established a permanent tax. Throughout Western
Europe, in the late Middle Ages, the theory had developed that
the king must obtain the consent of all people of any
consequence in his country before imposing a tax. In France, this
consent was obtained from large assemblies, local assemblies, or
towns. During the first part of his reign Charles had followed this
policy. After 1436, as his power increased, he imposed indirect
taxes *(aides)* without consent. No large assemblies met after 1439
to grant direct taxes *(tailles)* and, by the early 1450s, he imposed
these taxes every year without consulting local assemblies or
towns. The only exception was several large provinces, such as
Normandy and Languedoc, which retained their local assemblies, known as provincial estates, and maintained the right to
bargain slightly over their share of royal taxes.

During the Hundred Years' War, many towns had gained
considerable independence of action, including the right to tax
themselves without royal consent. In the latter years of the reign
of Charles VII, many of these towns began to lose their municipal
liberties before the rising power of the monarchy. Under Louis
XI this trend continued.

Weary of war, the people of France now asked only to be
allowed to live in peace, and gave up, without much resistance,
some of the political liberties which they had gained during the
long struggle with England when the crown had been forced to
bargain with them for taxes. The French monarchy, which had
been so weakened in the early years of the fifteenth century, was
now in a very strong position. It was supported by popular
sentiment for having finally brought the war to a successful
conclusion, and it possessed a permanent army and permanent
taxes. The monarchy alone, in the hands of a strong man, seemed
capable of pulling France out of anarchy and ruin.[3]

Louis XI was unquestionably a strong man determined to take
full advantage of the situation. Unlike his father, he succeeded in
maintaining a high degree of personal rule, with few significant
advisors.

What sort of man was this who now so confidently grasped the
reins of power? His personal appearance was not attractive. He

had a long nose, sunken but piercing eyes, thin legs, a pale face, but a rather strong chin. He dressed simply. He went bald early, and usually wore an old hat, decorated with a lead medal of a saint, and with a broad brim that protected his head from cold, sun, or rain.

Louis hated formality and was not interested in ceremonies, banquets, balls, and tournaments. There was little gaiety at the French court. His chief amusements were dining at the homes of his friends, often of the middle class or lesser nobility, in the company of pretty women, drinking heavily and exchanging slightly coarse jokes. He loved hunting and animals, and spent lavishly on both. He was extremely fond of dogs, and often asked for some that he specially wanted or was given some as a present. He even made an offering to St. Hubert for the health of his dogs. Their collars were more richly ornamented than the king's clothing. One had a collar containing ten rubies and twenty pearls. In addition to his dogs, Louis had a large collection of all kinds of birds, such as pheasants, owls, and herons. He was particularly fond of talking birds that would make vulgar remarks. He also had a zoo containing an elephant, two dromedaries, lions, and monkeys.

Actually, Louis was a man of few pleasures and much hard work. In a letter to the Duke of Milan in December 1465 the Milanese ambassador at the French court described a typical, long, hard day in the life of the king. He rose early in the morning, said his prayers, and attended Mass. He then went to a meeting of the royal council. Next he would go to his dining hall, where he remained until at least 2:00 P.M. conducting business. Later in the day, he would go out for some exercise, either on foot or on horseback. On his return, he usually met with some of his councillors until time for his evening meal. He dined quite early, but went to bed late.

Louis like to receive advice, although he did not necessarily accept it. One of the characteristics of his reign was the large number of consultative assemblies that he held. He summoned those groups best qualified to advise him or to give him the support that he required. Thus the composition of these assemblies varied considerably.

Louis had a passionate desire to see all and know everything personally. For this reason, in addition to summoning meetings to give him advice, he traveled constantly throughout France, wanting to see conditions first hand. He always traveled simply dressed with a small entourage. Foreign ambassadors frequently complained of the difficulty of catching up with him. He usually arrived unexpectedly in towns to avoid formal receptions. He would stay with a wealthy bourgeois or a royal official.

Even when not traveling, he was constantly seeking information. He developed a widespread service of spies. His famous Ordonnance of 1464 establishing the royal postal system was for the purpose of keeping himself informed. He had an intense curiosity. One chronicler says that no man ever listened to so many people, nor inquired about so many things, nor sought to know so many people. He was informed of all, had an excellent memory, and wanted to deal with everything personally.

Women played a rather small role in Louis's life. As we have seen, he had two mistresses as a young man in Dauphiné, and may have had a few more during the early years of his reign. If so, we know nothing about them. The contemporary historian Commynes, who became one of Louis's most trusted servants and knew the king probably better than any other man, reports that he heard Louis take an oath in July 1473, after the death of his year-old son François, never again to touch any other woman but the queen. Commynes remarks that it was highly praiseworthy that Louis kept this oath, as a king has so many women at his disposal and Queen Charlotte, although a worthy woman, "was not one to inspire great pleasure."

Louis XI was not a very loving husband. We have seen already his heartless treatment of Margaret of Scotland. He showed no great affection for Charlotte of Savoy either, and her life was lonely and sad. In 1464, the Milanese ambassador reported that he was very irritated that she had just borne him a daughter rather than a son, and complained that her cries in childbirth had disturbed him all night. In fact no woman, either queen or mistress, ever had any particular influence on his activities.

Louis did not have a very robust constitution. Much of his life he suffered from stomach disorders, hemorrhoids, gout, nervous disorders, and, in later years, a serious skin condition. He was a nervous and impatient man who could not relax. Commynes says that he never saw Louis free from care. In fact, he adds that, ever since his childhood, Louis had had nothing but trouble and he was certain that "if all the good days that he had had in his life, in which he had more joy and pleasure than trouble and work were counted, that they would be found to be very few; and it seems to me that he had at least twenty days of sorrow and work for every one of pleasure and ease."

All sources of the day agree that Louis was a man of great intelligence. In their reports to the Duke of Milan, three different Milanese ambassadors stress this point during the first year of Louis's reign. One refers to "that excellent mind and high intellect." The other two, although going on to make some unflattering remarks about Louis's miserliness, agree that he was a man of high intelligence. In January 1466, in a letter to his master, the Milanese ambassador expresses his admiration for Louis's wisdom as he dictated to his chancellor the terms and conditions of the surrender of Rouen in Normandy. He says that, if the Duke of Milan had been there, "he would have taken him not only for a consummate jurist, but for one of those emperors who founded and established laws, to such an extent did His Majesty show extraordinary wisdom." Commynes describes him as "quite well educated," and one of the Milanese ambassadors reported that Louis could read Italian. He said that Louis read the Duke of Milan's letter word for word "as easily as a true Italian could have done."

Louis XI has been accused of excessive cruelty, particularly in novels. In this regard, twentieth-century writers, such as Lawrence Schoonover, have carried on the tradition of Sir Walter Scott and Victor Hugo. Before reaching any conclusions on the truth of these allegations, it is necessary to remember that the fifteenth century was a rather brutal and callous age. Most of Louis's alleged acts of cruelty were done for a purpose, such as making an example of a traitor. Jean Hardy was convicted of trying to poison the king in 1473. He was decapitated and quartered: His head was placed on a lance in Paris and the four parts of his body were sent to be publicly displayed in four large cities in opposite corners of France. Occasionally he kept important political prisoners in iron cages. However, this practice was not uncommon at the time and was chiefly to make sure that they did not escape. Louis made relatively little use of this procedure. In short, although accused of cruelty by some of his enemies in his own time, Louis was by no means the monster of Sir Walter Scott's *Quentin Durward*, and was probably not unusually cruel for his day.

Louis had a rather cynical and malicious sense of humor. When planning the capture of the treacherous Constable de Saint-Pol, he dictated a letter to him saying that he was busy with very important matters and could use a head such as his. In an aside to Commynes, and several others present, he said, "I do not intend for us to have the body, but I mean for us to have the head and for the body to remain behind." When describing the execution of certain envoys from Arras to Mary of Burgundy in 1477, he said that "there was one among them, Master Oudart de Bussy, to whom I had given a seigniory in the parlement; and, so that everyone could recognize his head clearly, I have had placed on it a fine fur-trimmed cap, and it presides over the market of Hesdin." Louis even extended this rather cruel sense of humor to his own daughter Jeanne. She was a cripple and not very likely to bear children. He virtually forced the Duke of Orleans to marry her with the deliberate plan of extinguishing this powerful noble house. He then wrote to the Grand Master of the Royal Household telling him about the marriage and commented, "It seems to me that the children they will have together will not cost them very much to raise." Sometimes one is surprised to find a pun in his rather formal official correspondence with his ministers. For example, when writing to the Grand Master Dammartin in June 1473 Louis refers to the Burgundian herald as *Trahyson d'or* (Golden Treachery) instead of *Toison d'or* (Golden Fleece).

Louis's religious views have sometimes been described as cynical and hypocritical. This is not really true. According to the standards of his day, Louis XI was a deeply religious man, in a slightly superstitious way. He attended Mass every day and spent much time in prayer and pilgrimage. He was a firm believer in the potency of the Cross of Saint Laud at Angers. Those who violated an oath sworn upon it were thought to die within a year. He used it several times in having political treaties sworn. He was a great believer in the efficacy of the relics of the saints. He gave many gifts to churches. He regarded the Virgin Mary as his particular protector and frequently attributed his successes to her intervention. He even did feudal homage to the Virgin for the town of Boulogne-sur-mer. His favorite sanctuary was that of Nôtre-Dame de Cléry near Orleans, and he heaped gifts upon it. His piety was evidently sincere. However, the more superstitious and self-interested side of his religious views are also apparent. He believed that God, the Virgin, and the saints intervened constantly in his affairs, and he saw miracles everywhere. He saw piety as a means to gain his ends in this world as well as to secure salvation. He sought to win heavenly support by the same means that he won backers on earth—through costly gifts and bribes. He even tried to win away his rivals' celestial patrons. He paid special devotion to various saints regarded as the patrons of King René of Anjou and the Duke of Burgundy.

Louis was a great believer in the power of money. He believed every man had his price, even the celestial beings, and worked assiduously to buy those who could be useful to him. According to Commynes, he did not become discouraged at being refused once by a man whom he was seeking to win, but continued making him promises and showering him with honors and money. For years, as we shall see, he pensioned the King of England and many of his royal officials to keep them from invading and joining the great lords who were in rebellion against him in France. Those who served him well were handsomely rewarded. He also spent a great deal on maintaining a large and powerful army. All of these expenses cost a lot of money, and he raised the tax known as the *taille* to an unprecedented level.

Although willing to spend huge sums on bribes, pensions, and the army, he was almost miserly in his personal expenses. The Milanese ambassador, writing to Duke Francesco Sforza in 1461, said that his parsimoniousness with regard to his household expenses was incredible. He speculated that Louis was either avaricious or saving up for some great enterprise and commented that he used to be open-handed when he was dauphin. He often gave out public offices, which cost him nothing. Another Milanese ambassador, writing in the same year, also commented on his miserliness.

Louis's favorite weapon was diplomacy. He loved intrigue and was skillful at entangling his adversaries. He played upon the character and personal weaknesses of his opponents, such as Charles the Bold, whom he had known for years in Burgundy. His mind was fertile in schemes and combinations. His diplomacy was secret, and sometimes he used a valet or a barber for a special task. Whenever possible, he preferred to conduct his own diplomacy, however. He had a persuasive, cordial, and familiar manner which made him very successful in personal diplomacy. He had the subtlety of the Italian diplomats and their love for trickery and complicated intrigues. One of the Milanese ambassadors said in this connection: "It seems as though he had always lived in Italy and been raised there."

Louis was a man of violent passion. Nervous and impatient, he concealed with difficulty his desires and hatreds. He talked too much, and he knew it. According to Commynes, Louis frequently said "I know well that my tongue has done me great harm." Sometimes too his love of complicated political schemes and combinations got him into serious difficulties. He was at his most masterful, however, in freeing himself from entanglements. Commynes describes him as shrewd in adversity and says "of all those I have ever known, the wisest for extricating himself from a bad step in time of adversity was King Louis XI." In time of peace and security, however, he unnecessarily irritated people and made enemies. He was a man who inspired fear. He was admired by those who had benefited from his generosity and detested by those who had suffered from his hatred.

Louis was personally brave. He had demonstrated his courage several times as a young man. In a letter of December 1465 the Milanese ambassador describes Louis, while reoccupying Normandy, riding in full armor, scorning trouble and fatigue, as was his habit. He says that his vigilance, ardor, and application were indescribable. The same ambassador, reporting to his master in January 1466, describes Louis at the siege of Pont-de-l'Arche in Normandy during the same campaign. He approached to the very foot of the walls and ordered the placement of his cannons, surveying all and supervising everything without giving a thought to danger or fatigue.

And yet, in spite of his personal courage, and despite the fact that he had a large and well-equipped army, Louis always preferred diplomacy to war. He was completely uninterested in military glory and was unwilling to risk all on the fortunes of battle. Battles were sometimes decided by luck, and Louis was unwilling to risk all his carefully laid plans on anything so uncertain. When a powerful league of nobles was besieging Paris in 1465, Commynes reports that Louis was unwilling to do battle, although his power was great, "but his intention. . .was to treat for peace and to disperse the company without putting his estate, which was so great and good as king of this great and obedient kingdom of France, in peril with something as uncertain as a battle."[4]

This then was the shrewd, crafty, hard-working, but somewhat unlovable man who became King of France in 1461. A capable man, he lost no time in showing that he intended to be a strong monarch, and to correct what he believed to be some of the mistakes of his father's reign. In this connection, Louis had two immediate and drastic steps in mind; the dismissal of many of his father's chief advisors and a reform in his father's method of collecting taxes. Both of these projects turned out badly.

Louis dealt harshly and rather vindictively at first with some of his father's chief advisors and officials. A reward was offered for the capture of Pierre de Brézé and Antoine de Chabannes. Brézé gave himself up, Chabannes was captured, and both were imprisoned. Many of Charles's lesser advisors were dismissed. Some of them were replaced with Louis's companions from Genappe, or even from his days in Dauphiné. For example, Jean de Lescun, bastard of Armagnac, became Marshal of France and First Chamberlain. Louis granted him the county of Comminges and wrote the Chamber of Accounts in March 1462, ordering them to cease their opposition to this gift. The following month, he wrote the Parlement ordering them to register it. In January 1465 the Milanese ambassador reported to the Duke of Milan that Jean de Lescun had the most influence with the king of anyone at the court.

In spite of the mass dismissals, Louis did retain quite a few of the former royal servants and others were soon reinstated. The Parlement was largely untouched. Some of Charles's leading advisors were retained, such as the Bureau brothers and Tristan Lermite. Also, Louis soon realized his mistake in arresting some of the most capable of his father's ministers. Antoine de Chabannes was freed and became one of the king's chief military commanders. Pierre de Brézé was also released.

Louis also skillfully chose a number of new men of ability to serve him. Quite a few of them were foreigners, such as the Scot William Mennypenny and the Italian Boffille de Juge. He also won over some of the best servants of his great vassals, such as Commynes from the Duke of Burgundy, who became one of his closest advisors.

Louis chose his servants from all classes, but preferred the lesser nobility and the middle class. Some of them were men of shady background, such as Ambroise de Cambrai, who had forged a papal bull authorizing the incestuous Count of Armagnac to marry his own sister. Olivier le Mauvais, the king's barber, became one of Louis's chief royal servants and acquired a sinister reputation. He acted as royal spy, and enriched himself by extortion and bribery. He is even thought to have arranged the death of one or two of Louis's enemies.

The king required absolute obedience and ability. He was pitiless to traitors or incompetent men. It was the scaffold or prison for those who served him badly; rich rewards, in the form of lands, pensions, and profitable marriages, for those who served him well.

By 1464, Jean Bourré, a middle-class lawyer, had become one of Louis's chief officials. He signed many royal letters, and frequently served as an ambassador. Pierre Doriole, skilled financial administrator, was General of Finances. Pierre de Morvillier was Chancellor. Jean de Montauban was Admiral of France, and Jean de Lescun was still Marshal of France.

It is interesting to note that all these royal officials did as they were told and Louis dominated them all. What a contrast to the reign of Charles VII, who was nicknamed Charles the Well-Served! Most historians believe that the sweeping and valuable reforms carried out during the latter years of Charles's reign were more the work of his capable advisors than of the king himself. Now Louis XI would govern personally, and his ministers, beyond giving such advice as was requested, would merely serve.

Louis's household servants were almost exactly the same in number and duties as those of his father. He issued careful instructions regarding the food for the royal court. There must be absolutely no waste. He did insist on excellent wines, however.

Louis had six legitimate children, of whom three survived. The first two who lived were girls, Anne and Jeanne. Finally, in June 1470, the queen bore him the longed-for son and heir, Charles. He considered all his children instruments of his policies. We have already seen the callous manner in which he married the crippled Jeanne to the Duke of Orleans to extinguish that powerful family. He arranged the marriage of Anne to Pierre de Beaujeu, brother of the Duke of Bourbon, for political reasons. She was an intelligent woman who became regent after Louis's death. The education and treatment of his youngest child, the future Charles VIII, will be discussed later.

Louis's first plan of dismissing his father's chief advisors had proved unsuccessful, and he had recalled most of them. At the same time, he had promptly attempted his second intended reform regarding taxation. There was wide hope among the populace for tax reductions. Louis promptly undertook radical financial reforms. In provinces where there were provincial estates, such as Normandy, Languedoc, and Dauphiné, he replaced the old *tailles* and *aides* by a single tax that would yield an equal amount, but would be levied as the estates desired and collected by officials they named. In the *généralité* of Outre-Seine-et-Yonne he abolished *aides* in the country, and *tailles* in the towns. The attempted reform was a complete failure, however. Louis found himself with insufficient revenues and, in 1464, reverted to the system of his father without decreasing taxes at all.[5]

During the first four years of his reign, Louis traveled almost constantly. At this time, France did not have a fixed capital in the modern sense. It was, more or less, wherever the king chose to reside. Louis XI preferred to live in Touraine. He traveled most of the summer but settled down in the winter at Amboise, or Tours, or Montils, a nearby hunting lodge used by his father. He finally built a pleasant, comfortable, but strongly fortified castle at Plessis-les-Tours just outside Tours, and lived in it for most of the remainder of his life. Incidentally, most French kings from Charles VII down to the end of the sixteenth century lived in the Loire Valley rather than in Paris.

Even while traveling he was constantly at work organizing and administering the kingdom. In Guyenne, in 1461, Louis confirmed the privileges of many towns. He established a Parlement at Bordeaux. Bayonne was freed from all taxes, inasmuch as it had been ruined by war and plague. Louis established two fairs there to attract merchants. In August 1462 the king went on a pilgrimage to Mont Saint-Michel in Normandy. He visited Rouen and reinstalled Pierre de Brézé as Grand Seneschal of Normandy. Early in 1463 he visited Languedoc. He confirmed the privileges of many towns and ecclesiastical chapters and established fairs. He was in Paris in August 1463 to raise money for the repurchase of the towns of the Somme from Burgundy. In the summer of 1464, he visited Normandy and Picardy.

Early in his reign Louis XI made many enemies. In February 1462 the Milanese ambassador wrote to Francesco Sforza, Duke of Milan, saying that Louis was becoming much hated. He had

dismissed many of his father's officials, at least temporarily. He
even abolished the *Cour des Aides* (a financial branch of the
government) briefly from 1462-64. He treated the clergy
harshly. All ecclesiastics were forced to make a declaration of all
of their goods under the threat of confiscation for failure to do
so. He forced all those in Languedoc who held nonnoble land
(terres roturières) to pay the *taille* for the first time. He dealt
rudely with the University of Paris. He particularly antagonized
the nobles. Many of them were deprived of their pensions. He
forced them to stop wearing magnificent costumes at court. They
undoubtedly missed the gay court life of the later years of
Charles VII. They were even forbidden to hunt without royal
permission, and hunting was one of their favorite pastimes. One
Norman noble had his ear cut off for disobeying this law. Louis
freed or welcomed back treacherous nobles imprisoned or
expelled by Charles VII, such as the Duke of Alençon and Jean,
Count of Armagnac, both of whom would cause him much
trouble in later years. He antagonized some of the most powerful
nobles in the land, such as Dunois, Gaston de Foix, and the Duke
of Bourbon, from whom he took away the government of
Guyenne.

Louis was particularly antagonistic to Francis II, Duke of
Brittany, whose independence exasperated him. Francis was
second only to the Duke of Burgundy in his autonomy and
freedom from royal control. The activities of the royal officials
against the judicial, financial, and ecclesiastical independence of
Brittany were bound to provoke trouble. The main point of
conflict occurred over a dispute between the king and the duke
as to which of the two had the right to appoint men to high
ecclesiastical positions in Brittany. When vacancies occurred,
Louis appointed favorites as Bishop of Nantes and Abbot of
Redon. Francis promptly dismissed them in September 1462.
Francis finally agreed to arbitration by Charles of Anjou, Count
of Maine. During the dispute, incidentally, Louis accused Francis
of having entered into negotiations with the King of England,
thus conspiring against the French monarchy. Finally, in October
1464, the Count of Maine, under royal influence and threats,
naturally handed down his decision with regard to the right of
appointment to ecclesiastical offices in favor of Louis. Then, in
December 1464, the king persuaded an assembly at Tours of
princes of the blood and great nobles to support this verdict.

Louis's next step was the repurchase of several rich towns of the Somme Valley ceded to the Duke of Burgundy as part of the important Treaty of Arras of 1435. By this treaty the powerful duke had switched from the English to the French side, and this was one of the turning points of the Hundred Years' War. It was stated in the treaty that the towns could be repurchased by the French king for a large stipulated sum. At the time, it had seemed unlikely that the King of France would ever be able to afford such a transaction.

Louis had evidently resolved from the first to regain these towns. In a letter of October 1463 to the people of Amiens he said: "Since our recent advent to the crown, we have always had the desire and wish to have again and repurchase our towns and seigneuries of Picardy, engaged to our very dear and beloved uncle, the Duke of Burgundy, by the treaty and agreement made at Arras." France had recovered, to some extent, from the devastation of the Hundred Years' War, and Louis, with his wide taxing powers, felt that he could raise the stipulated 400,000 *écus.* The shrewd monarch was also aware of the great advantages, both economic and political, to be gained. The taxes that could be collected from this rich region would eventually reimburse him for the high purchase price. From the political point of view, Louis's ultimate objective was to beat down the powerful feudal nobles and make the monarchy supreme in France. Burgundy was obviously the strongest of the semiindependent fiefs, and the Somme River towns would provide a strategic line of defense against this inevitable rival.

As usual, Louis greased the wheels of diplomacy with gold. He bribed the powerful lords of Croy in Burgundy, who had great influence with Philip the Good. They persuaded the aging duke to agree to the sale. Had the young, ambitious, Charles the Bold, the next duke, been in control of the Burgundian state, he would doubtless have raised many difficulties.

Louis only had half of the required 400,000 *ecus.* He raised the remainder, in 1463, by forced loans, impositions on towns and monasteries, special taxes, and grants from provincial estates. The town of Tournai only sent 20,000 *écus* instead of the requested 30,000 but, in spite of such difficulties, Louis eventually raised the money and the towns were returned to him in September and October 1463.

Louis then went to meet Philip the Good at Hesdin in

Burgundian territory. As he and the duke rode through the town
the contrast between their appearance was striking. Philip, as
usual, was magnificently clad, while Louis, as usual, was simply
dressed. According to the Burgundian chronicler Chastellain, the
people asked each other:

Where is the king? Which one is he? *Benédicité*! Is that man a King of
France, the greatest king in the world? He looks more like a valet than
a knight. His horse and all his clothing are not worth twenty francs. Our
duke, our prince is a sunlike man and the image of a man of importance.

After heaping insincere compliments upon Duke Philip, Louis
returned home. The following summer he visited Amiens, one of
the richest of the repurchased towns. Here he received an
enthusiastic reception. Turning to the Milanese ambassador, who
accompanied him, he remarked, "Doesn't it seem to you that this
town alone is worth more than the 400,000 *écus* that I paid to the
Duke of Burgundy?"[6]

During the first three or four years of his reign the impatient
Louis XI had made some grave mistakes, such as his dismissal of
many of his father's advisors and his reckless new policy with
regard to taxation. He had the good sense to realize before long
that he had been unwise, and ended up by recalling most of his
father's ministers and going back to the previous system of
taxation. Actually then, there was much more continuity
between the reign of Louis XI and the latter years of the reign of
Charles VII than is sometimes realized.

In yet another sense there was some continuity between the
two reigns. Charles had spent his life fighting England. The war
had only been over for a few years when Louis ascended the
throne and he was faced with the constant threat of a renewed
English invasion. Throughout his reign, he was forced to keep a
watchful eye on the island kingdom across the Channel.

England had been France's most dangerous and persistent
enemy for several centuries. The Hundred Years' War had ended
without any formal treaty, and the Kings of England had not
renounced their claims to their lost lands in France. Moreover,
they continued to use the provocative title of King of France, and
still retained the town of Calais on French soil. Should the
powerful feudal lords in France whom Louis had antagonized
rebel against him there was a serious danger of the English
joining them.

The recovery of Calais and the weakening of England by taking advantage of the Wars of the Roses were part of Louis's policy during the opening years of his reign. In England, the Wars of the Roses had broken out in 1455 between the Yorkists and the Lancastrians. The insane king, Henry VI, was a Lancastrian. Next in line for the throne, after Henry's young son, was the Duke of York. The war was between their respective followers.

Charles VII, in the closing years of his reign, had supported Margaret of Anjou, daughter of King René, who was married to Henry VI. Margaret virtually controlled the English government during the king's periods of insanity. Louis, as dauphin, had supported the Yorkists, as did Philip of Burgundy.

When Louis became king, he continued his good relations with the Yorkists. He received the Lancastrian ambassador, however, leaving the situation open. Louis had no intention of allowing Philip the Good to act as mediator. He resolved to play this role himself. Therefore, in late 1461, he sent an ambassador to the Yorkist Edward IV, who had just seized the throne, offering to act as mediator to help arrive at an amicable solution of the Yorkist-Lancastrian struggle. His efforts were unsuccessful. Louis sought peace with England, not only for political reasons, but also in the hope of reviving Anglo-French commerce to the detriment of Anglo-Flemish trade.

In May 1462, Margaret of Anjou arrived in France to seek help against Edward IV. She and her husband had fled to Scotland when they had been overthrown. Louis met her personally at Chinon. The result was the Treaty of Chinon whereby Louis promised Margaret 20,000 *livres tournois*. For repayment, she pledged Calais, under certain conditions. This was followed by the Truce of Tours of June 1462, to last for 100 years, in the name of King Henry VI. Both kings agreed to help each other against all rebels. Of course, this treaty would remain a dead letter unless the Lancastrians were in power. Louis XI was now, for the first time, firmly allied with the Lancastrians against the Yorkists.[7]

These agreements seemed much more favorable to Henry VI than to Louis XI. Henry did not even abandon his claim to the French crown. Louis was primarily attempting to immobilize Edward while he seized Calais. As Calais was surrounded by Burgundian lands, Louis could not advance upon it without the consent of Philip the Good. Louis planned a military attack against England accompanied by a land and sea attack on Calais. Philip the Good refused to cooperate, however, because of his valuable trade relations with England.

Meanwhile, Edward IV, under all these provocations, was preparing an invasion. The English plundered the islands of Poitou in August and September 1462, but accomplished nothing of importance. The French retaliated with an invasion of England, under the command of Pierre de Brézé, from October 1462 to January 1463. Louis failed to give the invasion sufficient support, and it was unsuccessful. Louis then abandoned the idea of capturing Calais.

During the next two years, Louis sought to improve his relations with Edward IV. The immediate objective of his diplomacy was now the repurchase of the Somme towns, from the Duke of Burgundy. As Philip the Good still supported Edward, and as the latter seemed to be quite firmly ensconced on the English throne, Louis thought it advisable to come to terms with the Yorkist king. Louis, therefore, decided to allow Philip to act as mediator between France and England and stated his willingness to participate in conferences that Philip was planning to hold at Saint-Omer in June. Edward IV, on the advice of the most influential noble in England, Warwick the Kingmaker, agreed to send delegates. Louis was now about to conclude a pact, not with Lancaster, but with York. The efforts of Margaret of Anjou to participate in the conference were unavailing.

At a series of meetings at Saint-Omer and Hesdin in the fall of 1463, Louis met with both Philip the Good and English ambassadors. He succeeded in negotiating the repurchase of the Somme towns from Burgundy and in concluding a one-year truce with England. Louis and Edward promised not to aid each other's enemies. Louis specifically promised not to help Henry VI or Margaret of Anjou. The Milanese ambassador, reporting home in April 1464, said that Louis wanted peace with England more than anything else. He had achieved it, for the moment, at the expense of switching his support from the Lancastrian to the Yorkist cause.[8]

Plans had been made for another conference at Saint-Omer in the middle of 1464. In the meantime, Louis sought to strengthen his friendship with England through a marriage between his sister-in-law, Bonne of Savoy, and Edward IV. He arranged for

Bonne to come to France, in the summer of 1464, planning to present her to Warwick at the coming conference at Saint-Omer. The conference was postponed, however, as Warwick was fighting the Lancastrians in northern England.

The rescheduled conference never took place. Edward suddenly announced, in September that he was not free to consider marriage with Bonne as he had secretly married Elizabeth Grey in May. Warwick, who had virtually guided royal policy and had not been informed of the royal marriage, was astounded. Louis was disappointed as the conference, from which he had expected significant gains, was cancelled. This incident virtually marked the liberation of Edward IV from the influence of Warwick, especially seeing the new queen was an enemy of his family. By the fall of 1464, events were tending to separate Louis from Edward IV.[9]

During these same years in France, although he had rectified his mistakes regarding his advisors and his finances, Louis had made one grave error that he had not corrected. He had aroused the enmity of nearly all the powerful nobles of France, some of whom could have been of help to him in his impending struggle with his strongest and most dangerous vassal, the Duke of Burgundy. The latter was probably the richest and most powerful man in western Europe. In addition to Burgundy in France, the dukes, in the late fourteenth and fifteenth centuries, had accumulated, chiefly by marriage, large blocks of land in the areas that in modern times would correspond roughly to Holland, Belgium, and Luxemburg. These territories were nominally fiefs of the crumbling Holy Roman Empire, but the weak emperors of the period exerted virtually no authority there. The Low Countries were extremely rich due to a thriving textile industry, plentiful trade, and considerable agriculture. They provided the Duke of Burgundy with an income exceeding that of the King of France. If Louis XI was to be supreme in France, the overly mighty Duke of Burgundy must be weakened and his French fiefs brought under royal control. The fact that Philip the Good had sheltered Louis, protected him from his father, and done so much for him had no effect on the king's political plans. Gratitude was not one of his virtues, unless he saw future profit in it.

It should be noted, however, that the destruction of Burgundian power was a long-term plan in the mind of the French King.

During the early years of Louis's reign, the Burgundian alliance was an essential part of his diplomatic plans. Louis's political ambitions included the annexation of the Duchy of Savoy to France. To achieve this, he needed alliances, notably with Savoy's powerful neighbors, Milan and Burgundy. Hence his care to avoid an open break with Philip the Good and his signature of the Treaty of Abbéville, in late 1463, with the Duke of Milan. His negotiations and alliance with the Swiss in 1463–64 were in the same connection, and not intended as an immediate threat to Burgundy.

Strangely enough, the implementation of these French plans depended to a large extent on Burgundian help. The Marshal of Burgundy, Thibaud de Neuchâtel, was mainly responsible for the French alliances with Milan and the Swiss. Moreover, Duke Philip himself worked on Louis's behalf through much of 1463, with no permanent success, though, to bring about a rapprochement and an alliance between Louis and Burgundy's ally Edward IV of England.

Thus, Burgundy appeared, in the early years of Louis's reign, as an instrument of French foreign policy, while Philip the Good seemed to do all in his power to further the interests of France, even to the extent of ceding the important Somme towns. Philip's actions may have been due in part to his confidence in French intentions, especially his misplaced faith in Louis's friendship, gratitude, and integrity. Certainly his policy was also due in part to the advice of lifelong associates like Antoine, Lord of Croy, and Thibaud de Neuchâtel, who were in Louis's pay.

Philip of Burgundy's attitude toward France in the early years of the reign of Louis XI was also influenced by the fact that, for many years, he had sincerely desired to take part in a crusade against the Turks. As he grew older, this ambition was transferred into a veritable obsession. In the autumn of 1463 and the winter of 1463–64, the sixty-seven-year-old duke came nearer than ever before to setting out on a crusade. Certainly one of his chief reasons for restoring the Somme towns to Louis XI was to raise money for the project. On Christmas Day 1463, when the Milanese ambassador asked Louis if he thought Philip would go, the king replied in the affirmative.

Philip the Good and his son Charles were on bad terms at the moment, and it was rumored that the lord of Croy would act as regent of the Burgundian territories while Philip went on the crusade. But in February 1464 the quarrel was settled by the Estates General of the Burgundian provinces, and the lord of Croy, who was in Louis's pay, went immediately to France to tell the French king of this new development. Louis, fearful of what the warlike and ambitious Charles might do if his father appointed him regent, arranged for a personal meeting with Philip at Lille on February 23, 1464, to try to persuade him to delay his departure.

Louis's arguments at this meeting are interesting. He said that he relied on Philip to negotiate an Anglo-French peace. If war should break out with England, Philip's help, as Louis's most powerful vassal, would be essential. Moreover, he argued that it would not be honorable to help the "Emperor of Greece" to recover lands from the Turks while leaving France open to attack by the English who, Louis argued, had done more harm than the Turks in the lands they had conquered. Then he indicated his mistrust of Philip's allies, the Venetians. He said that they were only interested in capturing Morea in Greece for themselves and would then make a separate peace with the Turks. If Philip would wait until peace was made with England, Louis promised him a contingent of 10,000 French troops.

Louis succeeded in persuading Philip not to go on the Crusade at this time. How effective the French king's arguments were is uncertain. In any case, Philip felt too old, was short of money, and was worried about leaving his son Charles in charge of his lands. He decided to present his excuses to Pope Pius II, and to send an expedition under his bastard son Antoine instead. Antoine set sail in May 1464, but his expedition was delayed in Marseilles by the news of the death of Pope Pius II and was then canceled on the advice of Antoine, lord of Croy, and others.

There was only one notable exception to Louis's policy of maintaining good relations with Philip the Good during the early years of his reign. As early as 1461, Louis returned to Charles VII's policy of interference in Liège in the Low Countries, which was ruled independently by a prince-bishop, who was a nephew of the Duke of Burgundy. Liège, and other towns in the area, were important industrial centers, and many of them had fallen under the control of turbulent popular assemblies. The prince-bishop had lost most of his authority during the Great Schism (1378–1417) when Europe had been divided between two, and later among three, claimants to the papal throne. After the

Schism he regained some of his lost power with Burgundian
assistance. The popular assemblies had then turned to Charles
VII for help against their ruler. Charles had given them some
assistance and, in 1461, Louis XI continued this policy by
promising them support against the prince-bishop. It became his
consistent practice to stir up trouble in Liège against the
Burgundian supported prince-bishop. The Milanese ambassador
wrote to his duke in October 1464 that the people of Liège had
attacked several castles belonging to the Duke of Burgundy and
had revolted against their prince-bishop. The duke accused the
French king of having fomented these disturbances. The
ambassador added that relations between Louis and the Duke of
Burgundy were becoming strained.

The previous month, the same ambassador had written
describing the efforts of the Duke of Brittany to stir up
opposition against Louis. He believed that the duke had
organized a league against the king consisting of Charles, Count
of Charolais, the Duke of Orleans, the Duke of Bourbon, the
Count of Armagnac, and many others. He thought that the
league was defensive, however, and would not dare attack the
king. Nevertheless, he passed on Louis's request for some troops
from the Duke of Milan, whom Louis would pay, in case of war
against the great lords. Louis had always maintained a close
alliance with Francesco Sforza, Duke of Milan, whom he admired
greatly. The ambassador advised the duke to agree to Louis's
request as he believed that no other French king could be more
favorable to Milan. As late as October 1464 the Milanese
ambassador still did not believe that the great nobles would dare
to attack the king.[10]

Louis had antagonized so many powerful men in France by this
time that civil war was imminent. Edward IV of England was
watching the growing baronial unrest in France closely. If a
major uprising occurred against the French king, there was grave
danger that he might invade and support the rebels. Although
Philip the Good was still alive, he was old and sick, and his son,
Charles, Count of Charolais, was playing an increasing role in the
government of Burgundy. With Louis and Charolais (later to be
known as Charles the Bold), a new bitterness entered the rivalry
between France and Burgundy. Louis and Philip had personally
esteemed each other, but Louis and Charles did not.

Louis, of course, knew many of Charles's weaknesses from the days when they had hunted together at the Burgundian court. Charles was twenty-seven in 1461, making him eleven years younger than Louis. He was short, robust, and agile. He had clear blue eyes, a swarthy complexion, a dark beard, thick, black, curly hair, and a broad forehead. He was strong, well-educated, pious, sincere, and hard-working. He was a faithful husband and an abstemious drinker, always mixing water with his wine. His quiet, melancholy eyes were usually on the ground. He was a man of fixed ideals, stiff and arrogant. His ambition was limitless. Indeed, he even dreamed of joining up all his territories by the acquisition of Alsace and Lorraine and then having himself proclaimed king by the Holy Roman Emperor. This would roughly revive the old kingdom of Lotharingia created when the Carolingian empire was divided between Charlemagne's three grandsons. He spent his life hurling himself rashly into almost impossible projects such as this. Unlike Louis XI, he loved military glory. He was cruel and treacherous, quick-tempered and brutal. He lacked a cool head in his diplomacy. In fact, he was neither a good statesman nor a good general. Setbacks only irritated his great pride. Commynes commented on his boundless ambition and said that half of Europe would not have satisfied him. He believed that Charles attempted so many great projects that a lifetime was insufficient for them. Moreover, they were almost all overly ambitious. Commynes, who had served Charles before switching masters and joining Louis, concluded that he was bold enough for any undertaking, but lacked sufficient good sense to carry it out. Louis himself had a low opinion of Charles, and described him to the Milanese ambassador as a man of little sense, haughty, violent, and, in fact, just like a beast. The ambassador reported that Louis even imitated certain gestures of Charles which were those of a madman.[11]

Louis was destined to become deeply involved, for the next thirteen years, in a bitter struggle for power with Charles the Bold, frequently supported by other disaffected nobles. The striking difference in character of the two rivals is interesting and was destined to influence the outcome of the conflict.

CHAPTER 4

Baronial Reaction, 1464–1470

ONE of the chief characteristics of medieval feudalism was that the central authority broke down and royal rights of government were usurped by the barons in their own lands. This happened in France around the time of the break-up of the Carolingian Empire in the ninth century. French kings in the tenth and eleventh centuries had virtually no real power. Then, gradually, more powerful monarchs began to strengthen royal authority at the expense of the barons. Philip II and Philip IV made considerable progress. Whenever the feudal barons saw a suitable opportunity, or were pushed too far, they rebelled against the king trying to regain their declining authority. This was the general trend in French history down to the mid-seventeenth century when royal absolutism finally triumphed. Similar struggles between king and nobles occurred throughout most of western Europe, although the results and the timing were not always the same as in France.

A good example of these feudal uprisings was the rebellion of the French nobles against Charles VII in the *Praguerie* of 1440. They had been pushed too far by the rapid growth of royal authority in the previous year or two. Ironically, they chose King Charles's heir, the future Louis XI, as their nominal leader. Now he himself was to be faced by a similar uprising.

The previous chapter described how Louis had made enemies of nearly all of the great nobles in the realm, by 1464, by his unremitting attempts to assert his royal authority over them. The Milanese ambassadors had reported a conspiracy, but they did not believe that the nobles would dare to attack the powerful monarch.

They underestimated the determination of the barons, however. As early as December 1464, a large assembly was held of supporters of the conspiracy in Nôtre-Dame Cathedral in Paris

without the king's knowledge. By the beginning of 1465, a
dangerous coalition was forming. Louis XI had shown little
respect for the privileges of nobles and clergy. His attempts to
strengthen the royal government clashed with the ambitions of
the great feudatories. He had dealt harshly with the Duke of
Brittany over the Breton bishoprics. The duke then refused to
swear liege homage and negotiated with the Count of Charolais
and with England. Although the assembly of magnates at Tours
supported Louis in his dispute against the Duke of Brittany, and
although King René, Duke of Anjou, speaking on behalf of all the
nobles, pledged obedience to the king, the plans for the rebellion
continued.

Beside earning the hostility of the Duke of Brittany, Louis had
antagonized the House of Anjou by not giving them any
significant support in their claims to Sicily and Naples. Similarly,
the Duke of Orleans had a claim to Milan, and counted on royal
backing. It was not forthcoming. The editor of the valuable
Dépêches des ambassadeurs milanais considered this failure of
Louis to act in Italy to support the Houses of Orleans and Anjou
one of the chief causes of the forthcoming rebellion. He
emphasized particularly Louis's abandonment of the Angevin
cause. King René was too old and lethargic to act, but his
vigorous son, John of Calabria, played a leading role in the
conspiracy.

Although the barons who participated in the revolt of 1465
were each seeking exclusively their own ends, they had the
political wisdom to pose as champions of the people against royal
oppression. Thus they called themselves the League of the
Public Weal. They claimed to seek a remedy to the evils of a
tyrannical government. They complained of the king's infringe-
ments on the rights of nobles and clergy and of his heavy taxes on
the poor. To help the overburdened lower classes, and win their
support, they called for the summoning of the Estates General, a
decrease in taxation, and the suppression of the *aides*. Their
secret plans apparently called for the king's brother, Charles,
Duke of Berry, to become regent, and the Dukes of Berry,
Bourbon, Brittany, and the Count of Charolais to conduct the
reforms they sought and to control the army. They would
summon the Estates General, which they expected to control, as
a gesture to win support. They hoped then to control finances,
the granting of public offices, and the person of the king.

Just as in 1440, the rebels chose the heir to the throne as their nominal leader. In fact, in many ways, the whole movement was a repetition of the *Praguerie* of that year. This time the heir to the throne was the king's brother, Charles of France, Duke of Berry. Louis had no sons yet, and it had been established for many years that a woman could not inherit the throne of France. This ruled out Louis's daughters.

Charles, Duke of Berry, was eighteen years old, weak, homely, unintelligent, effeminate, and vain. He was also politically inexperienced, and did not play a preponderant role in the league. He was a figure-head leader and became a tool in the hands of the king's enemies.

The principal members of the league were the Duke of Alençon; the veteran commander Dunois; Antoine de Chabannes (all of whom had participated in the *Praguerie* of 1440); Charles the Bold, Count of Charolais; the Count of St.-Pol; the Duke of Brittany; Charles II of Albret; John, Duke of Lorraine and Calabria (the most active member of the House of Anjou); and Jacques d'Armagnac, Duke of Nemours. According to one contemporary chronicler, the army of the league contained twenty-one great lords and 51,000 warriors. The only great noble to support Louis was Gaston of Foix. The Count of Nevers, King René, and his brother, Charles, Count of Maine, rode the fence. Of these latter three, the Count of Maine seems to have favored the league, although he did not completely break with the king.

The lesser nobility were not anxious to forward the designs of the great magnates. Many of them sided with the king or remained neutral. Some fought rather reluctantly for the league. As for the clergy, a few bishops of Normandy and central France supported the league, but the majority remained uncommitted. The royal officials and the upper bourgeoisie generally refused to commit themselves. The latter were chiefly concerned about preventing an extension of the war, which would have disrupted business. The lower classes, especially in Paris, were openly hostile to the league. They were unimpressed and unconvinced by the great lords' manifestations of concern with the lot of the people.

The King of England was biding his time to see how events would turn out. He was possibly deterred from supporting the rebellion by the continuing pro-Lancastrian policy of Charolais.

Louis recruited mercenaries in Savoy. Galeazzo Sforza, son of his
old ally the Duke of Milan, also brought troops to his aid. In May
1465, Louis secured the alliance of Liège. He also had the
tremendous advantage of a well-trained, well-equipped permanent army, which his opponents lacked.[1]

The events leading up to the entry of Charles the Bold into this
war merit special examination. In the first place, it marked a
complete reversal of recent Franco-Burgundian relations which,
as we have seen, had been fairly cordial since the accession of
Louis XI. In the second place, this reversal proved to be long-
term, and the fighting between Louis XI and Charles the Bold in
the War of the League of the Public Weal was destined to be
merely the first round in a long and bitter struggle between
them.

A rapid deterioration in relations between France and
Burgundy in the second half of 1464 was closely linked to the rise
at the Burgundian court of Charles, Count of Charolais. The
affair of the bastard of Rubempré was an important factor in
these events. In September 1464 Louis XI sent the bastard
brother of the lord of Rubempré into Dutch waters with an
armed galley. The purpose was to arrest an emissary of the Duke
of Brittany, Jean de Rouville. The king had learnt from spies that
Rouville was instructed to arrange an alliance between Brittany
and England and then cross to Holland to inform Charles the
Bold and perhaps involve him in a plot against France. Louis
hoped to intercept Rouville on his way back from England to
learn the truth about these schemes of the Duke of Brittany and,
at the same time, to prevent him from reaching Charles to spread
the plot. The bastard was arrested after being found in
Gorinchem in Holland, where Charles was staying, making
enquiries about Charles's health and habits. Charles found that
he was under orders from Louis. The rumor rapidly spread that
he had been sent to arrest Charles. These rumors embarrassed
Louis XI. He sent ambassadors to the Burgundian court to explain
the bastard's presence at Gorinchem, denying any plot on his
part against Charles.

It seems that Charles exploited the Rubempré incident to
arouse the fears of his father, Philip the Good, and from then on
Charles enjoyed increasing influence with his father. This ended
a period of open dissension between them. This domestic
revolution at the Burgundian court brought about a diplomatic

change. From now on, Burgundian policy was no longer inspired by the powerful, pro-French Croy family but increasingly by Charles, and it became increasingly hostile to Louis XI.

It has recently been proven that Philip did not hand over all powers to his son in the spring of 1465, as some have maintained. The state continued to be ruled by Philip, assisted by his council, until his death. However, Charles began to play a vital part in the formulation of foreign policy while, in previous years, he had been virtually excluded from major decisions. He was now permitted to carry out his policy towards France, evidently aimed at regaining the Somme towns. He began to intrigue with French princes, signing a treaty in December 1464 with John of Anjou, Duke of Calabria.

Quite apart from his contacts in France, Charles established a series of personal contacts with other powers. Between September 1464 and June 1465, he signed agreements or treaties with the Duke of Cleves, the Duke of Bavaria, and Frederick, the Elector Palatine. In October 1466 Edward IV of England made a declaration of friendship with Charles, and promised not to assist any of his enemies against him. Some of these alliances were confirmed and reinforced by Duke Philip.

Philip placed Charles in command of military operations in France in April 1465 by appointing him lieutenant-general. The previous month, he had rid himself of his chief opponents at the Burgundian court, the Croy family, by seizing all of their strongholds while his father was seriously ill. They fled, abandoning their last vestige of power in the state. Charles's influence was now very strong.

The motives which impelled Charles to persuade his father to respond to the Duke of Berry's appeal for military help against the King of France were not sympathy with the French princes or personal dislike of Louis XI. It was his determination to seize the first opportunity of recovering the territories, forming part of his inheritance, of which he believed he had been unjustly deprived. These were Péronne, Roye, and Montdidier, which Philip the Good had ceded to Jean, Count of Étampes and Nevers, and the Somme towns, ceded to Burgundy in 1435 but repurchased by Louis XI in 1463.[2]

The signal for the uprising was given when Charles, Duke of Berry, suddenly fled from the royal court to Brittany in March 1465. Louis then wrote a series of letters telling of Charles's

flight and seeking support. Such letters were sent to the Duke of
Bourbon—instructing him to come immediately with 100 *lances*[3]
of troops, whom Louis would pay—the Duke of Burgundy, and
the towns of Amiens, Lyons, Auxerre, St. Quentin, and Abbéville.
A second letter to Lyons told them that he was assembling troops
in Dauphiné to fight against the Duke of Bourbon, and he
ordered the people of the town to be prepared to help.

The lack of coordination among the rebel leaders was evident
right from the start. The Duke of Bourbon started hostilities in
central France in March 1465 without waiting for his allies.
Louis, with a splendid royal army, moved promptly against him.
The Milanese ambassador, writing home in May, stressed the
strength of the royal army, describing it as large, well-equipped,
and with the finest artillery he had ever seen. In their letters
home in the spring of 1465, the Milanese ambassadors
emphasized the impecuniousness of the king's enemies and the
power of the king, and predicted a royal victory. They stressed
particularly the financial weakness of King René, the Duke of
Calabria, the Duke of Nemours, the Count of Armagnac, and
Charles d'Albret. They believed that these magnates were all
unable to support the expenses of a long campaign now that the
king had cut off their pensions.

Louis sought the support of the towns, justifying his actions
and making fun of the claims of the princes to be concerned with
the people. He offered amnesty to all if they would abandon his
brother's cause within a month. On April 10, he wrote to the
Royal Chancellor announcing the good news that the towns of
Picardy had pledged their loyalty to him and that King René of
Anjou had just swung his support behind him. In fact, King René
continued to play a cautious game and offered little real
assistance. Louis informed the chancellor that he already had
1,000 *lances* of ordonnance with him, and expected more. He had
sent an advance guard into Berry and would follow up with the
main royal army. He closed by informing the chancellor that
King René, acting as the king's representative, had met with the
veteran commander Dunois and the Dukes of Berry and Brittany
near Angers to try to negotiate a peace settlement.

In late April Charles the Bold formally announced his
impending campaign in France. Throughout May, he assembled a
large army and seized three of the Somme towns. Soon after the
middle of May Charles set out from Hainault with his main army.

Charles appeared in no hurry to march on Paris. His campaign seemed at first to be directed against the Count of Nevers, not France. In June he isolated Péronne and captured Nesle, Roye, and Montdidier from the count. He still made no move on Paris. He even tried to initiate negotiations with the Chancellor of France, and made several efforts to persuade the citizens of Amiens to declare for him. The townsmen sent his letters to the king. After two weeks' inactivity near Roye, Charles finally set out for St. Denis, not far from Paris, where the confederates had agreed to assemble. By July 5, his army had reached St. Denis.

Meanwhile, Louis was campaigning vigorously. His powerful army quickly subdued Berry and Bourbonnais. He made a truce with the Duke of Bourbon on June 30.

Louis's leadership and courage during this campaign in Berry and Bourbonnais were praised highly by the Milanese ambassador. He described how the king personally directed the march of his men as if he were a simple captain. At the siege of Hérisson, for example, the king, "who understood the matter very well," criticized the position of several badly placed pieces of artillery. He seemed to be indefatigable.

While the king was campaigning in Bourbonnais, the Marshal of France, Joachim Rouault, entered Paris with troops to help defend it against the Burgundians. The people of Paris were divided in their loyalties and, although probably the majority supported the king, Rouault's action was a wise precaution.

Charles the Bold attacked Paris unsuccessfully on July 7 and July 8. He then crossed the Seine. He announced his plans in a letter to his father dated July 14, 1465. The Duke of Berry had written him stating that he was near Chartres with the Duke of Brittany, Dunois, and a large army. He had urged Charles to join them so they could make a common front against the king, who was marching back from Bourbonnais. Charles wrote that he would do so.

As Louis hurried back from Bourbonnais toward Paris, in July, the Milanese ambassador reported that the king was extremely worried about the dangerous coalition in the field against him. In fact, the ambassador feared that Louis was about to seek peace and give in to nearly all the demands of the great barons.

The king knew that the rebels' plan was for the Dukes of Brittany and Berry to join the Burgundians near Paris. This

would have constituted a formidable fighting force that might
have overwhelmed him.

Charles advanced on July 15 to meet his allies. He reached the
village of Montlhéry only to discover that he was about to meet
the royal army head on while the Dukes of Brittany and Berry
had not arrived with their forces.

Louis took counsel and, in spite of much advice to the contrary,
pushed on as rapidly as possible in order to engage the waiting
Burgundians before their allies could join them. The army of the
Duke of Brittany probably could have arrived in time, but
delayed at Châteaudun, perhaps not wanting Charolais to win
too easy a victory. The rivalry between the allies was crippling
their cause. The Duke of Berry remained at Chartres and made
no effort to join the Burgundians in time for the battle either.

Thus Louis XI was able to meet the Burgundians alone in the
hard-fought, disorganized, and bloody battle of Montlhéry on
July 16. It was really a series of desperate skirmishes. Charolais
was wounded. Louis again showed his personal courage and
leadership and inspired his men. According to one account, he
fought all that day without eating or drinking, exposing himself
to great personal danger. Both the Milanese ambassador and one
of the Milanese commanders, sent by the Duke of Milan to help
the French king, agreed in describing the courage of Louis XI in
leading the attack and his presence of mind in reassuring his men
by charging forward with his sword in his hand when the rumor
spread that he was killed or captured. The ambassador, in the
flamboyant language of Renaissance Italy, filled with classical
allusions, even described his bravery as "worthy of Alexander or
of Caesar." According to Commynes, Louis's presence and
conduct at the battle prevented his men from fleeing.

Both the Milanese commander and the Milanese ambassador
described the cowardly flight near the beginning of the battle of
the Count of Maine, who was fighting on the side of the king. The
ambassador believed that, otherwise, the Burgundian army
would have been completely destroyed. It is possible that the
Count of Maine was really in league with the enemy and hoped
to throw Louis's army into confusion by his precipitous flight.

When night fell, Charolais remained on the field of battle
prepared to continue the combat in the morning. During the
night, however, the king's troops secretly stole away in the

direction of Paris. Charles was able, a few days later, to join his allies at Étampes.

Both sides claimed victory: Charles on the grounds that he had remained on the field of battle; Louis on the grounds that the Burgundian losses exceeded his own and he had managed to break through to Paris. The Milanese ambassador reported that, although Charolais claimed victory because he had remained on the field, his losses far exceeded those of the king. He declared that this battle did Louis honor. The Milanese envoy to Savoy, writing a week later, said that, after having investigated the conflicting stories about the battle, he believed that the Burgundians had suffered much greater losses than the king, even though they remained on the field, and would have been completely destroyed but for the defection of part of the king's army.

Charles, however, wrote to the Marshal of Burgundy and others claiming complete victory in battle. He said the king's army had fled during the night, abandoning their artillery to the victors. Louis, on the other hand, wrote to various towns of France claiming victory also. When writing the town of Amboise he claimed that the enemy lost 1,400–1,500 killed and 300–400 prisoners and that an additional 2,000 were killed or captured while fleeing. In his letter to Beauvais the king said that his losses were only one-tenth those of the enemy. When writing to Poitiers, he declared that he had lost only 150 men, killed or captured.

The Battle of Montlhéry is usually described as a drawn battle. Even contemporaries found it hard to decide who had won. Probably, in all justice, the victory should be credited to the king, however, since his opponents' losses definitely exceeded his own, and he gained the major strategic advantage of breaking through the enemy coalition to Paris. On the other hand, the battle enhanced Charles's prestige. He had faced the royal army without any assistance and fought them to a virtual draw. This fact impressed his allies and worried the king in the months to come.[4]

Louis XI entered Paris on July 18, 1465. He promptly sought support by decreasing the tax on the retail sale of wine in Paris from one-quarter to one-eighth and canceling a number of other vexatious taxes altogether. The news was greeted by rejoicing and bonfires in the streets. He also granted tax exemptions to the university and the clergy. He appointed some Parisian bourgeois as members of the Parlement of Paris and named some clerics from the university to his royal council. Known traitors were expelled or executed.

As the forces of the league closed in on Paris, Louis realized the city was going to have to withstand a siege, and lacked sufficient men and supplies. Louis, therefore, conducted a lightning expedition into Normandy to raise reinforcements and gather provisions. Many of the Paris bourgeoisie, particularly in the Parlement, favored the league during the summer of 1465 and were plotting to open the gates to them. Louis's efficient spy service found out about them in time, and they were imprisoned, expelled, or executed. Louis counted on Paris now to withstand any siege until he could return with reinforcements. His trust was well placed as the army of the league reached Paris before the king's return, and the city refused to open its gates.

Louis returned at the head of a large army with a plentiful supply of provisons after only eighteen days. He entered Paris, and was welcomed joyfully.

In the meantime, the various leaders of the league had finally joined forces and were encamped nearby. Charolais had at last been joined by the Duke of Brittany, Charles of France (the king's brother), the Duke of Bourbon, and others. Needless to say, the Burgundians felt bitter against the men of Brittany and those of Charles of France who had failed to join them in the Battle of Montlhéry. Had they done so, the outcome might have been quite different.

The league now began to besiege Paris, which eventually began to run short of supplies. The king then heard disheartening news from Normandy. The Grand Seneschal of Normandy had opened the gates of Rouen to the Bretons and the Duke of Bourbon, who then began to overrun the entire province. Pontoise also opened its gates to the rebels in September, and town after town in Normandy followed suit.

By early September, the Milanese ambassador informed his duke that Louis was growing discouraged and was thinking of negotiating peace. He had confided to the ambassador, however, that he had no intention of keeping any promises he might be forced to make. On September 29, the ambassador reported Louis's dismay over the various defections in Normandy. Louis felt that he would have to give in to the princes and probably

give Normandy to his brother Charles. In his letter to the Duke
of Milan on October 2 the ambassador told him that Louis had
come to terms with the barons through fear of the betrayals and
defections that occurred daily around him, and negotiations
were under way between the king and the princes.[5]

The result of the negotiations was the treaties of Conflans and
Saint-Maur-des-Fossés of October 1465, which satisfied the most
powerful members of the league. The king's brother and heir,
Charles of France, received the rich Duchy of Normandy instead
of his former apanage, Berry. The right of the Duke of Brittany
to appoint to Breton bishoprics was confirmed. Charles the Bold
received back the towns of the Somme without Louis being
compensated for the large sum of money he had spent to buy
them. They could only be repurchased after Charles's death. He
also received Péronne, Roye, and Montidier, and his friend and
supporter, the Count of Saint-Pol, was made Constable of
France. The Duke of Bourbon was made Lieutenant-General of
all the provinces of central France. Dunois and Chabannes got
back all of their previously confiscated possessions. Nemours,
Armagnac, and Albret, however, received nothing. Louis made a
particular point of showing friendship for Charolais, whom he
rightly saw as the military nucleus of the coalitions, and whom he
wrongly believed could be transformed into a loyal ally of the
crown. He entertained him royally and they seemed like old
friends. Louis even suggested the engagement of his eldest
daughter Anne to Charolais.

The so-called War of the Public Weal had certainly done
nothing to promote the welfare of the French people. Taxes
were increased to pay the various pensions promised to the
princes and their protegés. Morever, much damage was done by
the pillaging troops of the league in many parts of France.

As for the king, he was the temporary loser. He had been
forced to grant substantial concessions to the leaders of the
league. Nevertheless, he had dispersed a dangerous coalition and
kept the sovereignty of the crown intact. Moreover, the crafty
monarch had no intention of accepting all of his losses as
permanent.[6]

Even before the war was over, Louis made sure to reinforce
his friendship with the Duke of Milan. In June 1465, and again in
August, he wrote Galeazzo Sforza, the duke's son, thanking him
for leading Milanese troops to his help. As early as November,

the Milanese ambassador reported that Louis was firmly resolved not to suffer the loss of Normandy, which had been granted to his brother only as a result of force. He had already concluded an alliance against his brother with the Dukes of Bourbon and Nemours, the Count of Armagnac, and the sire d'Albret.

The chief reason Louis was so concerned about seeing Normandy in the hands of his brother Charles was that Charles's lands would then touch those of Brittany and almost those of Burgundy. They could easily help each other against the king and even possibly secure assistance from England. Therefore, Louis had every intention of taking back Normandy at the first opportunity. He soon had his chance. The Duke of Brittany and Charles of France quarreled over the spoils in Normandy. The former had hoped to secure the key positions and lands for his supporters in Normandy and dominate the weak Charles. Fighting broke out between the two, and Louis took advantage of the quarrel to invade Normandy, claiming that his brother was conspiring with the English. He then declared war on England in December 1465. He counted on the French barons being divided and King Edward backing down. His estimation was correct and Normandy was reoccupied by January. Charles of France then patched up his differences with Francis II of Brittany and fled to his court. Edward sought to renew the truce between England and France which was due to expire on September 1, 1465. A new truce was signed at Calais in May 1466, to last until March 1468. Another meeting was planned to reach a permanent accord. The diplomatic situation between England and France was now back to the point where it had been before the War of the League of the Public Weal.

Charolais, although still hesitating to abandon the House of Lancaster for that of York was concerned to see Louis strengthened by the truce with England. He was forbidden by the Treaty of Arras of 1435 to sign a separate treaty with England. Therefore, in order to justify his violation of this stipulation, he accused Louis of a plot with England whereby several pieces of Burgundian land would be ceded to the English. He began to propose seriously a marriage with Margaret of York, the sister of Edward IV, which he had suggested previously without conviction. Edward and Warwick were cool to the proposal, but the Woodvilles, the family of the new English

queen, supported it, and their influence was growing rapidly at
court.

Meanwhile, King René of Anjou was recognized by the
Catalans of northeastern Spain as their king. He and his son, John
of Calabria, were supported in Spain by Louis XI. Thus Louis was
antagonizing all those endangered by the ambitions of the
Angevin family, including Edward IV, who was menaced by
Margaret of Anjou. In spite of his truce with France, Edward
signed a formal alliance with Charolais in October 1466. A
menacing coalition was beginning to form against Louis as his
relations with England were taking a new turn.

With regard to the king's enemies in France, the Milanese
envoy, writing home about this time, described Louis as very
vindictive. He said the king ardently desired to avenge himself
against all those who had opposed him in the previous year and
determined to take back all he had been forced to give. This
would probably lead to a long struggle with the French barons
which would tie up the Milanese troops which the Duke of Milan
had left at Louis's disposal until the following spring. He warned
the duke not to rely too much on Louis's good faith and
friendship.[7]

In June 1467 the aged Duke of Burgundy, Philip the Good, had
died and was succeeded by the fiery young Count of Charolais,
Charles the Bold. Thanks to the errors of several contemporary
chroniclers, notably Philippe de Commynes, and generations of
historians, relations among France, Burgundy and England for
the next decade have been simplified into a clash of personalities
between Louis XI and Charles. They disliked and feared each
other, but relations between them were too complex to be seen
as a sort of duel. Louis was faced with three other enemies, each
as dangerous and powerful as Burgundy: dissident elements
among the French princes and aristocracy; the King of England
who still claimed the French throne; and the hostile and
dangerous John II of Aragon. Thus it was quite impossible for
Louis to concentrate exclusively on Burgundy.

Charles had gained everything he needed from France in
1465, the most important of which were the Somme towns.
Thereafter, his policy toward France was more or less defensive
until January and February 1471, when Louis recaptured two of
these towns, St. Quentin and Amiens. But throughout his reign,
although the fantasy of the destruction of French power

remained on his mind, his ambitions, field of action and dreams of conquest were all towards the lands of the German Holy Roman Emperor. This does not deny the mutually hostile position of France and Burgundy altogether. Their confrontation was a real one, but the policies of the two rulers were not derived merely from hatred, nor was the course of events after 1467 dictated by this animosity.

Charles the Bold became duke at a time when relations with France were strained. French royal officials were stirring up trouble in the duchy and county of Burgundy. They were similarly active in the Somme towns, which Louis was determined to regain. These provocations came to a head just when Charles was becoming preoccupied with serious troubles in Liège.[8]

We have seen that Liège was ruled by Charles's cousin, the prince-bishop Louis de Bourbon. A revolt against this unpopular prince had been combined in 1465 by a declaration of war against Philip the Good, which had been encouraged by Louis XI. Liège was, however, forced to accept the Peace of St. Rond in December 1465, and the Peace of Oleye in September 1466. The Duke of Burgundy was made hereditary guardian and protector of the principality of Liège, which was also forced to pay a large indemnity. The radical element refused to pay and prosecuted those responsible for negotiating the peace.

When Philip the Good died, in June 1467, Liège was in partial revolt against both the bishop and the duke. Earlier in the year, Louis XI had tried to mediate, hoping to replace Burgundian influence over the town with French. He rejected requests from Liège for military assistance in April and continued his efforts to mediate. Letters of July and August show Louis trying to avert war and urging moderation. Louis's ambassadors to Charles the Bold urged the same. There is no evidence to support the contentions of some historians that Louis was encouraging Liège to revolt against Charles. It was not Louis's intervention which determined events at Liège but the growing aggressiveness of the Liègeois themselves, increasingly dominated by extremists. They refused to pay the indemnity and executed the ex-burgomaster of Dinant. Then they arrested one of Charles the Bold's emissaries. Next they raided into Charles's Duchy of Limbourg. These acts of violence continued until a state of open warfare developed in September 1467. The Liègeois then captured Huy, to which the bishop had withdrawn for safety, and he was forced to flee.

Charles had been making preparations against Liège for months. His troops overran town after town in the principality in October and November, and finally Liège decided to negotiate. Charles entered the town on November 17 and imposed a severe treaty. The walls were demolished and a further indemnity was levied in addition to what was already owing under the terms of the treaty of 1466.

Liège was still not pacified, however. The departure of the duke's lieutenant-general in August 1468 emboldened the radical refugees to return to the town. They were convinced that Charles would soon be at war with Louis XI and would lose. They entered Liège in September 1468, massacred their opponents, and seized control. They promptly revolted against Charles. The duke prepared a punitive expedition. This was the situation with regard to Liège when Charles the Bold and Louis XI held their famous meeting at Peronne in October.[9]

During 1467, while Charles was involved in these troubles with Liège, both he and Louis XI were seeking English friendship. Edward IV attempted to conceal from Louis the fact that he was moving toward closer ties with Burgundy. Warwick was still favorable to Louis, but the queen's family, the Woodvilles, supported Burgundy. An English mission was sent to Burgundy in January 1467. England and France exchanged missions, each attempting to hide their real plans. As we have seen, Charles sought the hand of Edward IV's sister, Margaret of York. Louis proposed alternative candidates for the hand of Margaret, around whom diplomacy now centered. He also offered money for an alliance. Edward was tempted, but Louis's marriage candidates were not satisfactory. He sent Warwick to France to negotiate. Louis was delighted, believing that Warwick still ran English affairs, which was no longer the case. Two letters which Louis wrote to the town of Lyons in May and June 1467 show his high hopes for constructive gains from this meeting and his failure to realize that Warwick's authority in England was declining. Since the King of England had sent such a high dignitary as Warwick, Louis informed the town that he was going to send a distinguished embassy to England to continue the talks of peace and to work against the marriage of Charles the

Bold and Margaret of York. Warwick and his delegates were magnificently received by Louis personally at Rouen in June 1467.

While the official meetings were going on, Louis met secretly with Warwick. All members of the English embassy were showered with gifts and attention. When the English ambassadors returned home, a French mission accompanied them.

While Warwick was in France Edward had been very active. He removed Warwick's brother from the office of chancellor and signed a thirty-year truce with the Duke of Brittany. Edward opened negotiations with Charles the Bold, regarding the marriage alliance and a commercial treaty. The French embassy was treated coolly by Edward, and returned home unsuccessful in August 1467. Louis's sincere efforts for a rapprochement with Edward had failed.[10]

England now resolutely entered the orbit of the enemies of France. She signed a treaty with Castile in July 1467. The treaty with Burgundy was renewed. In September and October negotiations continued regarding the wedding of Margaret of York and Charles the Bold.

Charles was active, in 1467, in consolidating and extending his system of alliances, which already included Cleves, the Elector Palatine, and Francis II, Duke of Brittany. In March he negotiated a treaty with the King of Denmark, which included also Louis's brother Charles and the Duke of Brittany. In April Bern and other Swiss communities signed an alliance with Burgundy. In July he signed a treaty with Philip of Savoy. In October the Duke of Alençon concluded treaties with Charles of France, the Duke of Brittany, and Charles the Bold. It looked as though a new and dangerous coalition was forming against Louis, pledged to help Charles of France regain Normandy.

Throughout 1467, while Charles the Bold was competing with Louis for the friendship of Edward IV and negotiating other alliances, he was eying Louis with fear and suspicion, but made no effort to organize an attack against him. If the grand alliance that seemed to be forming against France had any guiding hand, it was not his. When the Duke of Brittany attacked Louis, in October, to try to help Charles of France recapture Normandy, Charles the Bold was tied up with Liège. He signed a six-month truce with Louis in November. Louis then signed a truce with

Duke Francis of Brittany in January 1468. He feared a renewal of the war in the spring, however, and his truce with England was due to expire.

The king decided that, before any possible resumption of war with the feudal barons, he had better secure his hold on Normandy. He concluded that the most effective way to do this was to mobilize the opinion of all the men of influence in France in favor of his seizure of Normandy. This could best be done by summoning the Estates General, which had not met since 1439. Louis felt strong enough to dominate the assembly. He could explain his reasons for recapturing Normandy to all the most important people in France and then count on the support of most of them for his action. The Estates General met at Tours in April 1468. After Louis had explained his position, the assembly declared that Charles of France could have only one apanage producing 12,000 *livres tournois,* plus an annual royal pension, but that he could not have Normandy, which they declared inalienable from the royal domain.

Meanwhile, conditions for the Anglo-Burgundian marriage had been finally fixed in February 1468, and a thirty-year truce signed between England and Burgundy. The following month, Edward ratified the marriage contract, the truce, and the alliance of the two states against all their enemies. He also signed a treaty with Brittany and declared his intention of making good his claim to the French crown. In July 1468 the marriage finally took place between Margaret and Charles the Bold, and Edward prepared to invade France. The wedding of Charles and Margaret, and the close alliance of Burgundy and England that went with it, was of great significance for Charles.

Louis made preparations for the impending struggle. In July, he wrote the Duke of Milan asking him to attack Savoy as soon as the duke received word that Louis had attacked Burgundy. He renewed this plea in August, and promised to help Milan against Savoy and to secure the further assistance of the Marquis of Montferrat in northern Italy. He followed up with several other letters expressing his thanks for the Duke of Milan's apparent willingness to fall in with this plan and urging him to be ready to act.

Two opposing armed camps now began to form. As in 1463, the House of Anjou was largely the key to the grouping. As Louis was supporting René of Anjou and John of Calabria in Catalonia, their rival, John II of Aragon, was forced into a coalition against the French. He became one of the most astute and powerful enemies of Louis XI.

While Edward was delayed with domestic troubles in England and Charles the Bold was involved in putting down a revolt in Liège, Louis struck rapidly, in July, against the weakest of Charles the Bold's major allies, Francis II of Brittany. Meanwhile, Charles the Bold remained militarily inactive. Even in July, when French and Burgundian troops were massing along the frontier of Picardy, Charles showed no enthusiasm to take the field in person. He showed little sign of the obsession with France or the fanatical hatred of Louis that has often been attributed to him. After his wedding, he made solemn entries into various towns of his lands for several weeks. It was not until August 10 that he set out on a campaign against France, after telling a number of contemporary observers that he was only doing this for the sake of his allies, the Dukes of Berry and Brittany, who had asked for his help against the king. The events of August and September 1468 showed that Charles only meant to keep up appearances and had no intention of fighting a serious war with Louis. Neither did Louis plan to attack Charles. The French remained at Compiègne while Charles remained on the Burgundian side of the Somme.

By early September, the Duke of Brittany was defeated and forced to sign the Peace of Ancenis. By the terms of the agreement, Charles of France was to receive a pension of 60,000 *livres* until a suitable apanage could be selected for him. Three arbiters were named to select a domain for him within a year. Francis II was given two weeks to secure the consent of Charles of France. The treaty was ratified soon after, with Charles of France, who was virtually a prisoner of the Duke of Brittany, accepting it reluctantly. Louis wrote the Duke of Milan telling him of this settlement but informed him that he was not yet sure whether peace with Burgundy would follow.

The Constable of France, Louis, Count of St. Pol, then acted as mediator at a peace conference with Charles the Bold at Ham. A Franco-Burgundian truce was signed for six months, to begin October 1. There were hopes for a firm peace, but Charles's conditions were unacceptable to the king. Cardinal Jean Balue, Bishop of Angers, now intervened on Louis's behalf and arranged a personal meeting between Louis and Charles at Péronne.[11]

The reasons why Louis XI planned this meeting are by no means obvious, and have often been misunderstood. The king found himself in a very favorable political and military situation in the fall of 1468. Some of the most important difficulties troubling the kingdom had been solved. The ownership of Normandy had been secured, the quarrel with his brother Charles had been settled, the opposition of the Duke of Brittany had been broken, the English threat had been dissipated, all hostile forces had been neutralized, and even the Duke of Burgundy had signed a six-months armistice and had been induced to give up his provocative position on the Somme. The French army was in a line of strongly fortified towns and outnumbered the Burgundians. Louis's military commanders urged him to attack.

Charles the Bold showed little enthusiasm for the meeting, and it took persistent negotiations by Cardinal Balue to obtain his agreement. Finally, on October 8, he issued Louis a letter of safe conduct and agreed to meet with him. The kings' councillors all advised him not to go. Some warned him that he could not count on Charles's good faith. He seemed to be going to Péronne against considerations of statecraft, military tactics, of certain risk opposed to uncertain gain, and contrary to the advice of his councillors, lords, and commanders. Louis did not see the danger to which he was exposing himself. He thought his guarantee of free and unhampered return was binding. Therein lay his biggest mistake. This matter of personal obligation and honor turned out to be unimportant to his opponent. Thus he rode off, accompanied by only about fifty unarmed lords and retainers, to put himself in the hands of his mightiest enemy.

Why would the intelligent and usually cautious king set out upon such an apparently foolhardy undertaking? The prize that he sought was great, and he believed that he could gain it. Louis's reason for going to Péronne was a desire for a firm and lasting peace settlement with Charles the Bold. This he hoped, would change the whole political situation in his kingdom and form a new power structure. A real alliance and friendship with Charles, and the availability of his armies, would provide Louis with an authority in the kingdom which could not be challenged. Instead of having, time and again, to use all his forces to keep the most powerful and unruly of his enemies in check, he would then have his support to overawe any potential dissidents in the kingdom. "To turn the prevailing rivalry into an intimate understanding, to change the deep enmity which hinders him at every step into an alliance before which everything will have to give way, to tie the power which he fears more than any other to himself and to have it at his disposal, . . .this is why Louis XI appears in Péronne."

The chronicler Commynes wrote a highly dramatic account of this famous meeting. He was a firsthand witness, being, at the time, one of the chief councillors of Charles the Bold. Virtually every historian of Louis XI has followed his description almost exactly. The German scholar Bittmann has recently proven, through many other contemporary sources, that Commynes's account is basically untrue with regard to both the facts and the apparently ingenious psychological interpretation that he drew from them regarding the characters of Louis and Charles. As his account has so strongly influenced historians of Louis XI ever since, not only with regard to the meeting of Péronne, but also with regard to their descriptions of subsequent events, and their opinions about the characters of the French king and the Burgundian duke, it is worth summarizing briefly before discussing what really happened.

According to Commynes, the meeting at Péronne was a remarkable case in which Louis, the "Spider King," became enmeshed in the complicated web of his own intrigues. He was confident of his mental superiority over Charles and believed that he could talk him into an advantageous treaty. He had forgotten, however, that at the very moment of these negotiations, his agents were in Liège stirring up the town against the Duke of Burgundy. While Charles and Louis were meeting, news arrived from Liège of an uprising, touched off by the king's agents. A force from Liège had seized nearby Tongres, capturing both the Bishop of Liège and the Burgundian governor. Charles flew into a towering rage over Louis's treachery and had the gates of the town and castle closed, thus imprisoning the king. Louis feared that he might be imprisoned indefinitely, or even be killed. Charles kept him locked up for two days and three nights without seeing him while he decided what to do with him. Louis made use of one of his favorite weapons, bribery, bribing some of Charles's chief councillors to persuade the duke to release him. Finally, Charles decided to free Louis, but only after forcing him to sign a treaty highly favorable to Burgundy, and forcing him to accompany Charles as a hostage while he destroyed the town of Liège. Louis returned from Liège deeply humiliated and, from here on, concentrated even more of his attention on the hated duke's destruction. Commynes contrasted the characters of Louis and Charles at Péronne, depicting Louis as relatively calm, collected, and shrewdly extricating himself from a difficult position, while Charles was intemperate, subject to passion, and deceived in the end by Louis's calculated concessions which could be nothing else but deceptions.

Now let us see what really happened at Péronne. Louis arrived on October 9, and was cordially received. Probably by sheer chance, this warm welcome was briefly marred by an unfortunate incident. Just as Louis was about to enter the luxurious house where he was to stay, a troop of horsemen galloped through the town gate. They were, in fact, the commanders of a force from the County and Duchy of Burgundy which Charles planned to send against Liège. They happened to include several old enemies of Louis's, and he was quite alarmed. They took up residence in the nearby castle of Péronne. Louis quickly informed Charles that, because of their presence, he wished to move within the greater safety of the castle walls. The duke promptly granted his wish and assured him that he had nothing to fear. Louis then moved into the castle with only twelve companions. The rest were sent to Ham.

No permanent harm was done by this untimely incident, and the first two days of the meeting were marked by the warmest cordiality on both sides. Very little progress was made in the negotiations, however. Both men met with the intention of settling their differences. However, each had very different peace terms in mind. Louis's aims were described above. Charles too saw great possiblities in an alliance with the king, and he also reached too hastily toward the gains which the new association would offer him. He could have paid back the Duke of Brittany for his denunciation of their old alliance by leaving him at the king's mercy. He could have seized the French possessions of the Duke of Nevers. He saw his greatest potential gain, however, in security. Concluding a firm alliance with Louis would have safeguarded him from further wars with France so that he could turn to Germany and expand his lands in the Empire. Charles made exorbitant demands, including considerable territorial expansion. Louis was willing to grant them all in return for the *one* thing he wanted most of all: an oath of unconditional fealty from Charles to serve him against any man. Charles objected. He wanted to exclude from the oath those who had served him loyally in the past. He also wanted his personal enemies to forfeit royal protection. Lively discussions occurred with no agreement in sight. Then, during the evening of October 11, came the news that Liège had revolted, captured Tongres, and imprisoned the Bishop of Liège and the Burgundian governor, the lord of Humbercourt.

The chronic revolts of Liège against the Duke of Burgundy, from 1465 until just before the meeting of Charles and Louis at Péronne were described earlier in this chapter. Radical elements had just seized control of the town and revolted again. Charles was planning a punitive expedition as early as September, and had placed the lord of Humbercourt in command of a force to march against Liège. Then the Liègeois captured Tongres. Contrary to Commynes's account, Louis XI had absolutely nothing to do with this event. Indeed, all of his correspondence with Liège for over a year had urged moderation. Just three days before the events at Tongres, Charles had sent a messenger from Péronne to the large Burgundian army already assembled at Namur and in Hainault ordering them to attack Liège.

It is perfectly clear then that Charles had known about the revolt of Liège before even agreeing to meet with Louis at Péronne and was making plans to deal with it. If he seriously blamed the king for the uprising, the meeting would probably have never taken place. The news from Tongres, while obviously an unpleasant surprise, was certainly no reason for his furious anger against Louis. The attack on Tongres was no secret uprising. It was a military action carried out in the course of an openly announced war. There was no scheming or treason. The only surprising thing was its success. Charles's anger was against Liège, not against the king.

Charles was indeed in a very angry mood after receiving the news of what had happened at Tongres. His troops had suffered an unexpected setback, and one of his ablest commanders, the lord of Humbercourt, had been taken by surprise. He had prepared everything for the attack on Liège and had intended to be in the field personally long before this. He had been delayed by the persuasive powers of Cardinal Balue who had talked him into meeting Louis at Péronne. After two days of hard bargaining, he had accomplished nothing. Now he had received this piece of bad news. His personal participation in the fighting was still being delayed by the frustrating discussions at Péronne. This explains the impact of the news from Tongres. He wanted immediate bloody revenge. He was very angry and ordered all available troops to prepare for a punitive expedition.

Although Louis had not stirred up the revolt in Liège, he feared that there might by some suspicion of his involvement, as the town had frequently sought his protection in the past. To dispel all suspicion, he pretended to be upset also about the news from Tongres and promised Charles his support in crushing Liège. He even offered his personal participation in a siege, at the head of French troops. It was agreed that Louis should accompany Charles to Liège.

The fiery duke did not want to stay in Péronne one hour longer. But first the alliance had to be concluded. As Louis and Charles met again for this purpose on October 12, the same difficulties as before emerged. The king still wanted a commitment from Charles to serve the crown against anyone without exception. Again Charles refused. Louis was deeply dissatisfied and he therefore declared that he would not accompany Charles to Liège after all. It was at this point that Charles's fury erupted against Louis. He lost control of his temper and threatened to imprison the king.

Why did Louis break his promise so soon? The Milanese ambassador speculated that he did not really expect that he would be taken at his word and obliged to accompany Charles. The latter, however, was completely unwilling to accept Louis's change of mind and was ready to force him to carry out his promise. The castle and town were sealed off. The king was isolated and kept against his will. Charles was master of the situation and ordered Louis to obey under threat of imprisonment. The uncontrolled anger of Charles was caused by Louis's breaking his promise to participate in the Liège expedition, not, as Commynes says, through the sudden revelation of secret collaboration of the king with the rebellion in Liège.

The situation seems to have reached its crucial point during the night of October 13-14. According to Commynes, Charles was profoundly upset. The well-informed Milanese ambassador to the court of Louis XI, Panigarola, says that Louis attempted to flee in disguise that night. No other source tells this story. Yet it

makes sense and gives a saisfactory psychological explanation for
the outcome of the Péronne meeting. According to Panigarola,
the duke discovered the plot. His long-standing hatred and
distrust of Louis was increased and he decided he could not wait
any longer. The moment of truth had arrived. Louis, in his
quarters, trembled for his life. During the night he received a
warning (perhaps from Commynes) not to provoke Charles any
more. He then decided to give in to save his skin and regain his
freedom.

The next morning, deputies from both sides negotiated the
conditions of the treaty. Charles then met with Louis and the
king agreed to all Charles's conditions. At noon on October 14, a
complete accord was reached. An oath of peace and reconciliation was sworn on the cross of Charlemagne. In addition to
agreeing to the terms of the treaty drawn up by Charles, which
will be described below, Louis consented to accompany Charles
to Liège. Both swore their friendship to each other. Charles
agreed to do homage to the king for his French lands, and Louis
promised him 100,000 crowns in reparations for his military
expenses in his previous war against France which he had
demanded at Ham. Louis paid over half of this sum immediately.
The two princes left Péronne together on October 15 for Liège.

The reason why Charles insisted on Louis accompanying him
to Liège was that he feared that, if he did not, Louis would attack
him from behind. It was to safeguard himself from this danger
that he forced Louis to go with him. It was not as a measure of
retribution or an attempt to humiliate the king, as Commynes
suggests.

Several conclusions remain to be drawn from the meeting at
Péronne. The brutality and violence in Charles's actions emerge
clearly when we realize that Louis did not, as has always been
supposed, catch himself in his own net, that he did not become at
Péronne the victim of his own too cleverly woven schemes which
were revealed at the wrong moment. Charles unhesitatingly set
aside all of the advantages which he might have gained from an
alliance with Louis because events at Liège took an unfavorable
turn. He lost interest in long-range possibilities. His entire
attention was directed toward his immediate objective, the
campaign against Liège. The destruction of Liège would make
the boundaries of Brabant secure. It would remove all threats to
the Low Countries to the east. The destruction of Liège would

help free his hands for expansion towards Germany. It would also serve as a fearful example of how princely might dealt with those who defied it. Once he received the news of Tongres, all that counted for him was to take strong action against Liège. When Louis went back on his promise to accompany him, he saw in him, as he always had, only duplicity and all his indignation was directed against his guest. No solution seemed possible to Charles but force and violence, and he unhesitatingly exploited the situation. We see Charles take a completely self-assured and confident attitude of inflexible will, as if the Duke of Burgundy were so powerful that he had nothing to fear and everything was permissible to him, even violating an obligation. He turned to intimidation and force, ignoring the prestige of the crown and his own promise of safe-conduct. In reality, Charles may have been guided by fear: fear for the falseness of the king, fear for the power of the crown which he might not be able to resist under other circumstances, and which had to be prevented from interfering with his plans by unscrupulously exploiting the situation. This explains his determination to take every advantage of the favorable conditions to take Louis with him in person as a hostage to Liège. By his abrupt treatment of the king, Charles diminished the value of the treaty they had signed. The peace to which they had both sworn could no longer be relied on. No obligation would prevent the coerced and insulted king from seeking revenge. Charles did not hesitate to throw possible friendship with Louis to the winds. Nothing else mattered to him but the destruction of Liège, and no one must prevent this.

Charles's attitude shattered the diplomatic art of Louis. He showed no particular cunning or cleverness at Péronne. His position did not allow him to make use of these talents. After he realized that his purpose for going to Péronne had failed, he had no other course but to do as Charles wished. He felt the injustice done to him by this coercion and the ignominy of his position. But he feared for his life. He made no well-considered concessions. He gave in because he could not do anything else. But immediately he began to plan his revenge.

Louis and Charles set out for Liège on October 15 with Louis a virtual hostage. The Burgundians captured the town on October 30, and the chronicler La Marche reported that Louis even entered the city wearing the Burgundian cross of St. Andrew on his cap and shouting, "Long live Burgundy." Charles permitted his soldiers several days of looting. Then he had the town systematically burned and demolished. Only the churches and a few houses were left. A Burgundian garrison was installed in a newly built fortress. Henceforth, Liège was under Burgundian control.

Although Louis wrote to the Count of Dammartin at the royal court that he was accompanying the Duke of Burgundy to Liège to suppress rebellion there entirely of his own free will and referred to the "good cheer" that he and Charles the Bold were enjoying together, it is doubtful if many people believed this version of the situation. Charles allowed Louis to leave after the conquest of Liège on October 30. Louis returned to Paris humiliated and indignant. His hatred of Charles was bitter and, from here on, he concentrated more of his attention upon the duke's destruction.

The treaty which Louis and Charles had signed at Péronne is of rather little political significance due to its unilateral nature and the kings' intention of repudiating it. Its chief interest lies in the fact that it shows some of the aspirations of Charles the Bold. This is especially true of the six points, the actual texts of which have not come down to us: The king promised to abide by the treaties of Arras (1435) and Conflans (1465); he permitted Charles to make alliances with England, provided they were not aimed at France; a general amnesty was declared for all Burgundian supporters in France; the king promised to give his brother the counties of Champagne and Brie as an apanage; restitution of conquered territory was promised to Louis of Savoy, who was to be included in the peace; the king agreed that, if he infringed on the treaties of Arras, Conflans, or Péronne, Burgundian territories dependent on France would be freed from all French jurisdiction.

These clauses were designed to guarantee Charles those grants of territories originally made by Charles VII in 1435 to Duke Philip the Good and confirmed to Charles in 1465: in particular, the Somme towns, Péronne, Roye, and Montdidier. Charles was anxious to reinforce his relationship with his two influential allies, Philip of Savoy and Charles of France. He hoped the latter would become a Burgundian puppet. The last clause probably shows Charles's main aspiration: the severance of all connections between France and Burgundy which reflected or maintained subservience of the duke to the king. This hope also shows in many of the other concessions expressed in surviving documents or letters-patent. For example, in one clause, the king exempted Ghent, Bruges, Ypres, and the countryside around Bruges from the jurisdiction of the Parlement of Paris. This underlying theme of diminishing wherever possible the crown's powers over Burgundian territories ran through the entire treaty. Also, every dispute between France and Burgundy was settled in Burgundy's favor.[12]

Louis had no intention of abiding by the terms of the Treaty of Péronne. Charles, on the other hand, was not content with the measure of royal control over his territories that the treaty permitted Louis to retain. Louis was just as determined to regain the Somme towns as Charles was to keep them. It is hardly surprising, then, that relations between them remained much the same after Péronne as before.

A change in the attitude of the French king had taken place, however. A desire for revenge, to efface the coercion he had been placed under, to retaliate for Péronne and Liège, and to avenge the humiliation he had suffered colored his future attitude toward Charles the Bold. His hatred for the Burgundian duke would never be quenched until Charles lay dead upon the frozen battlefield outside Nancy. However, unlike Charles, he did not let a personal wish for vengeance destroy his sense of balance. He gave top priority to his plan to seize strategic lands from the King of Aragon, and thus extend his southeastern frontier to the Pyrenees. He was constantly faced with the danger of an English invasion, which once actually occurred, instigated by the Duke of Burgundy. He also continued to fear the possibility of the formation of new feudal coalitions against him inside France, especially if encouraged and supported by Charles the Bold. Therefore he made no serious effort to crush Charles, as long as the Duke of Burgundy was alive. His Burgundian policy was largely defensive. Only after Charles's death was the opportunity too tempting to resist, and Louis seized many Burgundian lands. Charles the Bold, on the contrary, allowed his desire for revenge against those who had defeated and humiliated him to virtually guide his entire policy, during the last year of his life, and this led to his downfall, as will be described later.

At first, the emphasis was on apparent friendship between Charles and Louis. Burgundian embassies were well received at the French court in February and March 1469. However, ambassadors from Bern, visiting Louis in July, were told that the king had had the treaty forced on him, and would not rest until he had avenged himself on Charles. By the autumn of 1469 Milanese ambassadors at the French court were convinced of Louis's belligerent intentions toward Charles. They reported that he planned to attack Charles the following year.

Under the circumstances, it was not possible for Louis to take military action against Charles in 1469. Long, careful preparations were needed before he could strike decisively. Skillful diplomacy was necessary to pave the way. He could not depend only on his own actions and plans. He had to consider other political powers working near him or against him in order to gain the necessary freedom of action.

Since his alliance with Burgundy had failed, Louis directed his efforts toward gaining the support of the House of Anjou and the Duke of Brittany. The most active member of the Angevin family was Duke John of Calabria who, since 1466, had been trying to conquer Catalonia. If he should succeed, he planned to turn to Italy to make good his claims to Naples and Sicily. He also planned to attack Milan. The king promised to support him against Catalonia. However, Milan was the most reliable ally Louis had at the moment, so that he could not help John to the extent of allowing him sufficient success to be able to attack Milan. Thus, Louis's activities in Spain and Italy now became interrelated with his struggle against Burgundy.

Savoy also had plans against Milan. Yolande, sister of Louis XI, who virtually governed the duchy for her invalid husband the duke, getting no encouragement from Louis, became an ally of Charles the Bold in hopes of getting Burgundian help. So did Philip of Savoy, powerful brother of the duke. In the spring of 1469, an alliance was formed between Burgundy, Savoy and Venice.

Louis was faced with these complications when he prepared to undo the Peace of Péronne. He had to hold back his brother from joining Burgundy, and prevent a premature break with Charles the Bold. He had to gain the friendship of the Duke of Brittany and the Angevins, specially John of Calabria. He had to break the close tie between Burgundy and England. He had to reestablish his lost influence in Savoy. He had to try to weaken the alliance between Burgundy and Brittany and stir up the traditional rivalry between Burgundy and the Angevins. He had to keep the Angevin and Savoyard projects in Italy separated and prevent the renewal of the friendship between John of Calabria and Charles the Bold that had almost ruined him in 1465. Louis was prepared to attempt this complicated policy in the spring of 1469.

Charles the Bold too had ambitious plans in 1469, which had nothing to do with his personal dislike for Louis XI. Charles's projects encompassed much of Europe. He planned to act as the aggressor. He had just destroyed Liège. A constant threat to Brabant and Namur was now ended, and the Low Countries were secure. Charles also brought an end to continuous rebellion in the rich Flemish town of Ghent. The road to the Rhine was open. No power seemed capable of stopping Burgundian expansion there.

There were also some changes going on in the court of Burgundy. Everything was now aimed at the glorification of the duke. Whatever he did, he was surrounded by a splendid company of nobles and retainers. Under the resplendent duke, concentrated executive power, such as never had existed there before, had been extended over all the Burgundian provinces.

In the spring of 1469, Charles believed that he was in a position to expand and conquer. Germany, France, and Italy were all destined to be the scene of his activities. He enjoyed a specially cordial relationship with Pope Paul II. The King of England seemed to be completely at his disposal. An English fleet was cruising the Channel and English troops were encamped in Picardy. A concentrated English invasion of France appeared imminent.

Charles's next plan was to go to his ancestral lands of Burgundy, which he had not visited as duke. In the agreements of the previous year with Louis XI, another meeting had been planned to regulate questions left unsettled by the Peace of Péronne. It was to take place in May or June at the border of the Duchy of Burgundy. Charles planned to appear so powerful there, in the company of Philip of Savoy, and with his far-reaching alliances, that Louis, outflanked and isolated, would have to agree to all his wishes and demands.[13]

Had Charles of France taken possession of Champagne, as the agreement of Péronne called for, a compact system could have been created, comprising the north and east of France, reaching from England through Savoy to Venice and Rome, centered around Burgundian power. The crown of France would have been overawed. Hence, which apanage Charles of France received was a matter of great importance.

Charles the Bold urged Charles of France to accept Champagne as agreed. Louis had no intention of keeping this promise as his brother and Charles the Bold would then control a solid block of contiguous land. Instead, he offered his brother Guyenne, a larger apanage, but at the opposite corner of France. Charles hesitated, fearing to displease Charles the Bold, and not trusting Louis. It was at this point that Louis discovered the plot of two of his ministers, both high churchmen, Cardinal Balue and Guillaume de Harancourt, Bishop of Verdun, to persuade Charles to refuse and accept only Champagne. The two churchmen were imprisoned. Louis used all kinds of deceit, cunning, and elaborate diplomacy over this crucial issue of Charles's apanage. Bittmann describes this complicated maneuvering in some detail. Louis then won over by bribes and persuasion his brother's chief advisors, notably Odet d'Aydie, himself a Gascon. They finally persuaded Charles of France to accept Louis's offer, and in April 1469, Charles was granted Guyenne, plus Agenais, Quercy, Périgord, Saintonge, La Rochelle, and Aunis, to the great displeasure of Charles the Bold. This was indeed a large and rich apanage, but at least it removed Charles of France as far as possible from Charles the Bold.

In August 1469, Louis had his brother swear on the Cross of Saint-Laud of Angers never to conspire against the king's life or liberty, never to marry Mary of Burgundy, and to renounce permanently any claim to Berry or Normandy. It was popularly believed that anyone who broke an oath sworn upon this cross would die within a year. In two letters in early September, one to the chancellor and one to the town of Rheims, Louis announced that his brother had sworn complete obedience to him. On November 1, 1469, the king wrote to the Constable of France ordering him to see that the ring by which Charles of France had been ceremonially wedded to the Duchy of Normandy be publicly broken at the session of Exchequer of Normandy, which was then meeting. Thus, by the end of 1469, Louis believed that he had his weak, pleasure-loving brother safely out of the way.

The apparent permanent reconciliation between Louis and Charles of France was a great triumph for the French king. Its

importance has been overlooked by many historians. Milanese
dispatches show that this accord of the two brothers was directed
against Charles the Bold. They reported that the new Duke of
Guyenne showed more hatred for the Duke of Burgundy than
the king himself. It was decided that Charles would return to
Guyenne and prepare as quickly as possible for war.

To control France in this period meant to rely on the great
princes. To persuade them to support the crown was the king's
most important task in domestic affairs. Louis's reconciliation
with his brother was a crucial step. By the express wish of
Charles, the House of Foix was included in the treaties and
promised future loyalty.

The next important step was to persuade the second most
powerful prince in France, the Duke of Brittany, to join the
union. Louis and Charles sent a joint legation to Duke Francis II.
Francis replied in courteous and submissive terms. He sent a
letter from Charles the Bold calling for a renewal of their
alliance to Louis. He said that he rejected it and wanted to live in
peace with the crown.

Another result of the reconciliation between Louis and
Charles was a change in the king's relationship with Savoy. The
friendship that had always existed between Charles of France
and his sister Yolande now helped their brother Louis. Three-
way negotiations were started. Before long, a Savoyard envoy
delivered Yolande's declaration that, from then on, she would do
everything possible to please the king. Louis requested that she
give up her Venetian alliance and seek the friendship of Milan.
This was followed by a French mission to Savoy which resulted in
the breaking of the Savoyard-Venetian association and the
formation of an alliance among France, Savoy, and Milan. The
union of the king and his brother had led to the recreation of
French influence in Savoy.

It also affected France's relationship with Castile. Two months
before, Louis had persuaded the King of Castile to break off his
alliance with England and renew his alliance with France. Now it
was expected that he would arrange the marriage of his sister
and heiress, Isabella, with Charles of Guyenne, providing the
latter with the prospect of the Castilian throne. This would have
put Castile under French domination.[14]

Meanwhile, dramatic events had been occurring in England
which Louis watched with growing excitement. During the

summer of 1469, Edward IV had been planning an invasion of France. Suddenly, in June, his invasion plans were ruined as a revolt broke out in England headed by that incurable adventurer Warwick the Kingmaker. Next came the startling news that Warwick had married his eldest daughter to Edward's brother, the Duke of Clarence, defeated the king, and taken him prisoner. He wanted to crown Clarence and sought the help of Louis XI in August, 1469. Louis was unenthusiastic about Clarence, a weak man, and began to consider a more daring plan—the restoration of the Lancastrians. So he decided not to intervene and to await the outcome.[15]

Thus, in the fall of 1469, Louis XI seemed to stand at an important turning point. All internal and external conditions were in his favor. There remained one main obstacle in his way if he wanted to make his authority felt without serious restraint: Burgundian power. His goal was to destroy it, if he could, or at least to limit it drastically. The time seemed highly favorable to avenge the humiliation he had suffered at Péronne and Liège. He planned to celebrate Christmas with all the important princes gathered around him. The campaign against Charles the Bold would be discussed and definite plans made.

Meanwhile, in the autumn of 1469, Charles the Bold made another attempt to regain Charles of France as an ally. He offered him membership in his prestigious order of the Golden Fleece, and his daughter, Mary of Burgundy, in marriage. Charles, now firmly committed to his royal brother, refused.

The Duke of Burgundy now foresaw war, and made military preparations in the fall of 1469. By March, the Burgundian forces were ready to fight, but the duke was unlikely to attack unless Louis attacked him.[16]

In the meantime, the situation in England had changed again. By the fall of 1469 Edward had escaped and regained London. In April 1470 news reached Louis that Edward and Warwick were once again at war. A month later, Warwick and Clarence were defeated and forced to flee to France, where they were welcomed by Louis. On the way across the Channel Warwick captured some Burgundian ships. Charles the Bold was furious over the ships and over Warwick's warm reception in France.

Warwick's plans now closely coincided with the French king's. He hoped for a reconciliation with Margaret of Anjou. He then planned to secure French help, invade England, and restore

Henry VI to the throne. Probably Louis had already hinted at this project.

Warwick and Louis met at Amboise in June 1470. Louis had some misgivings about committing himself, partly because he feared that Warwick might fail, and partly because he knew that support of the plan meant war with Burgundy. Although he had intended to attack Charles the Bold that year, the time would no longer be propitious if he were also involved in supporting this daring invasion of England. He finally decided that it was worth the risk. The discussions between the king and Warwick lasted four days, during which time "the Kingmaker" and his retinue were lavishly entertained. Eventually they agreed that Warwick would restore Henry VI to the English throne, with the help of French ships and money, and Warwick's younger daughter Anne would marry Henry and Margaret's son, Prince Edward.

The next task, and a highly difficult one, was the reconciliation of Warwick and Margaret of Anjou. They had been personal enemies. Not only had Warwick been largely responsible for dethroning her but also he had made several remarks about her private life which she found difficult to forgive. They decided that it would be best if Warwick left Amboise for a while and allowed Louis to begin the negotiations with Margaret. Warwick would then return to conclude the agreement.

Two weeks after Warwick's departure, the haughty Queen Margaret arrived at Amboise from the Duchy of Bar, where Louis had established a small court for her. She readily agreed to a thirty years' truce between France and England in return for Louis's support of her husband, Henry, but she refused to have anything to do with Warwick and would not allow her son to marry his daughter. Louis turned on all his persuasive skill and charm.

During the negotiations, on June 30, 1470, a male heir was born to the French queen, Charlotte. He was christened Charles. Louis seized the opportunity to honor the House of Lancaster. He chose Margaret's son, Prince Edward, as godfather. He then immediately renewed his attempts to reconcile Margaret with Warwick. She finally agreed to the marriage of Edward to Warwick's daughter.

Louis then arranged the most congenial place he could think of for the meeting of Margaret and Warwick. He selected Angers, where Margaret had grown up, and promised that her father,

King René, and her cousin, Charles of France, Duke of Guienne, would be present. Louis and Duke Charles arrived at Angers early in July. On July 22, both Queen Margaret and Warwick arrived. Warwick humbly begged Margaret's forgiveness for wrongs he had done her in the past. She promised to treat him as a true and faithful subject. He then swore "to uphold the party. . .of King Henry." The oaths were taken on the cross of St. Laud.

Louis was careful during the summer not to provoke Charles the Bold into a declaration of war. Fearing an alliance between Edward and Charles against him, he adopted a conciliatory attitude toward Charles, who vigorously protested in letters and embassies against Louis's alleged connivance in Warwick's piratical actions against Burgundian ships. In July 1470 Charles made an angry speech to French ambassadors, allegedly saying that Louis was his "greatest enemy in the world."

On July 31, 1470, Warwick and Jasper Tudor, Earl of Pembroke, Henry VI's half-brother, set out to prepare for the expedition. Prince Edward, Margaret, and Warwick's wife and daughters remained in France. Louis had promised Warwick the sizable sum of 50,000 *ecus* and the support of the French fleet. In return, Warwick had promised to bind England to a war to the finish against Burgundy. The expedition was delayed about a month by a tight Burgundian naval blockade accompanied by raids on the Norman coast. Finally, in early September, the Burgundian fleet was dispersed by a severe storm. On September 9, Warwick's ships were able to sail, accompanied by a strong French naval detachment.

In mid-October, Jasper Tudor arrived from England with the welcome news that Warwick had marched through England almost unopposed. Edward VI had been forced to flee to Holland. Richard Neville, Earl of Warwick, calling himself the King's Lieutenant of the Realm, had entered London on October 6 and knelt before Henry VI, whom he himself had imprisoned five years previously. Tudor then gave Louis a letter from Warwick, dated October 8, saying that "this whole Kingdom is now placed under the obedience of the King my sovereign lord, and the usurper Edward driven out of it." Louis was jubilant.

Louis eventually received the papal dispensation necessary, because of distant consanguinity, and Anne Neville and Prince Edward were married on November 28, 1470. The wedding of

Warwick's daughter and the Lancastrian Prince of Wales was Louis's answer to Charles the Bold's marriage with Margaret of York.

Louis then prepared an embassy to send to Warwick to conclude a military alliance against Burgundy. Warwick would receive Holland and Zeeland as his share of the spoils. He held back his ambassadors, however, until December while he completed his preparations for war.

In the closing months of 1470, it appeared that Louis XI had accomplished one of his greatest diplomatic triumphs. The Anglo-Burgundian encirclement of France was broken. Burgundy was without a major ally and was now threatened by the Franco-Lancastrian alliance. England was no longer a dangerous enemy but a military ally. The relentless French monarch prepared to move in for the kill.[17]

CHAPTER 5

The Struggle with Charles the Bold, and the Fall of the House of Burgundy

LOUIS now lost little time in moving against Charles the Bold. The king held an assembly at Tours in November 1470 of nobles, prelates, and royal officials, at which he explained his grievances against Burgundy. They agreed that he was not bound by the treaties of 1465 and 1468, which had been imposed upon him by force. Then Louis declared war on Burgundy in December 1470, pronouncing all the duke's lands forfeit to the crown in retaliation for his having confiscated the belongings of French merchants going to the fairs at Antwerp and for his invasion of Normandy.

It is possible that, at this time, Louis was aiming at the total destruction of Burgundian power and the conquest of many of Charles's lands. He had peace for the moment on his southern frontier, and the Duke of Burgundy had not yet reached the peak of his power and military glory. Or, he may have had the more limited objective of reconquering the Somme towns. He began to move his troops up toward the Somme frontier, but intended to postpone his main campaign until the spring to give Warwick time to prepare. Suddenly he learned, in January 1471, that St. Quentin, one of the Somme towns, had opened its gates to the Constable St. Pol. The king then decided to strike at once. In February, Amiens surrendered to Antoine de Chabannes, Grand Master of the Royal Household. The French also captured Roye and Montdidier. The Duke of Burgundy then besieged Amiens. He was soon almost surrounded by the royal army advancing from the south. If the English came from Calais, to the north, the Burgundians would be trapped.

Meanwhile, as Louis campaigned, he anxiously awaited the results of his embassy to England. He already knew that his ambassadors had been welcomed in December 1470. He continued to receive encouraging but vague news regarding the anti-Burgundian alliance. Finally, in March, his envoys returned with only a trade agreement and a truce rather than a formal treaty. They also brought Warwick's verbal assurance that, as soon as the queen and Prince Edward arrived back in England to hold it in his absence, he would come with about 8,000 men. The queen and the prince were lingering uncertainly on the French coast at Honfleur. The envoys also brought word that, just as they were leaving, news came that King Edward was attempting to land in England. Warwick would now have to fight to retain control of England and Louis's hopes of an English army coming to his help and closing in like a vice on the Burgundians evaporated. Louis then opened secret negotiations with the Duke of Burgundy. Charles believed that his own military position was so precarious that he wrote Louis seeking peace and a three-months truce was signed in April 1471. From then until June, 1472, a state of armed peace and almost continuous negotiation existed between Charles, anxious to recover St. Quentin and Amiens, and Louis, made somewhat defensive by developments in England.

The news from England arrived slowly, but gradually the picture began to become clear. After Edward had been deposed, he had fled to the court of Charles the Bold. Charles had publicly ordered that no help be given Edward, but he secretly provided him with money and a fleet. Edward invaded England in March 1471. He defeated and killed Warwick in April. Margaret of Anjou and Prince Edward returned to England, where they were defeated by Edward IV at Tewkesbury in May. Prince Edward was killed in the battle, and Margaret and Henry VI were imprisoned. Henry died in prison soon afterward, possibly murdered. Louis had lost Warwick, who had always stood for Anglo-French friendship. He was now faced with a restored Edward IV, whose overthrow he had worked so hard for. His great diplomatic triumph had evaporated.[1]

By repudiating the treaties of Conflans and Péronne, Louis had provoked a new feudal coalition against him. It formed gradually in 1471, weakening Louis's position, while the Burgundian position grew stronger through Charles the Bold's negotiations.

Charles of France was dissatisfied with Guyenne, which had been ravaged during the last years of the Hundred Years' War and had not yet fully recovered. Moreover, all of his prospects for the future had been changed, as he was no longer heir to the throne since the birth of the Dauphin Charles in 1470. He still hoped to marry Mary of Burgundy, the daughter of Charles the Bold, in spite of his promise not to do so. Charles the Bold kept his hopes alive, as he did with all her other suitors. Therefore Charles of France requested the Pope to annul the oath he had taken never to marry her. Louis suggested other marriages to him, but without success. Commynes believed that Charles the Bold had no intention of marrying his daughter to anyone, as long as he was alive, but rather intended to continue to profit from her availability for his diplomacy. If so, Louis's strenuous efforts to prevent her marriage to Charles of France were unnecessary.

From August to December 1471 Louis wrote letter after letter attempting to block this marriage and showing an increasing awareness of the coalition that was forming against him. In August, he wrote six letters in this connection. Two were written to the seigneur du Bouchage, his special envoy to the Duke of Guyenne. Bouchage was to question the duke regarding the following points: reports of his willingness to restore confiscated lands to the seigneur of Armagnac; that he had been in contact with John of Calabria, the sire de Beaujeu, and various other royal servants; that he had sent envoys to the Duchess of Savoy urging her not to declare for Louis nor to aid him against the Duke of Burgundy (Louis had already been informed about this latter point by Philip of Savoy); and that Charles was seeking papal dispensation to renounce his promise never to wed Mary of Burgundy. Also, Bouchage was to remind Charles of his promises to Louis and to assure him of the king's desire for his continuing friendship.

In another letter in August Louis said that the Duke of Brittany had sent an envoy to the Duke of Burgundy informing him that Charles of Guyenne would join him and his allies against the king. Also in August, Olivier le Roux, the king's envoy, wrote him of his suspicions that Charles of Guyenne, the Duke of Brittany, and others were plotting against him. They were planning to act before next All Saints' Day. He was not sure whether the Count of Foix was involved or not.

Louis then wrote to Lorenzo de Medici, asking him to use his

influence with the Pope to persuade him not to absolve Charles
of Guyenne from his promise of loyalty to Louis XI and from his
oath not to marry Mary of Burgundy. Another letter in August
indicates that the king knew that the Duke of Burgundy had
received letters from Edward IV of England saying that Edward
planned to invade France to seize Normandy or Guyenne, and
sought Burgundian help.

In September 1471, Louis wrote two letters regarding the
coalition that was forming. The first was to the townspeople of
Lyons ordering them to guard their city well and stating that he
was sending them an envoy with special instructions in this
regard. The envoy informed them that the king was aware that
the Dukes of Guyenne, Brittany, and Burgundy, and certain
other lords, had formed an alliance against him and were raising
troops.

Louis's second letter in September was to Tanneguy du
Châtel, a trusted royal official, telling him that Yolande of
France, Duchess of Savoy and an adherent of Charles of
Guyenne, was facing a revolt from Philip of Savoy, her husband's
brother and an adherent of Charles the Bold. The royal official
was instructed to try to secure peace between Yolande and
Philip and to see which of the two would be the more valuable
ally for Louis.

Sometime during the fall of 1471 Louis received further word
that Charles of France was believed to be forming a coalition
with Brittany, England, and Burgundy against him. Charles had
sent envoys to Burgundy to negotiate a marriage with Mary of
Burgundy. Charles had also summoned the *ban* (the levy of his
feudal vassals) in Guyenne, but many nobles were reluctant to
serve him against the king.

Louis was fully aware of the danger of England joining a
hostile coalition against him. Both he and Edward IV were
willing to negotiate with each other to gain time. They
conducted secret bargaining while they both prepared for war.
The result was a truce signed in September 1471, to last until
May 1472. Edward, however, also renewed his thirty-year truce
with Brittany and kept up close friendship with Charles the Bold.

Meanwhile, on France's southern frontier, John II of Aragon
was continuing his diplomatic activity against Louis. The result
was a treaty, in November 1471, among Aragon, Burgundy, and
Naples.

In late 1471, both Louis and the English were attempting to negotiate a treaty with Charles the Bold. In a letter to his envoys to the Duke of Burgundy, Louis appeared very worried and anxious to conclude the treaty. Faced with a renewed coalition of princes against him Louis continued to seek a settlement. But Charles, even when offered the return of St. Quentin and Amiens, was unwilling to stand by while Louis crushed his allies. In November 1471, Charles declared all Burgundian territories exempt from the jurisdiction of the French crown and Parlement. Hence, Charles was unwilling to accept French suzerainty which Louis insisted upon as part of a peace settlement. Nevertheless, negotiations continued through the spring of 1472.

In actual fact, the coalition that had formed against Louis, by the end of 1471, consisted of the Duke of Brittany, Gaston of Foix, Charles of France, John V of Armagnac, Charles the Bold, John II of Aragon, Yolande, Duchess of Savoy, and Nicholas of Anjou, Duke of Lorraine, son of John of Calabria, who had died in 1470. They were still negotiating with Edward IV of England.[2]

In March 1472, Louis wrote to the people of Lyons telling them that he had received documents definitely proving that Charles of Guyenne had sent envoys to the Pope seeking dispensation from his promise of fidelity sworn to Louis on the Cross of St. Laud. In April, both Louis and the Duke of Burgundy began military preparations. In mid-May, the king launched a campaign against his brother, Charles of Guyenne, who was seriously ill, and quickly occupied his lands.

The chronicler Commynes has misled many historians regarding Louis's plans at this point. He overemphasized Louis's political skill. He portrayed the king extricating himself from the difficult situation caused by the menacing coalition against him. With precise calculation and masterly timing he is supposed to have struck against his opponents separately. Commynes was wrong when he said that Louis knew that Charles the Bold was so eager for the return of the two Somme towns that he would not dare anger the king. This would leave Louis the fifteen or twenty days he needed to capture Guyenne, and thus knock his brother out of the alliance. This calculating and cunning cannot be confirmed by the facts.

Actually, Louis started his attack on Guyenne too early. He had bribed the monk who assisted his brother in his devotions to keep him informed about Charles's condition. Thus he was well aware, by mid-May, that he was not expected to live. In fact, Charles died on May 24, just ten days after Louis attacked. As a matter of fact, the king announced Charles's death one week prematurely to the town of Bayonne in Guyenne. He told them he was sending a royal official to take possession of the town, and promised tax reductions and pardons. As soon as he realized that his negotiations with Burgundy had failed, he attacked Guyenne. His tactics consisted of hasty grabbing rather than weighing and considering the situation.

If Louis had waited only a few more days, it would have changed the whole situation. With the death of the Duke of Guyenne, the apanage would have lawfully reverted to the king. Taking it back would not have been considered a use of force. The armistice, which included the Duke of Guyenne, would not have been broken. Louis's hasty action gave Charles the Bold an excuse not to adhere to the armistice either, and to attack France. By launching his attack prematurely for a gain that would have come to him anyway without force, he called into play forces which changed the situation to his disadvantage. Contrary to Commynes's expectations, Charles the Bold did not delay. Without considering the possible delivery of the two Somme towns to him by the king through further negotiation, as soon as he heard that Louis had broken the armistice by attacking the Duke of Guyenne, he invaded Picardy.

The nature of Charles of Guyenne's death also proved to be important. The rumor spread that he had been killed by poison and sorcery at the instigation of the king. In actual fact, the accusation was untrue. Charles probably died of tuberculosis aggravated by syphilis. Charles the Bold seems to have really believed the rumors, however. On the day that he left Arras to join his troops, he told the Papal Nuncio, the Bishop of Sebenico, his motives for war. He accused Louis of causing Charles's death through poison and sorcery. He said that, if the king acted in this way against his own brother, he was likely to act even more treacherously against him. Indeed, many attempts had already been made on his life. He did not plan to wait for such an end. He said that he would rather live among the Turks than have to fear permanently for his own life. He saw only one way of defense against Louis's treachery. He was resorting to war to get rid of the malicious opposition of Louis forever. He tried to persuade the nuncio that, with a king like Louis, a man filled with falseness and deceit, no agreement was possible. Louis must be compelled to capitulate by force of arms.[3]

Louis had just signed a year's truce with Charles the Bold. As we have seen, as soon as the Duke of Burgundy learned of Louis's attack on Guyenne, he reopened hostilities. Early in June 1472 he announced his intention of avenging his late ally's death and crossed the Somme in a war of pillage and conquest. At the same time, his ally, the Duke of Brittany, attacked. Charles quickly captured the small town of Nesle, about thirty-five miles southeast of Amiens, and then massacred the inhabitants after the town had surrendered. He then captured Roye and Montididier. Northern France trembled before the power and ferocity of the Burgundian duke. The French commander, Constable St. Pol, wrote in desperation to the king, who was campaigning against Charles's ally in Brittany, urging him to rush his army up to oppose the Burgundians. Louis refused to panic and wrote back ordering him to defend only the strong towns and abandon the weak ones like Nesle. He said prophetically: "The first place that can resist him—that will be sufficient to undo him."

Louis continued to conduct personally the campaign against the Duke of Brittany. He was confident that he would meet little opposition here, and events proved him correct. He remarked humorously of the Bretons, "You never saw such poor Burgundians as they are." Duke Francis II was forced to sign a year's truce in October 1472.

On June 27, Charles the Bold besieged the large town of Beauvais. It was not very well garrisoned, but resisted courageously until royal reinforcements arrived. Charles continued the siege for nearly a month, bombarding the town with his excellent artillery and doing a great deal of damage. His own losses, however, were considerable. Finally, the frustrated duke was forced to abandon the siege. He marched into Normandy, burning and plundering. However, the main French army remained constantly between him and Brittany. Charles the Bold, without the only ally who had given him military support, since Louis's truce with Brittany, and running short of supplies, was forced to turn back. In November he agreed to a truce to last until April 1, 1473. After it expired, it was renewed for a year. This was the last campaign fought on French soil by Charles in person, and it ended in failure.

Louis's prophecy that the first town that could resist Charles would be his undoing had been proven correct by Beauvais. In July 1472 Louis rewarded the town of Beauvais for its brave resistance. He granted the town a charter entitling it to elect its own mayor, and all its inhabitants were freed from taxes. He had a particular word of commendation for the women of Beauvais, who had fought heroically during the seige. A certain Jeanne Laisné is said to have captured the Burgundian standard. The women of Beauvais, even the nonnoble, were granted the right to wear any clothing they saw fit. This was a novel concession because noble ladies usually went to great lengths to prevent other women from dressing above their station.

Louis made an indirect gain from the recently completed campaign against Burgundy. Philippe de Commynes, the most capable advisor of Charles the Bold, abandoned his rather rash and warlike master and slipped away from the Burgundian camp in Normandy in August. He fled to the royal court and sought service under Louis XI, the skillful diplomat whom he admired. Louis welcomed him with open arms. The king, who was always well informed, was aware of Commynes's ability. He made him a royal chamberlain and councillor and gave him rich lands and pensions. He soon became one of Louis's closest and most trusted advisors. Commynes later wrote his *Memoires,* to which we have referred so often, which established his reputation for centuries as one of the best historians of the fifteenth century. Recent scholarship, however, has proven him to be inaccurate on many important points.

The situation had been critical for Louis in the year 1472. An English invasion, in support of Burgundy and Brittany, had been imminent. Louis had negotiated with England and managed to delay them until he had forced both Brittany and Burgundy to sign truces. He had again gotten out of a dangerous situation, partly due to the slowness of England to act. Fearing to be left isolated, Edward IV negotiated the Truce of Brussels in March 1473, to last between France and England for a year.[4]

The nature of Louis XI's diplomacy and plans in late 1472 and early 1473 is of interest, and has often been misunderstood. He carefully sought to ensure the friendship of Duke Francis II of Brittany, with whom he had signed a year's truce in October 1472. He tried to honor him by assuring him that he alone could secure the peace of the kingdom by gaining the prolongation of the truce of November 1472, with Burgundy, which was due to expire the following April. Duke Francis would act as the peacemaker.

There were several reasons for this policy. The south was in a state of unrest. A rebellion by the Duke of Armagnac required the prompt intervention of the royal army. Gascony was seething with discontent. Louis feared an English landing in the spring. There was also a new menace from Aragon which would require French troops. Therefore, Louis desperately needed peace with both Brittany and Burgundy.

The Duke of Brittany agreed to negotiate with Charles the Bold on Louis's behalf. In January 1473 Louis gave him the authority to try to persuade Burgundy to extend the truce, and be included in the agreement between France and Brittany. An able Breton diplomat was sent. The Constable of St. Pol warned Louis of deceit. He said Charles was preparing for war and probably did not want a longer truce, especially one brought about by the mediation of the Duke of Brittany. Louis was well aware of the danger that the two dukes might only try to slow down his own military preparations, until they were sure of an English invasion, and then turn against him.

At this point, a landing of the English in France was certainly regarded by Louis as his gravest danger. News kept arriving from across the Channel of military preparations and grants of money by parliament for the war. Then news came that an English army was preparing to invade, under the personal leadership of the king. Louis is descibed as being unusually worried and depressed—almost out of his mind with despair. His fear of England was the main reason why, in the spring of 1473, all his efforts were directed towards coming to an agreement with his potential enemies in the kingdom. He diligently pursued an extension of the truce with Burgundy and continued to do his best to win the Duke of Brittany to his side. He offered the duke a large annual pension to do his utmost to bring about the prolongation of the Burgundian truce.

By March it was becoming clear that the English would not invade that year, because of internal difficulties in England. The king's brothers were making trouble for him, and the tense relationship with Scotland necessitated his presence in the north. The chief threat to France now came from an Aragonese invasion of Roussillon.

From the above account, it is clear that the truce extension
with Burgundy in 1473 was brought about quite differently from
the way it is described by Commynes. It was not the Duke of
Burgundy who requested the extension: it was the king, using
Breton mediation. Almost no price would have been too high for
him to assure peace. At first, he was threatened by an English
invasion. By the spring, the extension of the truce became
necessary because of the invasion of Roussillon by Aragon and
the need to safeguard the borders of the Pyrenees.

The intermission in fighting was intended by Louis to be
temporary: no longer than the war in the south required.
Commynes said that Louis's diplomacy called for a long period of
peace with Burgundy—a long-term truce with continuous
extensions to give Louis's complicated plans time to ripen. The
Milanese dispatches, on the other hand, show that the king did
not plan to give Charles more than one year's extension. He
needed this much time to deal with the Duke of Armagnac and
the King of Aragon. He expected to finish both enterprises in
that time, and would then have no other opponent but the Duke
of Burgundy, as he believed that the Duke of Brittany could be
won over to neutrality. At the end of the year's truce, he planned
to turn his full power against Charles the Bold.

Louis's intention to have only one year's truce is shown most
clearly in his conversation with the Milanese envoy in April 1473.
Contrary to the envoy's advice, Louis said that in no event would
he extend the truce with Burgundy. It is clear that he was not
planning any far-reaching, grandiose plans against Charles,
which would take a long time to prepare. He merely needed a
temporary truce due to the necessities of the moment.

On April 4, 1473, a secretary of the Duke of Brittany arrived
with letters from Charles the Bold agreeing to a one-year
extension of the truce. They were to be ratified by Louis. The
king hesitated because the contract contained one passage
totally in conflict with his plans. The King of Aragon was
included in the list of Burgundy's allies. Hence he would be
included in the truce and every military activity against him must
cease. The chief reason Louis now sought the truce was to attack
the King of Aragon. Finally, he ratified the contract anyway. He
did not intend this to prevent him from fighting the King of
Aragon in Roussillon, however.

By this time Louis had already dealt with Duke John V of

Armagnac. He was one of the most powerful nobles in southern France. When Charles of France held Guyenne, John had intrigued with him. Louis had sent an army which seized John's chief stronghold, Lectoure. John fled to Spain. While Louis was fighting Burgundy and Brittany in 1472, John returned to Lectoure. It was besieged by a royal army, and he was killed during the fighting, in March 1473. His extensive lands were then divided between Pierre de Beaujeu and a number of other royal supporters.

In February 1473 another of the king's enemies, the Duke of Alençon, was captured and imprisoned. By the spring of 1473 the period of the great feudal coalitions had ended. Charles the Bold had extended his truce with France until April 1474 and became involved in German affairs. Charles of France and the Count of Armagnac were dead, the County of Foix was in the hands of a child, the Duke of Alençon was in prison, and the Duke of Brittany became inactive.

By this time, Louis largely controlled the clergy and the upper middle class in the towns. Thus, with the great nobles weakened, his power over the three most influential social classes in the country was very strong and was destined to become even stronger by the closing years of his reign. French particularism and the remnants of feudal privileges were still too deeply entrenched, and the French monarchy not yet powerful enough, however, for Louis XI to be an absolute monarch like Louis XIV, two centuries later. If the idea of such absolutism ever occurred to him, he realized that it was impossible. In fact, he was very conscious of the importance of public opinion.[5]

As Charles the Bold turned his attention increasingly toward German affairs, it might be well to pause for a moment and see exactly what his ambitions were in the direction of Germany and what success he had achieved thus far. He probably hoped to join his northern domains in the Low Countries with the Duchy of Burgundy in Eastern France and the adjoining County of Burgundy in the Holy Roman Empire.

Actually, Charles was less active in territorial expansion in his early years as duke than previous dukes, such as Philip the Bold and Philip the Good. He seldom pursued aggression for its own sake; only when it furthered his major ambition, to secure the succession to the throne of the Holy Roman Empire.

We have seen that he seized Liège in 1468. Historians have

alleged that he was particularly anxious to gain control of Upper
Alsace as part of his plan to join his northern and southern lands.
There is little evidence that this is so. Geographically speaking, it
would not have linked his territories anyway. Even if he did have
such a desire, there is certainly nothing new in it. Previous dukes
had been interested in extending Burgundian influence in Alsace.

In the 1460s, the Emperor Frederick III ruled the eastern
Habsburg lands, centered around Austria, while his cousin
Sigismund ruled the western lands scattered along both banks of
the Upper Rhine. Both called themselves Duke of Austria.
Sigismund also claimed to rule the Swiss cantons, but they did not
recognize his suzerainty. Sigismund's lands were subject to
frequent Swiss aggression. In 1468, the Swiss invaded, defeated
the indolent Sigismund, and forced him to sign the Treaty of
Walshut. He had to pay them a large indemnity of 10,000 florins
by June 1469. He requested a loan from France, but Louis
refused. He was then forced to turn to the Duke of Burgundy. By
the Treaty of St. Omer, in May 1469, Charles the Bold took
Sigismund under his protection and gave him 50,000 florins, in
return for the Upper Rhine Vorlande in mortgage. This included
Upper Alsace and the County of Ferrette. Charles appointed an
arrogant bailiff to administer these lands, Peter von Hagenbach,
who soon made himself very unpopular.

Charles's rights in Upper Alsace and Ferrette were limited by
the fact that many areas had been mortgaged to local nobles or
towns. Also, the ten principal towns were imperial cities directly
under the Emperor. Upper Alsace was chaotically administered
at the time. Charles did little to improve it. He made no serious
effort to gain control over the imperial towns. Charles seemed to
have no primary interest in developing his power in Alsace. His
immediate political ambitions lay elsewhere. He never con-
verted Upper Alsace into a genuine territory fully incorporated
into the other Burgundian lands.

Much more important than Alsace as a possible link between
Charles's northern and southern territories was Lorraine. It was
French-speaking, but part of the Empire. It was not completely
annexed until 1475, but Charles the Bold gained virtual control
of it somewhat earlier.

Duke John of Calabria and Lorraine died in 1470. He was
succeeded by his son Nicholas. The latter was enticed into a close
alliance with Charles the Bold by the insincere offer of Mary of
Burgundy in marriage. In May 1472 he signed a treaty

of alliance with Charles which gave the Duke of Burgundy and his troops transit rights in the duchy and the right of entry into its towns and fortified places.

The death of Nicholas of Lorraine, in 1473, threw open the succession. As King René of Anjou had now outlived both his son and his grandson, and had no male heirs, not only the immediate succession to Lorraine was open, but the ultimate fate of René's other possessions, Anjou, Provence, Maine, and Bar, was an issue. Charles the Bold was deeply concerned with Lorraine, and had his eye on Provence. Louis XI was also interested in the succession in Lorraine, and hoped to acquire all of King René's territories.

There were two claimants to Lorraine. The provincial estates met in August 1473 and offered the duchy to one of them, Yolande of Anjou. She accepted and abdicated in favor of her son, René, cousin of Duke Nicholas and grandson of King René through his mother. Charles the Bold was involved with his imperial ambitions and plans to join England to crush Louis XI once and for all. Therefore he was not seriously interested in the conquest of Lorraine at the time. However, he did need to keep his lines of communication across it open. Charles signed the Treaty of Nancy with René in October. Each promised to help the other against French attack. Each also permitted the free passage of troops across each other's territories. This confirmed the previous grant of Duke Nicholas. Relations between Charles and René remained good.

Charles the Bold's other territorial gain during the period was greatly facilitated by his prolongation of the truce with Louis XI in the spring of 1473. When Charles abandoned his original plan to attack the French king again that April, and agreed to extend the truce by one year, he was guided by the same thought that was in Louis's mind. He too planned to use the truce for activity on another front. The battle with the French crown was not ended. A renewal of the war was certain at the end of the truce, if not sooner. Until then, Charles as well as Louis thought it highly beneficial to have a free hand for other projects which an immediate continuation of the war with France would have prevented. Conditions in England also left Charles free to act. If Edward IV had been determined to invade France in 1473, the truce extension with France could not have gone into effect. However, Edward was forced to postpone his invasion plans until the following year. Many Italian contemporaries thought Charles planned to take advantage of the truce extension to attack Milan and thus destroy the French-Milanese alliance. Actually Charles intended to conquer Guelders.

For several years, Charles the Bold had been continuing Philip the Good's policy of extending Burgundian influence in the Duchy of Guelders. At the end of 1471, Duke Arnold, in an effort to obtain Burgundian assistance against supporters of his son, who was trying to seize the duchy, offered Charles the guardianship of Guelders. Charles accepted. The towns and many nobles remained loyal to his son. Therefore, in December 1472 Arnold mortgaged Guelders to Charles, although he was to enjoy its possession for the rest of his life. He died in February 1473, leaving Guelders to Charles in his will. The Estates of Guelders and some towns denied the legality of the will. The truce extension with France left Charles free to take military action. He invaded and conquered Guelders in the summer of 1473. Throughout the rest of his reign, Guelders was under Burgundian military occupation. The conquest of Guelders helped round out Burgundian possessions in the Netherlands, and drove a wedge between Holland and Friesland.

Commynes describes the policy of Louis XI after the conquest of Guelders as one of cunning laissez-faire, aimed at allowing Charles to become involved in projects that would lead to his ruin. Some historians have seen both Louis's extension of the truce with Charles in April 1473 and his lack of intervention during the Guelders campaign as part of this policy. As seen before, Louis had good reasons for wanting to extend the truce, but this was certainly not one of them. Nor was his failure to act during Charles's conquest of Guelders part of his plans. Louis did not secretly approve Charles's campaign. He failed to realize that it was planned. When he learned of it, he considered himself outmaneuvered. A Milanese envoy later mentioned that the king saw himself as having been deluded and deceived by the truce. This explains how Charles succeeded in conquering Guelders in a few weeks undisturbed by any intervention against him.

In the case of Upper Alsace, Lorraine, and Guelders, Charles the Bold seems to have been by no means an overambitious, rash conqueror. His plans were carefully laid, his interventions were judiciously timed and limited in extent. He only really acted forcefully in Guelders. His royal or imperial ambitions took precedence over mere territorial conquests.

What were Charles the Bold's imperial dreams, already frequently mentioned? The loose federation known as the Holy Roman Empire, although containing some non-German lands, was German in its ruler, government, and its center of gravity. The Emperor was Frederick III, head of the House of Habsburg, Duke of Austria, Styria, Carinthia, and Carniola. He had ruled since 1440, although his official coronation in Rome had not taken place until 1452. His interests were chiefly dynastic, not imperial. The princes who were really influential in the Empire at the time were the King of Denmark, Norway and Sweden; the King of Bohemia; the King of Hungary; and Charles the Bold. Two-thirds of Charles's lands lay within the Empire.

As imperial princes, the Dukes of Burgundy in the fifteenth century had always taken part in imperial affairs, sending deputies to meetings of the imperial Diet (a kind of parliament), and maintaining a network of alliances in imperial territory. Philip the Good had annexed Brabant, Holland and Luxembourg within the Empire. Charles was active in Alsace, Lorraine and Guelders. The Dukes of Burgundy also had economic interests in the Empire, particularly the wine trade down the Rhine River. Because of both territorial and economic activities within the Empire, the Dukes of Burgundy naturally had ambitions there.

In 1463, the Emperor Frederick III disclosed that he would not be opposed to a marriage alliance between Mary of Burgundy, daughter of Charles the Bold, and his son, Maximilian, and to the promotion at the same time of the Duke of Burgundy to the royal dignity. The projected marriage was again under negotiation in 1467, and there was talk of the duke becoming vicar of the Empire. It is hardly surprising that this project should become the dominant theme of Charles's diplomatic relations with the Emperor. Like most of his other ambitions and policies, it had been taken over from his father.

The chief pawn in Charles's diplomacy with the Emperor was his only child and heiress, Mary, born in February 1457. She was the bait used to tempt the Habsurgs to cede some, or even all, of their imperial power in return for Maximilian gaining all the rich Burgundian lands. Charles made good use of her, as he did in his diplomacy with many other princes. He seems, however, to have been unable to part with his daughter while he lived, unless perhaps it would lead to the accomplishment of his imperial dreams.

Charles enlarged the scope of his father's imperial ambitions. He wanted Frederick to name him King of the Romans (Vice-Emperor) and successor to the imperial throne. He made several diplomatic overtures through German princes, in 1469, trying to obtain this position in return for the marriage of Mary to Maximilian. There is considerable evidence that many felt, in 1469, that the elevation of Charles to the position of King of the Romans would be desirable. It would place him at the head of Christendom's defences against the Turks and would restore the Empire's unity and strength. Sigismund of Austria, as part of an agreement with Charles, negotiated intermittently in 1470 with the Emperor on Charles's behalf. Frederick refused at the time. He believed that it would have entailed the partial, or even complete abdication of his own imperial authority. Also, in 1471, Charles was the principal ally of Frederick's enemy, the Elector Palatine of the Rhine.

This coolness between Frederick and Charles was followed by a rapprochement in 1472–73. The initiative came from Burgundy. It was a three-sided affair. Charles wanted the imperial crown; Frederick hoped for the marriage alliance to bring the Burgundian lands into the hereditary Habsburg possessions; Duke Sigismund still needed Burgundian help against the Swiss. The trouble was that Charles had no intention of fighting the Swiss and the Emperor had no intention of abdicating imperial authority to Charles.

Early in 1473, Charles sent an ambassador to Frederick. He was to tell him that Charles sought to be made King of the Romans to succeed Frederick but that, contrary to the Emperor's fears, Charles would serve him loyally and strengthen his authority rather than weaken it. Then, on Frederick's death, Charles would name Maximilian King of the Romans. The envoy was to propose a personal meeting between Charles and Frederick. Frederick agreed to a meeting at Trier.

The meeting took place on September 30, 1473, outside Trier. Each had splendid retinues, but Charles dazzled everyone with the magnificent costumes of his entourage and the richness of his treasure.

The opening meeting was very friendly. The first few days

were taken up chiefly with feasts and tournaments. The climax was a magnificent banquet given by Charles for the Emperor. When the serious discussions got under way, Frederick refused to grant Charles his main objective, to be crowned King of the Romans and promised the succession to the imperial throne, in return for the marriage alliance. Instead, he offered an imperial vicarate and a territorial kingdom dependent upon the Empire. Finding his main ambition thwarted, Charles proposed his investment with Savoy, as guardian of the young duke, reconciliation between the Emperor and the Elector Palatine, and his investment with the Duchy of Guelders, which he had already occupied. He was duly invested with Guelders on November 6.

Charles then lowered his sights from the Kingdom of the Romans to a kingdom of his own lands, which he had at first refused. The duke was within a hair's breadth of wearing a crown. Workmen prepared the Cathedral of Trier for the coronation for November 18, later deferred until November 21. The crown, the scepter, and costumes are said to have been made ready. The exact title which Charles was to receive was probably King of Burgundy. But no coronation took place. On November 24, Frederick announced his intended departure. The next morning he slipped away unobtrusively down the Rhine in spite of the efforts of one of Charles's senior negotiators to detain him. He did not even see Charles in person.

The exact reason why no coronation took place has yet to be found. It had nothing to do with Louis XI's letter to the Emperor requesting that Charles not be crowned, and offering his own daughter to Maximilian instead. There were probably two fundamental difficulties in the way of the creation of Charles's kingdom. In the first place, the duke was not happy with what to him was second best, and kept making new proposals. This irritated Frederick. In the second place, the imperial electors were opposed to the idea. They feared the added prestige of the powerful duke within the Empire. Also, Charles may have demanded the place in the college of electors that belonged to the King of Bohemia, who was in revolt at the time because he supported the heresy of John Huss. This would have been too much for Frederick and the electors. Moreover, Frederick was probably annoyed at Charles's refusal to abandon his ally, the Count Palatine. Perhaps significant was Upper Alsace. Sigismund urged Frederick to get it back for him, but Charles refused to restore it. Finally, the character and attitude of Frederick was probably a factor. His diplomacy was habitually tortuous and evasive. He always moved slowly and uncertainly. He may have been unwilling to accept Charles as a king within the Empire.

Charles left Trier empty-handed. He failed to gain the succession of the Empire; he failed to obtain the crown of the Romans; he failed to establish his lands as a kingdom. However, his person and court had been displayed at Trier as the most splendid in Europe. He still had his widespread circle of supporters and allies. He had completed the creation of a new army. Contemporaries speculated on the next move of this frustrated, powerful, and ambitious prince.

During the last half of 1473, while Charles the Bold held the center of the stage, Louis XI appeared relatively inactive. He was largely incapacitated by illness for two months during the summer.

In spite of his bitter disappointment at Trier, the Grand Duke of the West (as Charles the Bold was often called by then), did not abandon his project. He resolved to form his kingdom all by himself, with or without the approval of the emperor. He meddled openly in German affairs by announcing his intention to seize Cologne, whose prince-archbishop had been driven from the city and had sought Charles's help. The occupation of Cologne would give him another piece of Rhine territory. He then marched through Lorraine and Upper Alsace, attempting to overawe the inhabitants with a demonstration of his military might. In January 1474 he reached Dijon, capital of the Duchy of Burgundy, and announced to an assembly of nobles and prelates that he intended to recreate the old Kingdom of Burgundy— Lotharingia.[6]

Charles the Bold's expansionist policy toward the German area inevitably aroused hostility from the regions threatened by it. His partial control of Upper Alsace and the County of Ferrette, since he had obtained them in 1469 by mortgage, was resented by most of his new neighbors. It aroused the mistrust of his ally Frederick, Elector Palatine of the Rhine, and of the two most powerful and populous cities on that river, Strasbourg and Basel. Strasbourg exercised strong economic and political control over the Rhineland from Frankfurt and Cologne to Basel. She became consistently anti-Burgundian after Charles's intrusion into Upper Alsace.

The treaty of St. Omer between Sigismund of Austria and Charles the Bold, in 1469, was a direct provocation to the Swiss. Sigismund had signed it to get Burgundian military help against them, and had become a Burgundian ally. This could be interpreted as an infringement of a treaty signed by Charles two years before with Bern, Zurich, Soluthurn, and Fribourg.

Exactly what was meant by the term "the Swiss" in the fifteenth century requires a brief explanation. The narrower term "Swiss Federation," the *Eidgenossen,* consisted of five rural communities and the three towns of Lucerne, Zurich, and Bern. The broader term "the Swiss" also included their allies and dependencies. They were expansionist and aggressive. Perhaps the most militant was the town of Bern. She expanded westwards, and several towns, such as Fribourg, became her allies and virtual satellites.

The situation in Neuchâtel and Vaud, both dependencies of Bern, was unfavorable to Burgundian-Bernese friendship. Both the Count of Neuchâtel and the Baron of Vaud were loyal and trusted supporters of Charles the Bold. Peter von Hagenbach, the arrogant Burgundian bailiff appointed by Charles in Upper Alsace in 1469, was hostile to the towns and to the Swiss. So were the Alsatian nobles. Both would have gladly joined with Duke Sigismund of Austria in making war against the Swiss, but Charles the Bold refused to support any such plan. He was concerned about possible war with France, and he urged Sigismund not to provoke the Swiss.

In June 1470, a meeting was held of those concerned by Charles's acquisition of Upper Alsace. It was attended by Frederick, Elector Palatine of the Rhine, Strasbourg, Colmar, Basel, and the Swiss federation. This was possibly the beginning of a plan to expel Burgundy from Alsace. This meeting coincided approximately with Louis XI's first treaty with the Swiss in August 1470, by the terms of which each promised to remain neutral if the other were attacked by Charles the Bold.

By 1471 Sigismund was losing hope of recovering his ancestral possessions from the Swiss with the military help of Charles the Bold. Until the fourteenth century, his family had controlled

virtually the entire Swiss region, and in the fifteenth century
they had lost two more pieces of land to Swiss aggression.
Sigismund now turned from plans of attacking the Swiss to
attempts at negotiation. A peace conference was held in October
1471 aimed at achieving a lasting settlement with the Swiss. The
latter proposed that Sigismund regain possession of his lands in
Alsace mortgaged to Charles the Bold. Little was achieved at
this meeting, but it was a step toward the formation of a grand
alliance against Burgundy, without any encouragement from
Louis XI.

Charles the Bold was aware of these developments, and tried
unsuccessfully, in 1471, to negotiate a treaty of friendship or
alliance with the Swiss. Actually, he preferred a settlement with
Sigismund. Both men were playing a double game. Sigismund was
negotiating with the Swiss while seeking Burgundian help against
them. Charles was negotiating with the Swiss while discussing
with Sigismund the possibility of a joint attack on them. The
Swiss sent a cordial reply to Charles's embassy in the spring of
1472. However, the actions and statements of Charles's bailiff,
Hagenbach, in Upper Alsace, continued to antagonize them.

In early 1473, the blustering, aggressive activities of von
Hagenbach provoked further moves toward an anti-Burgundian
alliance. He ordered the independent, imperial city of Mulhouse,
for the third time, to open her gates to Duke Charles. In
February the Swiss diet (a sort of parliament of the federation),
after seeing a copy of Hagenbach's threatening letter to
Mulhouse, resolved to work for an alliance of the imperial towns
of the Upper Rhine against Burgundy. The imperial towns were
those that were under the direct authority of the Holy Roman
Emperor, without any intermediate territorial ruler. Also in
February, deputies from Strasbourg, Basel, Colmar, and Sélestat
met and agreed that Burgundian rule in the County of Ferrette
must be brought to an end, by force, if necessary.

The climax came at a meeting in Basel on March 14, 1473. A
project for a ten-year alliance was drawn up between the
Bishops of Strasbourg and Basel, Colmar, and Sélestat on one side
and the Swiss and Mulhouse on the other. If any "foreign people"
should "try unjustly by force to take away the liberties of or
detach from the Holy Empire one or more members of the
alliance," the others would help them. The four imperial towns
agreed to raise the money for the redemption of mortgaged

Alsace from Charles the Bold. All of the main elements of a grand alliance against Charles had emerged by the spring of 1473, but the project was not yet completed.

In June 1473 Charles sent envoys to the Swiss proposing an alliance with Burgundy, but they were not interested. They felt themselves threatened by Burgundian power. Also, Charles did nothing about the provocations to which Hagenbach was subjecting them in and around Alsace. Meanwhile, Duke Sigismund of Austria was becoming increasingly disillusioned about the value of his alliance with Charles the Bold. Both Sigismund and the Swiss were in contact with Louis XI. Both hoped, since all else had failed, that an agreement between them and the redemption of Alsace could be achieved by French diplomacy. Charles's determination to retain Alsace, however, was publicly displayed by his visit there at Christmas 1473. Wherever he went, he insisted on the inhabitants swearing oaths of fealty to him.

In January 1474, the Duke of Burgundy received two important embassies. The first was from the Swiss complaining of Hagenbach's boast that he would soon conquer many Swiss lordships and would soon be lord of Bern. The second was from Duke Sigismund attempting to explain his negotiations with Louis XI. Charles's reply showed his anger and demonstrated that the Austro-Burgundian alliance was no longer in effect.

As usual, the initiative in the next round of negotiations for an alliance against Burgundy was urban. Strasbourg raised the matter with Bern at the end of 1473. In January 1474, at Basel, Swiss ambassadors, returning from Alsace, agreed to a revival of the scheme which had been discussed there in March 1473. In the talk that followed, the redemption of Alsace was once more proposed, partly because Louis XI insisted that Sigismund break his alliance with Charles the Bold and regain Alsace, in return for his helping to mediate between the parties involved. But Louis's role was limited. Instead of using French diplomats in the negotiations, he allowed the Swiss and Austrians to undertake them by themselves. He was still unprepared to pay for the redemption of the Alsatian mortgage. This had to be undertaken by the towns. Basel, Colmar, Sélestat, and Strasbourg raised the necessary money. All that was still necessary was for Bern and Zurich to persuade the rest of the Swiss federation to agree to the general alliance that had now been virtually created against

Charles the Bold. This task was completed by Bern. Her ambassadors finally persuaded Schwyz to join, after most of the rest of the Swiss federation had agreed to an alliance with the Alsatian towns and Sigismund in March 1474.

Later that month, at a conference at Constance, the various negotiations reached a definitive stage. The documents sealed on March 31 and April 4 contained the four main points of agreement which created the League of Constance. First, a "Perpetual Peace" between Austria and the Swiss was proclaimed in principle, with final arrangements to be settled through the arbitration of Louis XI. Second, a ten-year defensive alliance of the Upper Rhine powers was created, under the name of the Lower Union, the term being used to distinguish them from the Swiss federation, which called itself the alliance or league of Upper Germany. The original members were Duke Sigismund, the Bishop of Strasbourg, the Bishop of Basel, and the four imperial towns of Strasbourg, Basel, Sélestat, and Colmar. In July 1474, five Alsatian towns joined, followed in October by the town of Montbéliard. Finally, in April 1475, René, Duke of Lorraine, joined the Lower Union.

The third point of agreement in the formation of the League of Constance was the redemption by Sigismund of his lands and rights in Upper Alsace mortgaged to Charles the Bold. The money was to be paid by the towns. The final point was the formation of a ten-year defensive alliance between the bishops and towns of Basel and Strasbourg, with Colmar and Sélestat, on the one side (the Lower Union except Sigismund), and the Swiss federation and the town of Soluthurn on the other.

Thus was formed gradually the League of Constance, a grand alliance against Charles the Bold. It was defensive in nature, except for the possible use of force to secure the return of Upper Alsace to Sigismund. It was primarily urban, the towns having taken the initiative. It was loosely organized and geographically scattered, making it almost incapable of concerted offensive action. It appeared to pose no serious threat to Burgundian power, until internal events in Alsace gave it an opportunity to intervene decisively.[7]

The League of Constance was destined to bring about the downfall of the powerful Charles the Bold of Burgundy. Therefore, the role of Louis XI in forging this alliance is very significant in judging his diplomatic achievements.

According to virtually all previous historians of Louis XI, basing their opinion directly on Commynes, the French king played the leading part in bringing about the "Perpetual Peace" between the Duke of Austria and the Swiss. He supposedly worked diligently, sparing no expense, to achieve the very difficult task of reconciling these sworn enemies. Moreover, he persuaded other mutually hostile powers on the Upper Rhine to form an alliance with them. His purpose was to use them all against Burgundy. Allegedly this was the most successful and brilliant accomplishment of the king's reign.

Commynes's picture is shown by original sources to be incorrect. The role of Louis XI in the whole formation of the alliance system was very small. When his help was finally requested by Sigismund of Austria, he had no new plans. He merely fell back on the conditions of the agreement already drawn up at Constance in 1472, in the formulation of which he had played no part at all. Claims that Louis cleverly gained decisive influence over the Swiss with a lavish distribution of gold to make them act in his interest are completely false in the years before 1473. His activity was confined to a brief period from the summer of 1473, when he became involved in the peace negotiations, until March 1474, when the League of Constance was formed. Even then, there is no evidence of a grand plan or masterful politics on Louis's part. A treaty that had been in existence for some time was recognized as the basis for peace, and one party was forced to make concessions for the benefit of the other. Louis had been requested by the participants in the League of Constance to complete the negotiations between Duke Sigismund and the Swiss. He forced the Duke of Austria to accept everything the Swiss demanded without suggesting any concessions in return. His only guideline was the wishes and goals of the Swiss. Instead of leading them, he followed them. Louis's intervention in the reconciliation was limited to little more than putting previously determined peace conditions into royal letters patent. His embassy to the Swiss in mid-March 1474 arrived when the general alliance against Charles the Bold had already virtually been created.

The ransom of Duke Sigismund's lands in Alsace, pawned to Burgundy, has often been regarded as the immediate motive for French participation in the growing alliance system that became the League of Constance This is not true. It already had been demanded by the Swiss from Duke Sigismund in 1471 as the basic condition without which they would not enter into any peace agreement with him. The initiative did not come from Louis XI. It was, above all, the wish of Bern, so that their expansion towards the Upper Rhine would not be limited. It was the price for which Bern was willing to have peace with Austria It was also of the utmost importance to Strasbourg which, along with the imperial towns of Alsace, wished to be freed from the Burgundian threat as soon as possible. It was a point of common interest which united Bern and Strasbourg. The fears and the dangers which resulted from Burgundian rule in the Upper Rhine region drove the other powers in this area, and those dependent upon Burgundy, together. This alliance was not guided from afar. Its history, from its beginning until its conclusion, shows how small a part Louis XI played in its formation. Even when he finally supported it, he did not change it.

During the spring of 1473, while the alliance was slowly forming, the French king's policy toward its members was distinctly negative. In May the Swiss diet resolved to write Louis complaining of the passage of Charles's Italian mercenaries through their lands. The same month, the Milanese ambassador at the French court reported that Strasbourg had sent an envoy to seek help from Louis against Charles the Bold. Also in May Duke Sigismund, fearing Swiss attack but still getting no help from Burgundy, applied to Louis for protection and an alliance. Louis turned down his request and informed his Swiss allies of it. He made no effort to exploit the opportunity of stirring up trouble for Charles. He sent no help to either Strasbourg or the Swiss and did not encourage them to attack Burgundy. All Louis did was suggest the redemption of Sigismund's mortaged lands in Alsace from Charles, but he did not offer to pay for it. He also suggested a reconciliation between the Swiss and Sigismund. He had no far-reaching plans, no subtle intentions, and showed no brilliant diplomacy.

When Bern informed him of the conclusion of the Peace of Constance and the early victories of the League, in May 1474, Louis wrote a calm letter congratulating his friends on their success. The wording certainly did not seem to be that of a man who finally saw something he had long worked and planned for coming true.

When the Confederates felt themselves threatened, Louis suggested that they seek some allies within the Empire. He offered to participate himself in such alliances. In reality, these proposals of May 1474 probably had as their primary purpose the concealment of his own peace negotiations with Burgundy.

Louis's diplomatic relations with the Swiss were by no means new. They had been increasingly active and had been marked by a growing friendship. There were constant exchanges of information and expressions of goodwill. There was considerable correspondence between the king and Bern, as well as frequent exchanges of ambassadors.

Louis XI explained his real motives for retaining close relations with the Swiss to one of his envoys to the Duke of Austria in the summer of 1474. He did so in order to make it clear why he had to wait for a full reconciliation between Duke Sigismund and the Swiss Confederation before he could conclude a treaty with Austria. France had long maintained friendly relations with the House of Habsburg, and especially with Sigismund. However, these relations had been broken while the Duke of Austria was an ally of Burgundy. That is why Louis had sought even closer ties with the Swiss. In view of the constant unrest in France, often instigated by Burgundy, it seemed necessary to Louis, just as it did to Charles the Bold, to enter into German alliances for greater security. Therefore, Louis had undertaken to strengthen his old alliance with the Swiss. This made any close relationship with Austria impossible because of the long-standing animosity between Austria and the Swiss, in addition to Sigismund's Burgundian alliance. It was only after Louis had heard that the treaty between Sigismund and Charles the Bold had been dissolved, and that the Austrian duke had entered into negotiations with the Swiss, that he was able to renew his old friendship with Sigismund. Louis was carrying on negotiations with Sigismund and had promised him both protection and an alliance. However, the truce between France and Burgundy had just been extended for a year, and Louis had not included Sigismund as an ally in this agreement. Therefore, he had not really provided him with any protection against Burgundy at all. The royal instructions to the above-mentioned envoy to the Austrian duke tried to hide this fact.

Most historians have seen Louis's Swiss alliance as aggressive, aimed at turning them against Burgundy. On the contrary, it was

for defensive, not offensive, reasons. Louis advised the Swiss to
stay in their mountains for their security. He was quite content to
renew their old agreement of neutrality, rather than urging them
to war. In the middle of 1473, the king was still at the same point
as in 1469. His behavior toward the Swiss was one of reserve and
self-control. He reached no decision involving their interests
unless he was sure it would be acceptable to them. He followed
their will instead of guiding them. Their wishes, not the king's
cunning calculations, determined their relationship until the
signing of the "Perpetual Agreement."

The animosity of the Swiss against Burgundy originated chiefly
in Bern. It was not kindled by Louis XI, as many have claimed.
On the one hand, Bern tried to pull the rest of the Swiss
federation into this hostility; on the other hand, she tried to win the
support of the King of France as an old and powerful enemy of
Charles the Bold. She proposed an alliance to him that would go
far beyond the existing agreement of neutrality. She wanted the
availability of his power if she should take up arms against the
Duke of Burgundy.

In these negotiations, French gold did not play a major part.
Until they accepted Louis's arbitration terms, which were
basically their own, regarding the final conclusion of the
"Perpetual Agreement," there was no question of a generous
distribution of French gold amongst the Swiss. It was not Louis
who tried to make the Swiss serve his aggressive interests. On
the contrary, it was Bern who sought to persuade him to serve
her warlike plans. The carefulness and reserve of the king stands
out in contrast against the stressed preparedness for war of Bern.
He remained cautious about entering into the new and more
binding treaties urged by Bern. Aggressive thought as a basis for
French politics toward the Confederates is in contradiction to
the evidence. Thoughts of defense lend the Swiss policy of Louis
XI cohesion until, and even after, the conclusion of the
"Perpetual Agreement."

It is an old mistake to see Louis XI as necessarily aggressive in
all his planning. Even within his kingdom, his actions against the
French princes were more often defensive than aggressive. For
years he had to use all his strength to preserve his power and the
sovereignty of the crown. The man whom he regarded as his
most consistent opponent, in both internal and external affairs,
was the Duke of Burgundy. It was therefore necessary to isolate

Burgundian power, once it became clear that he could not overcome it alone. His constant preoccupations were to protect himself from Burgundian attack, to work against continuing Burgundian expansion, and to avoid having himself surrounded by Burgundian allies.

The association of Louis XI with Bern and the Swiss Confederacy was part of his defensive action against the continued threat from the Duke of Burgundy, both within and without the kingdom. He was particularly anxious to prevent an alliance between Burgundy and the Emperor, or, if it should occur, balance it by keeping the sworn enemies of the imperial house, the Swiss, as his friends and allies. He recognized the fact that they were militarily strong. Their lands also bordered directly on those of Burgundy.

In the early years of his reign, Louis had his alliance with Liège, which enabled him to keep Charles the Bold in constant difficulty. He had taken Liège, which was very hostile to Burgundy, under his protection. Although he did not plan Liège's revolt against Charles, he was able to take advantage of this hostility, and her constant threat to invade Brabant and Namur. The value of this alliance for Louis lay in the possibility of provoking war for Burgundy in the Low Countries if Charles should attack France. The defeat of Liège by Charles, in 1468, robbed him of this valuable protective weapon.

To make up for this loss, Louis XI brought the Swiss Confederates into his politics in place of Liége. When the animosity of Bern against Burgundy was presented to him, just as that of Liège had been, he slowly entered this new alliance. But he did not rush to give aggressive direction to the union. When he unleashed his great attack on Burgundy, in 1471, he let the Confederates stand neutral on the sidelines. This was the only time during the formation of the League of Constance when Louis was the aggressor against Charles. His campaign was one of limited objectives, however. He had no hope of completely smashing the Duke of Burgundy at this time and annexing some of his lands. He merely sought to inflict a serious enough military defeat upon him to keep him from sending his armies into France again, in support of feudal coalitions against him, as Charles had done consistently since 1465. The Confederates did not participate either in the war of 1472, which broke out against Louis's expectations. This time, it was Charles who attacked him.

Nevertheless, the association was very important to Louis in the field of general politics. It completely fulfilled its defensive purpose. It presented a constant threat to the ancestral Burgundian lands of Burgundy and Franche-Comté. From then on, Charles the Bold had constantly to take into very serious account the hostile influence of the King of France. He was worried by this alliance, and tried by every means to dissolve it. These efforts by Charles caused Louis to be even more careful to do everything he could to keep the Swiss as allies. Even when Bernese policies worked openly against him, as in Savoy in 1471, he ignored it. His assurances of faithfulness to the alliance sounded more and more sincere. However, it still retained its loose character of mutual obligation to neutrality.

When the Duke of Austria sought to switch his alliance from Burgundy to France, Louis would have liked to agree. He held back, however, as his association with the Swiss must at no cost be weakened. Only after the "Perpetual Alliance," when the Swiss and Austria reached agreement, did Louis send negotiators to Duke Sigismund.

One may well wonder why Louis XI wanted the Duke of Austria as an ally in spite of his relative weakness. His alliance constituted one more blow at the Duke of Burgundy. It allowed France to get a firmer footing in Germany and to gain, in addition to the Swiss, one more ally within the Empire. It was an addition to Louis's rather small system of alliances. Despite the weakness of the House of Austria, the strategic geographical position of its possessions was useful. They included one of the great connecting links over the Alps, the one to Venice. This route for his Italian diplomacy, and for bringing in his Italian mercenaries, was now closed to Charles. It exposed Franche-Comté to attack when the mortaged lands in Alsace were Austrian again. Sigismund had promised, when he sought French protection, to attack Burgundy from Germany if France should find herself at war against Charles again. The alliance fitted in with Louis's plans for protection and defense against Burgundian expansion with every possible alliance within the Empire. Peace between the Duke of Austria and the Swiss meant that Louis could have the help of both, if he needed it.

It is not true that Louis XI planned to hurl these new allies without delay at Burgundy, that he had worked diligently for peace between them in order to build a war machine, that he had shrewdly precalculated this alliance of old enemies with the express purpose of attacking Charles the Bold and bringing about his downfall. The way in which he basically let events run their course, and essential matters were wound up without his intervention, contradicts the usual image of Louis as the overseer of the "Perpetual Alliance." There was no preconceived plan, no refined psychological insight no purposeful calculation. His famous methods of diplomacy: clever persuasion, intrigue, subversive activity, incitement, and bribery were not applied. No particular diplomatic technique was even used. No high political art was practiced. It was not Louis's intention. The "Perpetual Alliance" was not formed in the way which Commynes described.[8]

In the spring of 1474 the course of events in Alsace was largely dependent upon the behavior of the Burgundian bailiff, Peter von Hagenbach. The interested parties at Constance had agreed that he must go. In May Charles the Bold sent an embassy to Basel complaining about her alleged plan to join an alliance against him. Basel answered that her acceptance of the extension of Burgundian power into the immediate environs of her city had been nullified by the insulting and intolerable behavior of Hagenbach. She sent a long list of complaints against him.

Meanwhile, Hagenbach's conduct in Alsace became increasingly arbitrary and offensive. It included alleged sexual offenses against nuns, and other sexual crudities. Perhaps his biggest mistake was his failure to pay his troops. They mutinied at Breisach in April 1474. The citizens of the town, who had lost their civic liberties and institutions to Hagenbach, supported the soldiers. Hagenbach was arrested and held prisoner.

Meanwhile, on April 6, Sigismund of Austria formally renounced his alliance with Charles the Bold and sent a herald to him to announce that he was resuming his rule in Alsace. He had deposited the money for the redemption of the mortgage in Basel. He arrived in Basel with troops on April 20. The towns of the League of Constance were equally aggressive. In mid-April, Strasbourg captured several places in Alsace. Basel and Strasbourg sent Charles the Bold a polite but firm note saying that they were bound to help Sigismund recover his Alasatian territories. Bern was actively preparing for war. Bern and others insisted on Hagenbach's trial and execution. He was tried by representatives of the League of Constance in early May 1474 and put to death.

For Charles the execution of Hagenbach and the loss of Alsace were critical events. They were his first serious reverses. As one historian says, they may have made a lasting impression, "arousing perhaps an irrational desire for revenge and the obstinate, emotional, violent and aggressive side of his character which was to become increasingly apparent in the months and years that followed." In April, even before the execution of Hagenbach, he swore to the Neapolitan ambassador that he would avenge himself on the Duke of Austria or lose his life and state. He planned to arrange an alliance with Venice for a joint attack on Sigismund and made military preparations.

Other things interfered with Charles's intention, in the summer of 1474, to regain his control of Alsace and avenge himself on Sigismund, Strasbourg, and Basel. The most important was his decision to restore the authority of his ally, Ruprecht of Bavaria, in the archbishopric of Cologne first. He expected to deal with this situation quickly, and then attack Sigismund and his allies. His involvement with Cologne turned out to be long and complicated, and will be discussed in more detail later. The renewal of his truce with France for another year in June left him free to continue his German projects.

The theory of generations of historians, basing their opinion on the words of Commynes, that it was the shrewd and deliberate policy of Louis XI to leave Charles alone in 1474, as it had been in 1473, and to encourage him to invade Germany so that he would be embroiled in the feuds and complications of the Empire, and thus dissipate his strength forever, is simply not true. Commynes, writing years later, was probably attributing in retrospect to the king a farsightedness that he did not have. It was not until the fall of 1474, when Charles's campaign in Germany had bogged down at the the siege of Neuss, that Louis adopted this policy of "laissez-faire" toward Burgundy, and even then he was motivated by other considerations as well.

As part of his campaign in favor of the Archbishop of Cologne, Charles besieged the town of Neuss. It was not until mid-August, after he had begun the siege of Neuss, that Charles took any action in Alsace. Burgundian troops engaged in a four-day raid, destroying, burning, or removing everything in and around three Alsatian towns.

In September Charles was still optimistic about finishing the siege of Neuss. He wrote to Dijon that he would be on his way before long to punish his rebellious subjects in Alsace as soon as he had dealt with the Archbishop of Cologne's rebellious subjects in Neuss. This is the last mention of plans to restore Burgundian rule in Alsace. The siege of Neuss dragged on till the summer of 1475. By that time, new projects had intervened. Charles the Bold never did avenge himself on Strasbourg, Basel, or Sigismund, and Burgundian rule in Alsace was never restored.[9]

During the next year, from the late summer of 1474 to the late summer of 1475, the mutual antagonism between Charles the Bold and the powers that formed the League of Constance continued. The aggressive and conflicting policies of Charles, on the one side, and Strasbourg, Basel, and Bern, on the other, were largely responsible.

The Treaty of Constance of April 1474 had proclaimed an everlasting settlement between the Swiss and the Austrian Habsburgs, but many outstanding difficulties had been set aside for French mediation. Louis XI was involved with the Swiss in another connection in the summer of 1474 because Bern, anticipating war with Burgundy, had turned to him as a possible ally. However, Louis wanted a settlement with Charles. He had nothing to gain at the moment from an offensive against Charles. He refused to encourage Bern, and also rejected proposals received from the Emperor Frederick III, about the same time, for a Franco-Imperial alliance aimed against Burgundy. Louis was involved primarily that summer in the reconquest of Roussillon from Aragon, which he put off until late in the year. During the winter of 1474–75, while Charles besieged Neuss in vain, Louis besieged Perpignan successfully.

Although it was Bern and some Lower Union powers, not France, which hoped to attack Burgundy in 1474, Louis was anxious to keep on good terms with his Swiss and Austrian allies, and not to abandon the potentially valuable diplomatic situation then enjoyed by France in the Upper Rhine region. In June he announced his arbitral decision on Swiss-Austrian problems. As stated previously, it was wholly favorable to the Swiss. After pressure from the French ambassador, in October, Sigismund

signed a treaty with France accepting eternal friendship with the
Swiss, French protection and a French pension. Why did the
Duke of Austria agree to such unfavorable conditions which he
had previously rejected as humiliating? He agreed because of his
critical position at the moment. He had switched alliances. His
fear of Burgundian retaliation left him no choice but to accept
the immediate protection of France. Therefore, he had to
comply unconditionally with Swiss demands, which Louis XI
insisted upon, fearing to lose their valuable alliance.

Louis then offered the Swiss what Bern had been urging: an
offensive alliance against Charles the Bold. It did not take its
definitive form until January 1475, two months after the Swiss
had declared war on Charles and the League of Constance had
attacked Burgundian territory. According to the terms of the
alliance, Louis was to pay the Swiss 20,000 francs per year for
the rest of his life and help them in their wars, especially against
Burgundy. If he was unable to give them military assistance when
required, he would pay them an extra 80,000 francs per year
while they were involved in war without his help. In return, the
Swiss promised to send him troops wherever he required them,
at his expense.

These French diplomatic successes were of rather limited
impact. It is untrue to say that Louis XI persuaded the Swiss to
attack Charles the Bold. This was the work chiefly of Strasbourg
and Bern. But French diplomacy had pressured Sigismund into
accepting an alliance on rather unfavorable terms, and French
cash had helped bring the less aggressive members of the Swiss
federation into line with Bern. Pressures for a campaign against
Charles had been building up ever since Strasbourg and Basel
had sent him virtual declarations of war in April 1474. Following
the Burgundian raid into Alsace in August, Bern prepared troops
to attack at once. The Lower Union assembled forces and
appealed to Sigismund to join them in an immediate campaign.
By September Frederick III had joined the Lower Union in
pressing for an attack by the League on Charles, hoping that it
might cause him to abandon the siege of Neuss.

A Swiss declaration of war on Charles the Bold was issued on
October 29, 1474. Frederick III, not Louis XI, was named as the
instigator.

The opening attack was made almost immediately against the
strategically placed castle of Héricourt on the frontier of

Franche-Comté. The troops were provided chiefly by Sigismund and the Lower Union, not the Swiss. Bern, and other members of the Swiss federation, did participate, however. This attack, apart from the execution of Hagenbach, was the only major act of aggression on the part of the League of Constance as a whole. A large army besieged and captured Héricourt in early November. This military operation was merely a raid, not a large-scale invasion. It did not interrupt Charles's siege of Neuss. There was no enthusiasm at this time for major military action against Charles on the part of the allies. Louis's much-vaunted diplomacy then met with complete failure. In the spring of 1475, he was finally trying to organize a combined attack on all Burgundian lands by all Charles's enemies at once. They resisted his bribes and exhortations and refused to move.

When Franche-Comté was again invaded, in July 1475, it was neither at the instigation of Louis nor the Swiss. Once again, as in October 1474, it was the Lower Union, above all Strasbourg and Basel, which organized the attack. The largest single contingents were sent by Sigismund. By the end of the campaign, in August, they had captured about a dozen castles in Franche-Comté.[10]

All of the above confrontations between Charles the Bold and the members of the League of Constance were the result of Charles's interests in Alsace. He also came into conflict with some of the allies in two other geographical areas, Savoy and Lorraine.

Savoy had been strong under Duke Amadeus VIII. After his death, in 1451, a period of decline occurred which was exploited by Savoy's aggressive neighbors. Burgundy and Savoy had common borders from the Saône River to the Lake of Neuchâtel. The Dukes of Milan coveted southern Savoyard territory. Louis XI hoped to bring the duchy into the French orbit, or even acquire it outright. Louis had married Charlotte of Savoy, and his sister, Yolande, was married to Amadeus IX, who became duke in 1465. Earlier Burgundian interest in Savoy was increased after 1467 by the personal ambitions of Charles the Bold and the growing Burgundian sympathies of many of the princes of Savoy. In that same year, Amadeus and Yolande signed a treaty with Charles and his ally, Charles of France. The most powerful of Amadeus's brothers, Philip, entered into the service of Charles the Bold as his lieutenant in the two Burgundies (the duchy and Franche-Comté).

The most dangerous and aggressive of Savoy's neighbors was Bern. The intervention of Charles the Bold in Alsace had blocked her expansion to the northeast. It was not surprising that Bern should turn her ambitions westwards towards her weak neighbor Savoy. In the 1460s she intervened there increasingly. Duke Amadeus was an epileptic invalid. Yolande was named regent in 1469, and her regency was confirmed after her husband's death in 1472.

Between 1472 and 1475, Charles the Bold managed to win Yolande over to a Burgundian alliance. He succeeded in establishing a virtual Burgundian protectorate over Savoy. His motives were to protect his frontier and to expel French influence from the area. Perhaps he was already planning to annex Savoy. This policy led to a clash with Bern, as he was intervening in her sphere of influence.

Bern also objected to the increasing flow of Italian mercenaries, recruited by Charles after 1473, which passed through Savoy. She felt herself directly threatened. She sent an ultimatum to Yolande in January 1475 stating that the passage of Charles's mercenaries through her territory must cease, or Bern would invade Vaud. The hostility of Bern increased when Charles the Bold brought about the alliance of Savoy, Burgundy, and Milan in January 1475. This was a blow to France's influence in Italy as Milan had been her principal ally there. It also was a threat to Bern who felt herself encircled and menaced.

Bern and her ally Fribourg then began a private, undeclared war against Savoy, without the support of the rest of the Swiss federation. The object was to seize certain strategic places and castles. By April 1475 Bern gained control of a ring of castles which had limited her power at the southern end of the Lake of Neuchâtel.

In September 1475 the scene was set for a major offensive against Savoy which would, at the same time, strike a blow against Charles the Bold. Even if he could have extricated himself from the commitments resulting from his penetration of Alsace, Charles could scarcely have avoided the clash with Bern toward which his policies in Savoy had led him.[11]

No attempt to explain the origins of the campaigns of 1476, which brought about the downfall of Charles the Bold, would be complete without some mention of Lorraine. Here, as in Alsace and Savoy, his policies led to confrontation with his powerful urban enemies that would end in war.

Although the Duchy of Lorraine was part of the Empire, Frederick III had no effective authority there. René II, when he became duke in 1473, was faced with the need to protect himself from his more powerful neighbors by an alliance with either France or Burgundy. He applied first to Louis XI in September 1473, but his demands were unacceptable. Instead, he signed the treaty of Nancy with Charles the Bold in October 1473. By the terms, Charles was assured the free passage of his troops through Lorraine, and the friendship of Duke René.

These friendly relations continued until they were upset, in the first half of 1474, by the depredations of Burgundian troops in Lorraine. At the same time, René was influenced to switch alliances by several other factors; the efforts of Louis XI to win his friendship; requests and threats from the League of Constance; and a growing distrust of Charles the Bold who, by June 1474, had probably made definite plans to incorporate Lorraine into the Burgundian state. René finally signed a firm alliance with Louis XI in July-August, secretly renouncing his treaty with Burgundy. He continued to allow the passage of Burgundian troops, however, and refused requests from the Lower Union to take sides openly against Charles.

Finally, in May 1475, René sent a formal declaration of war to Charles, who was besieging Neuss by then. He must have grown tired of the damages caused by Burgundian troops passing through Lorraine. Also, he felt more secure because of his alliance with France and Louis's apparent promise to come to his aid in person, if necessary. In April 1475 he had joined the Lower Union. In May, he signed a treaty with Frederick III in which each promised not to make a separate peace with Burgundy. It was, therefore, with the assurance of the support of Louis XI, the Lower Union, and Frederick III that Duke René sent his challenge to Charles the Bold.

At the time of René's declaration, Charles was involved in three urgent projects: the siege of Neuss, a planned joint attack with England against France, and the intended punishment of Sigismund and the Lower Union for their role in driving him from Alsace. Nevertheless, he decided that the conquest of Lorraine must be given high priority. René was massing troops on

the Luxembourg border. Also, Lorraine was an essential route
for the mercenaries he was still recruiting in Italy, as well as for
his diplomatic activities there. He wrote to his lieutenant in
Luxembourg that, as soon as he had finished the siege of Neuss,
he would move his entire army against Lorraine.

At this point, Duke René was treacherously abandoned by two
of his chief allies, Louis XI and Frederick III, both of whom made
a separate peace with Charles the Bold in the second half of
1475. Although Louis had promised René in August 1475 that, if
necessary, he would personally lead 10,000 troops to defend
Lorraine, he made a secret bargain with Charles giving him a
free hand in Lorraine in return for the surrender to him of the
treacherous Constable St. Pol.

Charles invaded Lorraine in September 1475. A few weeks
later, Bern invaded Vaud, a fief of Savoy. Both events were part
of the struggle between Burgundy and the League of Constance.
The eyes of contemporaries were riveted on Neuss, and on the
dangerous Anglo-Burgundian threat to France, which will be
described shortly. Modern historians have tended to concentrate
on these same two issues. In fact, however, the destiny of
Burgundy was being settled by the events which had led to the
formation of a grand alliance against Charles the Bold, the
League of Constance, comprising the Lower Union and the Swiss
federation. It was the towns, rather than princes like Louis XI,
Sigismund, and René, or the rural peasantry of Switzerland,
which formed the backbone of the resistance to Charles. A long
tradition of urban cooperation in the area made the League of
Constance possible. But Charles's confrontation and eventual
defeat by the League was not just the result of opposition to
Burgundian expansion in one area of the Upper Rhine. It was also
the result of his policies in Lorraine and Savoy: policies of
keeping his lines of communication open through them to Italy,
and his ambition to eventually annex them. Charles the Bold's
policy from Cologne to Italy threatened the independence of the
princes and the very existence of the towns.[12]

Charles's involvement with Cologne, and his siege of Neuss,
from the summer of 1474 to the summer of 1475, have already
been referred to frequently. His objectives and actions in this
region deserve a brief examination.

There is little likelihood that Charles the Bold planned to
conquer the entire River Rhine, as some have suggested.

Probably, in 1474, Charles's Rhine plans were limited to the conquest of Cologne and Strasbourg, and the restoration of Burgundian power in Upper Alsace.

It was Philip the Good, not Charles, who began the policy of Burgundian interest in the archbishopric of Cologne. In 1463 Ruprecht, brother of the Elector Palatine of the Rhine, was chosen archbishop. Philip soon made him a Burgundian ally and client.

In 1467–68 Charles the Bold first appeared as a mediator in a series of quarrels between the Archbishop of Cologne, on the one hand, and the city, Estates, and cathedral chapter on the other. More important still was the antagonism between the archbishop and the towns of the archbishopric. Neuss was the center of the opposition to Ruprecht. She hoped to gain complete independence from his authority over her.

In March 1473 most of the cathedral chapter, some nobles, and four or five of the towns of the archbishopric, including Neuss, withdrew their obedience from Archbishop Ruprecht. In June the city of Cologne joined the rebels. It was just at this time that Charles the Bold conquered Guelders, which made him a neighbor of Cologne. He was already an ally of Archbishop Ruprecht. His interest in Cologne was intensified by the failure of his negotiations with the Emperor at Trier regarding his promotion to the imperial, or at least royal, dignity. He was no longer interested in maintaining friendly relations with Frederick III. In December 1473 he announced that he was taking over the guardianship of the archbishopric on Ruprecht's behalf. Charles had now committed himself to assisting Ruprecht, by force of arms if necessary.

A treaty between Charles and Ruprecht was signed before the end of March 1474. Charles agreed to act as protector of the archbishopric for life, to help Ruprecht regain control over rebellious places, such as Neuss, and to help him recover his rights over the city of Cologne. In return, the archbishop agreed to pay Charles 200,000 Rhenish florins, granted him the right of entry into all of his places and ceded three towns to him. Charles then tried to persuade Neuss to put itself under his protection and to frighten Cologne into cooperating with himself and Ruprecht.

The final decision to embark on a large-scale military expedition in the archbishopric of Cologne was delayed by

Charles until the question of his relations with Louis XI was
settled temporarily by the truce of Compiègne, to run from June
13, 1474, to May 1, 1475. Then Charles issued letters-patent
announcing an expedition "to bring the rebellious subjects of the
Archbishop of Cologne back to his obedience." He then laid
siege not to the powerful, well-prepared city of Cologne, but to
the smaller town of Neuss, which he expected to capture easily.
However, Neuss withstood the siege, which lasted from July 30,
1474, to June 13, 1475. Even in September, Charles expected it
to fall soon. By mid-November he must have resigned himself to
a lengthy siege.

The courageous resistance of the town was amazing as, month
after month, it withstood the terrible bombardment of the
Burgundian artillery. It was partly due to careful preparations, as
well as to a large garrison of soldiers from Hesse. Charles
stubbornly refused to raise the siege.

By March 1475, the importance of the siege of Neuss was
becoming clear. An Italian at Geneva wrote "that the affair of
Neuss is of great importance. If the duke does not take it, the
Germans will become more enthusiastic to attack him." Frederick III's ambassador to the Swiss federation said that "should
Neuss be lost, such destruction would result to all German lands
that nobody can conceive of it."

In the meantime, the Emperor Frederick III was organizing a
large army to relieve Neuss. The project turned out to be a sort
of comic opera affair which might well have been entitled
"Much Ado About Nothing." The idea of armed intervention by
the Emperor began as early as the opening of the siege. On the
day before the siege began, Frederick wrote Cologne promising
support against Charles. There was a long delay due to
Frederick's habitual procrastination and the time needed to
gather an army. In August 1474 he sent an imperial summons to
the electoral princes (the seven who elected the Emperor)
ordering them to assemble troops in Koblenz in September.
Some parts of the empire were enthusiastic: some refused help.
Frederick's slowness can be explained, in part, by his desperate
financial situation. He began to march slowly towards Neuss in
the spring of 1475.

The chief enthusiasm for the campaign was from towns like
Strasbourg and Frankfurt. They were aware of the Burgundian

threat to themselves. Their enthusiasm was neither imperial nor German; it was urban and self-interested.

During Frederick's slow preparations to relieve Neuss, he had gained an ally in the person of Louis XI. The treaty of Andernach, signed in December 1474, promised French help. The agreement was renewed in April 1475, and both did lead armies against Charles the Bold in May. René, Duke of Lorraine, was added to the alliance in May 1475.

There was a remarkable lack of urgency and aggression among the imperial leaders, although they commanded an army of about 30,000 men. They were content to wait for Louis XI's promised attack on Luxembourg with 30,000 men.

The imperial forces finally arrived before Neuss on May 23. There were a few indecisive skirmishes. Charles had already tried to negotiate with Frederick in March and April. Finally, on May 29, a truce was agreed to, and provisional terms for a peace treaty were decided upon. The Burgundians began to withdraw. There were still difficulties, however, over the exact timing of the mutual withdrawals. After minor incidents, fighting broke out when the Germans attacked Charles's rear guard on June 16. Charles inflicted heavy casualties on the Germans. He pulled back on June 27, but stayed nearby until informed that the Emperor was also striking camp.

Charles the Bold now, at last, prepared to end the siege of Neuss. He did so because he was being urged by his allies, England and Brittany. Also, Louis XI was already attacking him with a terrific onslaught on two fronts; to the north in Picardy, Artois, and Hainault, and to the east in Burgundy and Franche-Comté. This campaign will be described shortly.

The damages suffered by Charles the Bold at Neuss were greatly exaggerated by contemporaries. Actually, the siege of Neuss made very little difference to Charles's military potential. He had been checked but not decisively defeated.[13]

It must be remembered that Charles the Bold had expected his campaign against Cologne, including the siege of Neuss, to be brief. Therefore, when he launcheded this attack in the summer of 1474, he was already planning other activities. We have seen that he meant to recapture Alsace. He was also preparing a decisive blow against France.

Charles's primary ambitions continued to be directed towards

the Holy Roman Empire, even though his attempt to secure the
succession to the imperial throne or to gain imperial recognition
as ruler of a territorial kingdom had failed. A large proportion of
his inherited lands lay within the borders of the empire, and most
of his territorial gains were within its western fringes.

As long as Charles's old enemy, Louis XI, remained strong and
hostile, he could never concentrate all of his attention on his
German projects. He had to be constantly on his guard against a
French attack from behind, and France was always likely to
assist his German enemies. Also, it will be recalled that, at
Péronne, in 1468, Charles had sought to free himself from any
French authority within those lands that he held as fiefs from the
King of France. While he had limited this royal control by the
Treaty of Péronne, he had not eliminated it, and he would never
be satisfied until he had. He therefore concluded an alliance
with England which he hoped would smash the power of Louis
XI forever.

The truce between France and Burgundy was due to expire on
April 1, 1474. Its renewal until May 1, 1475, allowed Charles to
launch his attack against Neuss. In the meantime, he completed
his negotiations with England, which culminated in the signing of
the Treaty of London in July 1474. Charles recognized Edward
as King of France and promised to support him with 10,000 men.
Edward promised to invade France with 10,000 men before July
1, 1475. Possibly foreseeing a French defeat, Louis's old ally, the
Duke of Milan, signed a treaty with Burgundy in January 1475, as
already mentioned.

Relations between France and England, at this time, were
apparently good. The truce of Brussels of March 1473 had called
for peace between the two countries for a year. When it expired,
it was renewed until May 1, 1475.

Louis's truces with both England and Burgundy were due to
expire on the same day, May 1, 1475. Just as Louis was using this
time to prepare his defenses, the King of England was making use
of the truce to prepare for war, and was assembling a large army
and navy.

While awaiting the English invasion, Louis was in pretty firm
control of France. He had little fear of a feudal uprising. The
most dangerous barons were dead, in prison, or intimidated. The
situation was bad enough, however. The resources of the Duke
of Burgundy were great. A large English army, commanded by

Edward IV, one of the best soldiers in Europe, was preparing to invade. If Louis suffered a major setback, there was a chance that the French feudal barons might rebel.

Aware of the imminent English invasion called for by the Anglo-Burgundian treaty, Louis now prepared at last for military action. During the spring of 1475, he raised the largest and most powerful army of his career. On April 25, six days before the expiration of his truce with England, Louis moved his troops to the borders of Picardy to await the English invasion.

We have seen that the purpose of Charles the Bold's treaty with England was to deliver a crushing blow to France. In fact, it was Louis XI who struck first. He had taken no military action against Charles since 1472, largely because he was too involved in his war with Aragon. This project had been brought to a successful completion in March, 1475.

One difference between Louis XI and Charles the Bold was that Louis's political actions were less motivated by desire for revenge. It is true that he had never forgiven Charles for the humiliation of Péronne, and had vowed to avenge it. His renewal of military action against Charles was probably caused even more, however, by his hope to deliver a severe enough blow to Charles so that he would be less able to assist the English, when they arrived. He also hoped to devastate some of the Burgundian lands in Picardy, through which the English army must pass, so that they would not be able to live off the land. As in 1471, it was a campaign of limited objectives, not aimed at crushing Charles completely. These were the only two occasions on which Louis XI departed briefly from his usual defensive policy toward Burgundy from the treaty of Péronne, in 1468, until the death of Charles the Bold.

The spring of 1475 was a propitious time for Louis to attack. Charles was still bogged down in his lengthy siege of Neuss, and the English had not yet invaded. The truce with Burgundy expired on May 1, and Louis promptly attacked on two fronts. The king personally led the bulk of the French army against Picardy, the Somme towns, and Artois and Hainault. The advance was swift and successful. Montdidier, Roye, and Corbie fell in early May. Then the French troops penetrated as far as Hesdin, Arras, and Valenciennes in Hainault. Louis ordered that any place captured on the frontier that was not strong enough to withstand a siege be destroyed. Throughout May, the French systematically devastated the lands of Picardy. When the English came, they would find very little food or supplies. Meanwhile, two other French armies pushed into Burgundy and Franche-Comté. Like the campaign in the north, this was largely a war of devastation rather than conquest. No strongly fortified places were taken. There was only one pitched battle, at which a Burgundian force was routed, and the governor-marshal of Burgundy, Antoine de Luxembourg, was taken prisoner. The French attack on both fronts seems to have had little permanent effect. The French forces were much too dispersed to achieve a major conquest, and Louis could not concentrate all of his efforts on the attack as he had to be prepared to meet the expected English invasion.

In June 1475, the first English troops began to land in Calais. King Edward followed soon afterward but, before leaving Dover, sent the chief herald of England to Louis's headquarters in Normandy with his formal declaration of war. Louis took the herald aside and gave him a number of reasons why the war was not to England's advantage. He also gave the herald 300 crowns and promised him more if a truce were concluded. The herald, carried away by the lure of gold and by Louis's affable manner, told him the key men among Edward's advisors to contact regarding a truce after the English had invaded.

The King of England arrived in Calais on July 4, 1475, to take command of his well-equipped army of about 20,000 men. Charles the Bold had finally abandoned the siege of Neuss in June and had begun a leisurely march toward Calais to meet him. Charles finally arrived in Calais in mid-July, but accompanied only by his household and his guard. He told Edward that he had already invaded Lorraine and that he would return to his army there. He would then push westward from Lorraine into Champagne. He proposed that the English march east to Champagne and that the two armies meet at Rheims, the traditional coronation site of French kings. There Edward would be crowned King of France. The English tentatively agreed.

Edward marched across Picardy and crossed the Somme at Péronne in early August, thus entering French territory. The French army marched parallel to them all the way and encamped about forty miles from the English near Péronne. Louis had left a long, powerful line of defense along the way. He now meant to carry the war to the English. Using his fortresses as bases, he intended to operate against their flank and rear.

The war was not going at all to King Edward's liking. He had counted on an uprising of the French feudal barons, which did not materialize. Even his ally, the Duke of Brittany, did nothing. Worse still, he had received little help from Charles the Bold. With bad weather coming on, the pleasure-loving king began to long for the comforts of London. Early in August, he sent word through a released French prisoner to Louis indicating that he might be interested in discussing peace. Negotiations followed, and the terms of the Treaty of Picquigny were worked out by August 23. Louis arranged for the treaty to be sealed at a personal meeting with Edward.

Commynes described the careful preparations for the meeting of the two kings. Each side chose two representatives to decide on the location. Commynes himself was one of those selected by Louis. They chose the town of Picquigny, and built a bridge over the Somme River with a wooden trellis dividing it from end to end. The holes in the trellis were only big enough for a man's arm. They had in mind the murder of Duke John of Burgundy on the bridge at Montereau in 1419 during his meeting with the Dauphin Charles, the future Charles VII.

The two kings met on the bridge, on August 29, with twelve followers each. Both swore on a prayer book and a holy relic to uphold the treaty. They then dismissed their retinues and spoke privately together.

The result of the conference was the Treaty of Picquigny. It called for a seven-year truce. Commercial advantages were promised for the merchants of both countries. Edward IV was to receive the large sum of 75,000 *écus* to return to England. A committee was set up to settle any differences between the two kings by negotiation. Each monarch swore to help the other against any rebel. The five-year-old Dauphin Charles was to marry Elizabeth, the nine-year-old daughter of Edward, when they reached the age of puberty. Louis XI promised a substantial dowry. He also promised an annual pension to Edward IV of 60,000 *écus*.

In the meantime, Louis provided huge quantities of food and wine for the English soldiers at nearby Amiens. For three or four days, the English ate and drank whatever they wanted in the taverns without paying anything. Louis said laughingly that he had chased the English out of France more easily than his father because he had done it by having them eat venison pasties and drink good wines, while his father had done it by force of arms. The English army returned to England in September.

In further negotiations with England, the liberation of Margaret of Anjou was arranged. Louis paid a ransom of 50,000 écus, and Margaret renounced all claims to the English throne. She was then transferred to the custody of Louis, who only released her in return for the renunciation of all her rights to the succession of her father, King René of Anjou, and her mother, Isabelle of Lorraine.

In addition to the pension to Edward IV, promised at the Treaty of Picquigny, Louis also considered it expedient to secretly pay regular financial grants to several influential English courtiers to keep their goodwill. Louis was in no hurry to hold the promised meetings to settle any further differences between the two kings. Pensions were keeping the English happy, and he was afraid of "rocking the boat."[14]

Charles the Bold was very annoyed about the signing of the Treaty of Picquigny. As soon as he had heard of the Anglo-French negotiations, about August 17, he had tried his best to persuade Edward not to come to terms with Louis, but he had failed. He now had little choice but to negotiate a settlement with France, too. The result was the Treaty of Soleuvre, of September 13, 1475, which was made public, and some related agreements which were kept secret. The settlement proved to be important, as it was maintained by both sides for the rest of Charles's life.

The Treaty of Soleuvre, and the related secret documents, called for a nine-year truce. The allies of both signatories were given until January 1, 1476, to accept the truce, if they had not made war on either party in the meantime. Bern, the Swiss, and the Duke of Lorraine were named among Louis's allies, but not the Lower Union. If either signatory were attacked by an ally of the other, he was free to defend himself. Louis was permitted to conquer Roussillon and Cerdagne from Charles's ally, the King of Aragon, if he ceded St. Quentin to Burgundy and Charles was permitted to recover Upper Alsace. If the Swiss helped Upper Alsace, Charles was free to attack them, even though they were Louis's allies. Charles was permitted to move troops freely between his northern and southern territories by the most convenient route, provided his men were peaceable. Charles promised to hand over Louis de Luxembourg, Count of St. Pol and Constable of France, if he could get his hands on him. Both he and Louis regarded this man as a traitor. Louis agreed that Charles could proceed with the conquest of his ally, Lorraine, if Charles did turn over the treacherous St. Pol.

Thus, Charles the Bold's plan to smash the power of Louis XI, once and for all, had failed. Had the major enemies of France effectively combined in the summer of 1475 to launch simultaneous attacks, French royal power might have suffered a serious setback. They failed to do so. The threat from Aragon had been effectively met by the French conquest of Perpignan, in March 1475, which was followed by a six-month truce. This was before the Anglo-Burgundian alliance was even completed. Edward IV of England seems to have sincerely planned a major campaign and perhaps really hoped to secure the French crown. Had he received full cooperation from Burgundy, Louis XI would have been seriously threatened. It was Charles the Bold himself who must be held chiefly responsible for the failure of the allies. Preoccupied with the conquest of Lorraine, he sent Edward virtually no help. Left alone to fight a strong French army, with winter approaching, and running short of cash, he was persuaded to accept a favorable peace treaty with France.

Charles the Bold now turned all his attention to the conquest of Lorraine. He seems to have been interested in this project as early as the summer of 1474, if not before. Duke René's declaration of war on him, in May 1475, led him to make up his mind, and provided him with an excuse to attack. In July he sent an ultimatum to René warning him to cease his military actions or accept the consequences.

Like most of Charles's campaigns, the conquest of Lorraine was a carefully planned military operation. Before the invasion, René was stripped of his two chief allies, Louis XI and Frederick III, partly by Burgundian diplomacy. The attack was launched on two fronts in early September 1475. There was no organized or large-scale resistance, and René received only token help from the Lower Union. The campaign was accompanied by a number of acts of brutality on Charles's part designed to discourage opposition. The conquest was completed by November 30.

December 1475 possibly marks the peak of Charles the Bold's political fortunes, the high point of Burgundian power. He had conquered Lorraine, made an advantageous peace with Louis XI,

and, on November 17, concluded a peace treaty with the
Emperor. He was inaugurated Duke of Lorraine on December
18, with great pomp and ceremony. He did not linger long in
Lorraine, however, but set out on January 11, 1476, on an
expedition in support of Savoy against Bern and her allies, which
would lead him, step by step, to disaster.[15]

Meanwhile Louis XI was dealing with the French feudal lords
who had plotted rebellion against him in 1475, while he was
faced with the dangerous Anglo-Burgundian coalition. The
Count of St. Pol, Constable of France, had attempted to organize
the uprising. He had entered into negotiations with the Dukes of
Brittany, Bourbon, and Nemours and King René of Anjou, as well
as Charles the Bold. None of them, except Charles, had dared to
attack the king, however, and the plot had fizzled.

Louis had had enough of these feudal coalitions. In September
1475 the Duke of Brittany was forced to swear on the cross of St.
Laud that he would aid the King of France against his enemies.
The Count of St. Pol fled to the Duke of Burgundy. Charles, as he
had promised in the treaty of Soleuvre, turned him over to Louis
XI, and the treacherous Constable was executed in December
1475. Jacques d'Armagnac, Duke of Nemours, was captured in
March 1476. Many of his lands were given to Louis's son-in-law,
Pierre de Beaujeu, the husband of Louis's eldest daughter, Anne.
He was imprisoned, tried, and eventually executed for treason in
August 1477. In April 1476 King René, Duke of Anjou, was
forced to swear never to form an alliance with the Duke of
Burgundy.[16]

While Louis XI was taking care of domestic problems, in late
1475 and early 1476 Charles the Bold was planning and
launching his ill-fated expedition in support of his ally, Savoy,
against Bern and her allies. During the summer of 1475, while
Charles was besieging Neuss, Bern and her associates seized the
lands of the Burgundian vassals in the barony of Vaud in Savoy. In
the fall, Franche-Comté and the lands of his ally Savoy were
exposed to further acts of aggression by Bern.

There were several reasons for Bern's increasing hostility
toward Charles. She resented growing Burgundian influence in
Savoy. She was still anxious to stop the movement of Italian
mercenaries through the Alps to join Charles's armies, fearing
that they might be used against her. In addition, she was

determined to extend her sphere of influence southwest toward Lake Geneva and west toward Burgundy.

Charles was well aware of Bern's hostility and expansionist policy. However, he was unwilling, until late in 1475, to divert forces from his other projects to attack her.

In October 1475 Bern and Fribourg invaded Vaud. By the end of the month, all of the county had been captured. The allies returned home, laden with booty and ransom. They retained only the well-fortified and stategic town of Morat (Murten).

Charles the Bold could not ignore the invasion of Vaud. Yolande of Savoy was his ally. Other Swiss acts of aggression in the autumn of 1475 strengthened his resolution to intervene. On several occasions they cut the route through Savoy for his Italian mercenaries coming to join his armies. In November the Bishop of Sion, a Bernese ally, conquered much of Lower Valais. This once again blocked the route from Italy, and Savoy had lost more territory.

A brief truce was signed from the end of November 1475 to January 1, 1476, between Charles the Bold and Savoy on the one side and Duke Sigismund of Austria, the powers of the League of Constance, and the Bishop of Sion on the other. Shortly after its expiration, on January 11, Charles set out from Nancy to defend the House of Savoy from further aggression.

As usual, Charles had prepared the way diplomatically. He had deprived his enemies of their most powerful allies. He had made an agreement with Louis XI in the autumn of 1475 and negotiated an alliance with Frederick III in November. Louis tried to talk Charles out of his campaign, fearing that Savoy would fall into Burgundian hands. While his opponents were thus isolated, Charles had as allies Milan, Venice, and Savoy.

To use the term "Swiss," as many writers do, for the enemies of Charles the Bold in 1476, is misleading. Actually, his opponents were a collection of small powers, including towns like Strasbourg, Basel, and Bern, rural communities like Uri, Schwyz, and Unterwalden, the Bishops of Strasbourg, Basel, and Sion, and two important secular rulers, Duke René of Lorraine and Duke Sigismund of Austria-Tirol. This alliance was, in fact, an enlarged League of Constance. Bern appealed to the others for help against Charles in Savoy. They agreed to come to her assistance, and Bern emerged as the chief leader of the alliance.

Constant appeals from Bern to her various allies, during February 1476, organized the resistance against Burgundy. The assumption of leadership by Bern in the League, accompanied by the emergence of the Swiss federation in a primary role, altered the prospects and policies of the entire alliance. Previously their campaigns had been aggressive raids by one or two members. Now the entire alliance became united in its determination to concentrate all of its military resources to check the impending Burgundian attack. Both sides intended to stake everything on one major battle.

In February 1476 Charles the Bold attacked Grandson in Vaud, which had been seized by Bern the previous year. The town and castle were captured, and the defenders of the latter massacred. This form of calculated terrorism seems to have been characteristic of Charles. He had already carried it out on several occasions. The capture of Grandson all but completed the Burgundian conquest of Vaud.

Bern then summoned her allies to assemble near Neuchâtel, which they began to do in late February. On March 2, the allies set out to attack a small castle garrisoned by Charles on Lake Neuchâtel. Charles set out the same day from Grandson. While one portion of the allied army besieged the castle, another sizable detachment pushed on ahead and collided with the advancing Burgundians. The ensuing battle was known as the battle of Grandson. The allied advance guard was joined by the rest of their army and Charles's troops were routed.

The fleeing Burgundians left nearly all their baggage and heavy equipment behind. There was rich booty for the victors, including many jewels, Charles's privy seal, his throne, and his jeweled hat. In spite of the one-sided nature of the battle, the Burgundian casualties were very light, probably amounting to only a few hundred men. The allies took Grandson, but did not pursue Charles's retreating army far.

Charles did not seem to have been particularly discouraged by his defeat. He immediately began to round up the fugitives, raise more troops, and collect new artillery. He planned to take the field again soon. In mid-March, he assembled his forces outside Lausanne.

Charles's move to Lausanne showed that future hostilities would be in Vaud, already largely under Burgundian control. Advancing against Bern from Lausanne, Charles would have to capture either Morat or Fribourg, for these were the two outer bastions of Bern against attack from the southwest.

Charles encamped near Lausanne from mid-March until late May 1476. Crucial to his whole position was the attitude and actions of Louis XI, who was at Lyons at this time, no great distance away, with troops readily available. Louis had no intention of attacking Charles, however, as Bern hoped. He was there to safeguard Savoy from both Burgundy and Bern. Possibly he hoped to obtain it for himself. The rebellion which broke out in Lorraine against Charles in April was instigated by its duke, René, rather than by Louis. His contact with Bern was limited to a letter congratulating her on her victory at Grandson, "about which he is so joyful that he could not be more so, and he could have had no better news in all his life." He did not reply to Bern's appeal of April 11 for military intervention to prevent Savoy from falling into Charles's hands.

Louis made no response either to secret anti-Burgundian overtures from Charles's supposed ally, Galeazzo-Maria Sforza of Milan. The latter offered Louis 200,000 crowns, and suggested that they divide Savoy between them.

Instead of organizing hostilities against Charles in the weeks after Grandson, as he was urged to do by Bern and Milan, Louis negotiated with him. He sought a personal meeting with Charles to settle their differences, particularly those concerning Bern and Savoy. The negotiations for the meeting broke down. Although officially maintaining his alliance with Burgundy, Louis ignored Charles's requests for military help, and secretly encouraged the Swiss federation to attack Piedmont in Savoy. In the meantime, Charles proceeded to virtually take over Savoy while the other interested parties, Louis XI, the Duke of Milan, and Bern did nothing to prevent him. Yolande of Savoy now joined Charles in Lausanne as his active supporter.

Charles then reinforced his friendship with the Emperor Frederick III. In April 1476 he published their treaty of the previous November, and he signed an agreement of engagement between his daughter, Mary, and the Emperor's son, Maximilian.

Yolande of Savoy, the Duke of Milan, and the Count Palatine of the Rhine all warned Charles not to risk his army against the Swiss again. Even if he should succeed in defeating them and conquering all their lands, they would yield him very little revenue. However, the only thing that made him hesitate was his fear that he might be attacked by Louis XI. He even considered fighting Louis first. Finally he decided to proceed against the Swiss and, according to the Milanese envoy at his court, "he vowed to God that he would either die with his men or conquer." A serious illness delayed Charles's departure on campaign for about a month that spring. Finally, in late May 1476, Charles set out from Lausanne with about 12,000 men. His immediate target was Morat, which barred the approaches to Bern, his principal enemy. The general alliance which had confronted him at Grandson had disintegrated. The *Eidgenossen* (Swiss Federation), for the moment, refused to help Bern against him.

Charles explained to the Milanese ambassador why he was so determined to attack the Swiss. It was partly a point of honor to avenge his defeat at Grandson. It was chiefly essential, however, in order to prevent the Swiss from continuing their raids on his territory, to regain possession of Upper Alsace, and to snatch complete control of Savoy from under Louis XI's nose. He knew that he was risking "his state, his life, and everything."

Charles the Bold besieged Morat on June 11. Although he knew that Bern's allies would not help her defend the town, he did not take advantage of this situation to concentrate all his efforts on the siege. Instead, he pushed on directly toward Bern, perhaps because he sought a decisive battle and knew that Bern's allies would come to her aid if she herself were attacked. Sure enough, a general mobilization of Bern's allies resulted. Now Charles could expect an attempted relief of the siege of Morat, not just by Bern, but by about 20,000 additional men from the League of Constance.

Charles expected the attack on June 21, and had his army drawn up in order of battle. When no attack came, he made a fatal error in judgment. He thought that Louis XI had asked the Swiss not to attack and decided that they must have accepted this advice, and would fight a defensive war only. As usual, he overestimated the hostility and influence of the man whom he regarded as his arch-enemy. He should have realized that the *Eidgenossen* and their allies were incapable of fighting a defensive war. It was very difficult to keep their army in the field for any length of time. They were short of provisions and supplies. Once gathered in strength, they had to attack or disband. They were merely awaiting a contingent from Zurich. A small force from Lorraine, commanded by Duke René in person, also arrived at the last minute.

The allied army of about 25,000 men advanced on Morat on June 22. The Burgundian army was taken completely by surprise. Their scattered resistance was easily overcome, and a general flight began. The allies killed all they could and took no prisoners. Several thousand of Charles's men died. The Burgundian defeat was much more decisive than at Grandson. Charles lost at least one-third of his army.

The defeated duke withdrew into Franche-Comté, where he spent July, August, and September preparing for a third campaign against the Swiss. He did not appear to be very discouraged. If anything, he seemed more self-confident and arrogant than before. He was more obsessed with avenging his defeats and restoring his military reputation than ever. He intended to march again against the allies, but the situation in Lorraine had so deteriorated by August that he was forced to change his plans and prepare to lead his troops there instead.

The fate of Savoy had been settled by the Battle of Morat. Had Charles won, it would have been his. He had even arrested the Duchess Yolande in June. Instead, it was Louis XI who gained virtual control over the duchy by his prompt intervention. While still negotiating with Charles as a supposed ally, he appointed his partisan, Philip of Savoy, his lieutenant in Piedmont, with the support of French troops. In October, he achieved the dramatic rescue of his sister Yolande from Rouvres castle and brought her to Tours. In early November, she formally renounced her Burgundian connections.

After Charles's defeat at Morat, Galeazzo-Maria Sforza of Milan completely abandoned him and signed a treaty of friendship with the King of France. Louis still showed no open signs of hostility to Charles, however, and he still had alliances with the Empire and England. His defeats had not led to complete diplomatic isolation.[17]

The end was not far off, however, As the English historian Richard Vaughan says: "The sudden collapse of Burgundian power and the swift extinction of the Burgundian state which, . . . had been an important element in the European political scene for almost a hundred years, was to all intents and purposes a direct result of the personal follies and failures of Charles the Bold." After severe defeats at the hands of the League of

Constance at Grandson and Morat, he led his army into the
Battle of Nancy in very unfavorable circumstances against the
same determined enemies. He can justifiably be blamed for
failing to provide his daughter Mary with a husband who would
have been able and willing to act as his lieutenant and thus be
trained and prepared to succeed him. He can rightly be blamed,
too, for his extravagant and unpopular policies.

A basic question in analyzing the downfall of Burgundy is to
what extent was it caused by Charles's military defeat and death,
and how far was it due to a process of internal disintegration? A
detailed examination of this issue lies beyond the scope of this
book. All evidence seems to indicate, however, that, during the
last year of his reign, he was neither facing financial ruin nor
large-scale rebellion. In spite of the pressures placed on it by his
policies, the framework of the Burgundian state remained firm
until his defeat and death. It was Charles's last and most
catastrophic military disaster in January 1477, rather than
internal disintegration, that led to the rapid and permanent
decline of the power of the Burgundian state.[18]

Therefore, Charles the Bold's last, disastrous campaign must
be examined briefly. As mentioned before, he would have
preferred a campaign of revenge against the allies of the League
of Constance who had just defeated him, but several more
pressing affairs intervened. In the first place, the project of a
meeting with Louis XI, which he and the king had discussed off
and on for several months, became an urgent priority for Charles
in July. Charles now took the initiative in these negotiations, but
Louis was unenthusiastic. He told the Milanese ambassador, in
fact, that he was suffering from a heart tremor, a headache, and
piles which he attributed to not having had sexual intercourse
recently. The ambassador wrote to the Duke of Milan that
Charles was Louis's "Turk, the Devil he loathes most in this
world." The meeting never took place.

At this time, Charles still held Yolande of Savoy prisoner, and
considered attempting to reconquer her duchy. However, Louis
XI's virtual takeover of Savoy and rescue of his sister frustrated
this plan. Then, as mentioned above, the situation in Lorraine
forced him to turn his attention there instead of carrying out his
war of revenge against the Swiss and the League of Constance.

Charles the Bold had conquered Lorraine in 1475 and
expelled Duke René. He had had himself proclaimed duke by

the three estates, and established a governor and garrisons. His control of the duchy began to slip when René's partisans, encouraged by the news of the Burgundian defeat at Grandson, seized the castle and county of Vaudemont in April 1476. Duke René, by fighting at the Battle of Morat, had shown his firm commitment to the League of Constance. After Charles the Bold's defeat at Morat, in July, René's supporters continued the reconquest of Lorraine until, by the end of the month, Nancy was almost the only important place remaining in Burgundian hands. Duke René arrived in August and organized the siege of the town.

Charles the Bold could hardly be expected to have remained inactive while the Duchy of Lorraine was snatched from him by a small army which, at that time, had no allies. In August he decided to march into Lorraine in person at the head of his troops. He delayed his departure, however, and Nancy fell to Duke René before he finally arrived in early October. Most of René's ill-disciplined army then largely melted away. Leaving garrisons in most of the principal places of the duchy, the Duke of Lorraine again went to seek the help which the League of Constance had previously refused him.

Charles the Bold began the siege of Nancy on October 22, in spite of the fact that many of his captains urged him to withdraw for the winter. He continued the siege through November and December, although his forces were weakened by hunger and disease. Charles resolved to take Nancy whatever the cost. He hoped to accomplish this before René could obtain assistance.

Louis XI seemed too involved in the affairs of Savoy to pay much attention to Lorraine. He was busy reinstating Yolande there under a French protectorate. He had refused to help René in the past and appeared willing to continue to honor his truce with Charles. The latter was further encouraged to continue the siege when he succeeded in renewing his alliance with the Empire. His daughter Mary and the Emperor's son Maximilian became engaged in November.

The Swiss countered Louis XI's suggestion that they should continue the war with Charles by suggesting that it was high time Louis himself declared war on Burgundy. When Duke René appeared before the Swiss diet in November, they refused again to grant him any direct assistance. René had to be content with an unofficial army of Swiss volunteers, who were to assemble at

Basel by December 15, and various contingents from members of the Lower Union, who were more willing to help than the Swiss. Probably Louis XI was among those who helped provide the money used by René to pay his Swiss mercenaries. René had been receiving a pension from the king for some time.

Meanwhile, the siege of Nancy dragged on. Charles showed an increasingly obstinate determination to continue come what may. He received reinforcements from his northern territories in November, and had sufficient cash to pay them.

The main body of Swiss, disciplined veterans under experienced commanders, set out from Basel in late December. Duke René ordered his men from his garrisons to join them on January 4, 1477. The allies approached Nancy the following day. Charles moved most of his army from the trenches around the city and drew it up ready for battle in a fortified, defensive position.

Charles the Bold's army was hopelessly outnumbered at Nancy. Estimates vary, but the best evidence indicates that he only had about 5,000 men. The army attacking him had no single commander-in-chief. It consisted of separate contingents of his various enemies. It included Duke René and his Lorrainers, the mercenaries he had raised among the *Eidgenossen*, and men from Basel, Colmar, and Strasbourg. There were at least 6,000 Swiss, and probably a grand total of 19,000–20,000 men. Charles's cold, exhausted, demoralized, and unpaid troops had little chance against this army, many of them veterans of Grandson and Morat, fresh and determined. The resultant Burgundian military catastrophe was a foregone conclusion, once Charles rejected the advice of his captains to withdraw, showing once again his inability to admit and correct his own errors. His entire army was killed or fled in confusion. It took two days of searching through the frozen corpses littering the battlefield before the body of the forty-four-year-old duke was found. It had been stripped of clothes and jewels. His death was a decisive event, which was followed by the rapid dismemberment of the Burgundian state.[19]

The completion of the downfall of Burgundy took a few more years after the death of Charles the Bold. According to Commynes, just before learning of Charles's death, Louis had been planning to secure control of Burgundy by arranging the marriage of the Dauphin Charles with Mary of Burgundy, Charles the Bold's only child and heiress. If this plan were unacceptable, because the dauphin was only six and she was

The Struggle with Charles the Bold

163

nineteen, he would try to bring about her marriage to some other French nobleman. Commynes considered this a wise plan.

As rumors of Charles's slaying began to reach the French court, Louis decided to take more positive action to seize some of his rival's lands. On January 9, 1477, even before he was certain of Charles's death, Louis wrote to his general, the seigneur de Craon, saying: "It is now time to use all five of your natural senses to place the Duchy and County of Burgundy in my hands." He was then to announce Louis's intention of marrying the dauphin to Mary of Burgundy. The same day, Louis wrote to the councillors and people of Dijon, capital of the Duchy of Burgundy, telling them that, if the rumor that the Duke of Burgundy was dead proved to be true, they were not to accept any authority but his own, as he was the duke's suzerain and Mary's godfather. He promised to respect her rights.

As soon as Charles the Bold's death was confirmed, Louis abandoned his plan to marry his son to Mary of Burgundy. For the first time, he decided to turn to outright military aggression. He resolved to simply annex the Somme towns, Artois, Flanders, Hainault, Burgundy, and Franche-Comté. With Charles removed from the scene, he believed that he could seize these lands by prompt military action and avoid the uncertainties of attempting to negotiate a marriage settlement. He wanted the remainder of the Burgundian possessions to go to some German princes who would be his allies. His only excuse for the entire annexation was the alleged felony of his vassal Charles. Franche-Comté and Hainault were parts of the Holy Roman Empire and not France, so Louis had no legal claim to them at all.

Louis paid off the other claimants to Burgundian territory— René II of Lorraine, Sigismund of Austria, and the Swiss. He also bribed the chief servants of Charles the Bold to support his claims. As usual, Louis was counting heavily on bribery to achieve his ends. In Burgundy and Franche-Comté, he made concessions to the towns, offered bribes to the chief nobles, and had his annexation accepted by the provincial estates of the two provinces before the end of February. The brutality of the occupation troops soon produced a general uprising, however. Burgundy was quickly subdued but Franche-Comté only after four years of fighting.

In the meantime, King Louis himself was leading his troops in the northern campaign. Heedless of his advancing years and delicate health, the fifty-three-year-old monarch set out on horseback, in bitterly cold weather, on January 18, 1477. He chose men with local connections and sent them ahead to the towns of Picardy, Artois, Flanders, and Hainault. They were to promise many concessions if the towns would open their gates to the king. Among these men was Louis's notorious Flemish barber, Olivier le Daim, whom he sent to the great Flemish town of Ghent. By the time Louis entered Péronne, in February, almost all the lands bordering the Channel and the towns of Picardy had yielded to his representatives. He then received the news of the capitulation of Burgundy and Franche-Comté.

Mary of Burgundy was now in a desperate position. She lacked money and support. In fact, she was virtually a prisoner of the people of Ghent, who had chafed under the oppressive rule of Charles the Bold. She was forced to summon the three Estates of Flanders and to grant them the right to meet whenever they pleased. On February 11, she had to restore all the liberties to the town of Ghent which Charles the Bold and Philip the Good had abolished. Mary's councillors all agreed that she must marry, as soon as possible, some foreign prince able to bring her powerful support. There were several possible candidates.

Meanwhile, Louis continued to advance. In early March, he approached Arras, the chief stronghold guarding the entry to Flanders. The town was divided into two parts; the *cité*, under the bishop, and the main town. He entered the *cité*, delivered to him by its commander, but had to negotiate with the main town. It accepted his overlordship but refused to let him enter it with troops.

Louis then learned of the failure of his envoy, Olivier le Daim, in Ghent. He had made himself so unpopular that he had been forced to flee from the town. The Estates of Flanders, dominated by Ghent, then sent envoys to negotiate with the king. Louis tried to exploit the ill will between Mary's court and the people of Ghent. He showed the envoys part of a letter from Mary stating that she intended to have all her affairs managed by two or three of her councillors and not by the Estates of Flanders. The delegates returned to Ghent in anger and had her two chief advisors executed.

Louis had become impatient with the delay caused by these

negotiations and led his troops into battle once more. He swept through Artois, and besieged and captured Hesdin. He then reached the Channel and captured the port-city of Boulogne, which he offered to the Virgin Mary to hold from her as a fief.

Meanwhile, Arras decided not to keep the truce it had made with the king and sent envoys to Mary of Burgundy asking for help. They were captured by royal troops, brought before Louis, and executed. Louis then besieged Arras. A Milanese envoy described how Louis personally saw to every detail of the siege. He risked his life repeatedly and was slightly wounded. On May 4 Arras capitulated.

By this time, Mary had chosen a husband. The man she selected, from several suitors, was Maximilian of Habsburg, son of the Emperor Frederick III, to whom her father had previously betrothed her. The marriage arrangements were negotiated in April. Maximilian arrived in Ghent on August 18, 1477, and the marriage took place the same day.

Meanwhile, in late May, Louis joined the Grand Master, Antoine de Chabannes, on the borders of Hainault. In June, the king conducted a campaign of devastation in that province. He wrote to the Grand Master: "I am sending you three or four thousand devastators [*faucheurs*: literally mowers or reapers] to carry out the kind of destruction that you are familiar with. I beg you, put them to work, and do not complain about using five or six casks of wine to make them drink well and make them drunk." His purpose, in this ruthless destruction of the crops, was to force the important town of Valenciennes to come to terms and to decrease the food supply of the Low Countries. By September, Hainault was forced to sign a truce.

In late June, while Chabannes continued the devastation of Hainault, Louis had returned to Artois to resume his campaign in that region. In August, he routed a Flemish army at Cassel in Flanders.

In late September Louis established garrisons in the towns he had captured in Artois and Hainault. In October he withdrew to the valley of the Loire for the winter.

In April 1478 Louis led his armies back into the field. In June, Mary and Maximilian requested a truce. A year's truce was signed in July. Louis then returned to the Loire. It was the last campaign in which he would participate personally. Even while taking part in this military expedition in the spring and early summer of 1478, Louis was building up a legal case to justify his actions. In May he wrote to the royal proctor and the royal advocate in the Parlement of Paris stating that Charles the Bold was guilty of lese-majesty. He instructed them to see that Parlement rapidly drew up letters authorizing the seizure of his lands. On the same day, he wrote to Jean Bourré asking him to send the safe-conduct letter which Charles had given him before his trip to Péronne. This letter was then shown to the Parlement. Louis then wrote the Parlement ordering them to issue letters, without any further delay, declaring the Duke of Burgundy guilty of lese-majesty and calling for the confiscation of his lands.[20]

During his campaigns of 1477–78 Louis had to keep a watchful eye on England. When Charles the Bold was killed, his daughter and heiress, Mary, and his widow, Margaret, sought the help of King Edward IV. It should be remembered that Margaret was Edward's sister and Mary his niece. He was unwilling to see Louis annex the Burgundian Low Countries, as they were England's ally and best customer. Also Calais, the only place the English retained in France since the end of the Hundred Years' War, would be threatened. The danger of English intervention was very real and might well spoil all of Louis's plans for seizing Burgundian territory. The French king devoted all of his diplomatic skill to preventing this threat from materializing.

Edward made the first diplomatic move. He sent ambassadors to the French court in February 1477 with a proposal that the Truce of Piquigny (1475) be prolonged for the lifetime of the two kings and for one year after whichever died first. The annual payment from the King of France to the King of England would continue throughout this period. Actually, as Louis knew, even while making these friendly overtures, Edward was conspiring with Brittany and Spain against France.

Louis received the English ambassadors well and agreed to Edward's proposals. He was stalling for time while he proceeded against Burgundy. In return, he sent ambassadors to England bearing his written agreement to the prolonged truce. The envoys also sought Edward's help against Burgundy and suggested a partition. Edward was evasive.

Immediately after the marriage of Mary of Burgundy and

Maximilian of Habsburg, in August 1477, Louis sent an envoy to England to try to find out whether this new development had affected Edward's plans regarding Burgundy. The envoy also suggested to Edward that his brother, George, Duke of Clarence, had been plotting to marry Mary of Burgundy and then seize the English throne. Edward arrested Clarence and put him to death (by drowning him in butt of Malmsey wine, according to some accounts). In view of this alleged treason, the envoy repeated Louis's proposal that Edward help him against Burgundy. Once again the English king turned down this suggestion.

In November 1477, Louis sent the Bishop of Elne as a permanent ambassador to England. This was one of the first times the French had made use of permanent ambassadors. The bishop had a delicate task as both Flemish and Spanish missions were there urging Edward to support Maximilian Edward decided on neutrality.

Hoping to keep at least the neutrality of the English king while he was seizing Burgundian lands, Louis agreed to go ahead with the meetings of the committee which was to settle by arbitration all remaining differences between the two monarchs. Louis had been "dragging his feet" on this issue. When the committee met, trouble soon arose over the fact that the French armies, which were attacking Mary of Burgundy, had burned or captured various towns which had formed part of the dowry of her mother, Margaret of York. The English protested and demanded damages. Louis sent envoys to temporize. This was the situation when Louis and Maximilian signed a year's truce in July 1478.

Commynes sums up very well Louis XI's policy with regard to England from 1477-78. Louis's objective, of course, was to stop England from interfering while he was seizing Burgundian lands. Louis continued to pension Edward IV, as well as his chief ministers. Lord Hastings, Grand Chamberlain of England, was given 2,000 *écus*. He refused to sign any receipt for it, fearing to compromise himself. He continued to receive his payments anyway without signing anything. Edward IV, who was growing fat and liked his pleasures too well to engage in a war in France, resisted pressure in England to send aid to Mary of Burgundy. He was also glad to keep receiving his pension from Louis. English ambassadors to the French court were always showered with gifts and sent home with promises that Louis would soon satisfy

Edward regarding the projected marriage of Edward's daughter
with the dauphin. Louis would then eventually send envoys with
vague promises. Louis had no intention of carrying out this
marriage. He was still merely stalling for time while he occupied
the Burgundian lands. Louis again offered to partition these
lands with England. He suggested that Edward take Flanders
and Brabant. Edward refused, saying that these two areas would
be too difficult to hold, and also that England had good
commercial relations with them. He asked for Boulogne and
some towns in Picardy instead. No agreement was reached, and
Louis continued with his campaign against Burgundy.[21]

By the summer of 1478, Edward concluded that he could
increase his pressure upon Louis for the price of his neutrality.
Sentiment in England favored aid to Maximilian, and he knew
that Louis feared another Anglo-Burgundian alliance. He
therefore presented the French king with a new set of demands.
They called for Louis to start immediately making annual
payments on the dowry of Edward's daughter Elizabeth who was
to marry the dauphin when they came of age, the prolongation of
the Treaty of Picquigny, and the inclusion of Maximilian and the
Duke of Brittany in the amended treaty as allies of England.
Louis's ambassador in England, the Bishop of Elne, found himself
subjected to great pressure to sign a treaty embodying these
demands. English crowds jeered him everywhere he went, to the
point where he actually feared for his life. After delaying the
negotiations as long as possible, the shrewd bishop finally signed
the agreement in February 1479, knowing that Louis could still
refuse to ratify it.

English ambassadors then took the treaty to France for the
French king's ratification. Louis received them well and
expressed general satisfaction with the terms, but he said there
were a few minor points that needed revising. He had his council
debate for a month the matter of the dowry for Edward's
daughter, Elizabeth. Meanwhile, he appointed Boffille de Juge,
one of his most trusted advisors, and another high official, to
sound out the English ambassadors regarding Edward's real
intentions. Boffille de Juge reported to Louis that one of the
English envoys had told him that Edward sincerely desired
peace and was anxious to see the long-discussed marriage
between his daughter and the dauphin take place. The envoy
also added that Edward was surprised and irritated that Louis

had not sent him the usual pension recently.

On receiving this information, Louis concluded that he could continue to hold off England by diplomacy and turn his attention once again to Maximilian. The year's truce with Burgundy expired in July 1479. As Maximilian and Mary showed no signs of accepting his peace terms, King Louis refused to extend the truce and decided to exert military pressure against them. He moved first to recover Franche-Comté on his eastern frontier, which had been seized in 1477, had rebelled and had been lost, as mentioned above. Skillful military operations under a new commander, accompanied by wise royal diplomacy, regained much of the county by the end of the summer of 1479.

On the northern front, toward the Burgundian Netherlands, Louis intended to remain chiefly on the defensive but to exert steady pressure and constant harassment on the enemy. By these means, he hoped to bring Maximilian to terms. However, one of his commanders, finding that Maximilian had advanced with an army into Artois, attacked him with a large French army on August 7, 1479, at the Battle of Guinegate. His cavalry quickly routed the enemy's mounted squadrons; but then, instead of turning on the Burgundian pikemen, the French commander led his horsemen in pursuit of the fleeing enemy cavalry. The Burgundian footmen stood firm and inflicted heavy casualties on the French infantry. The French thus lost an excellent opportunity for a decisive victory.

First accounts of the battle reaching Louis led him to believe that his troops had suffered a defeat. Further news was more reassuring, however. In effect, the battle was indecisive. Also, Maximilian could not afford the losses he had sustained while Louis could. The French forces were now so powerful, and their border towns so strongly fortified, that Maximilian could conduct no further effective military action.

Throughout the last half of 1479 and the early months of 1480, Louis continued to keep England neutral by diplomacy and by the continued payment of pensions to King Edward and his chief councillors. In February 1480 Louis sent ambassadors to England headed by the Bishop of Elne. He instructed them to tell Edward that he favored the continuation of a truce between them to last for one hundred years from the death of whichever of them died first, as well as the marriage of the dauphin and Edward's daughter. Maximilian of Austria and the Duke of Brittany were not to be included in any treaty that might be signed. Louis would make an annual payment to Edward of 50,000 *écus* as long as the English king kept the terms of the truce. The ambassadors were to do everything possible to prevent the rupture of the truce with England. They were also to negotiate regarding the marriage of Elizabeth and the Dauphin Charles, and to propose the marriage of the Prince of Wales and the daughter of the Duchess Bona of Milan, widow of Duke Galeazzo-Maria and regent for her young son, Giangaleazzo.

On their arrival in England, the French embassy acted according to the above instructions. By so doing, they were submitting Louis's refusal to ratify the act to which the Bishop of Elne had been forced to consent the previous year. They agreed to compensate Margaret of York for damages done to her dowry lands and renewed the offer of a pension to Edward's daughter Elizabeth. Edward again refused to accept the latter offer. He was unwilling to go to the point of a complete rupture, however, as he would lose his pension.

Nevertheless, Edward was getting fed up with Louis's delaying tactics which were giving the French king a free hand to continue his military pressure against Maximilian. Public opinion in England was urging him to take a firmer stand. Therefore, he wrote Louis demanding an immediate end to the war and insisting that he himself be selected as an arbiter. Louis promptly rejected this proposal, which would obviously be harmful to his interests. Edward then threatened to help Maximilian if the French king refused to accept his offer of arbitration. By the summer of 1480, Louis learned that this was no idle threat. Margaret of York, widow of Charles the Bold, was in England negotiating an Anglo-Burgundian treaty with her brother King Edward.

Louis decided to stand firm. In July he made it perfectly clear to an English embassy in France that he would never ratify the treaty signed by the Bishop of Elne and would continue to try to enforce peace terms on Maximilian. He then turned to England's traditional enemy, Scotland. In return for a small amount of French aid, the King of Scotland agreed to invade England.

Edward now feared diplomatic isolation and the loss of the advantages he had obtained at the Treaty of Picquigny. In August he signed a treaty of alliance with Margaret of York. In return for a pension as large as the French one, he promised a substantial loan and a contingent of fifteen hundred archers. As part of the treaty, a marriage was agreed to between Edward's third daughter, Anne, and Philip, the young son of Mary and Maximilian.

However, just as Margaret was concluding this treaty in London, Maximilian signed a truce with Louis XI. It called for a peace conference to be held in October. If the conference was unsuccessful, the truce would continue until the end of March, 1481. This and future events show that Maximilian was a very indecisive man whose dreams usually far exceeded his resources. Despite the good news that Duchess Margaret kept forwarding him from London about the progress of her negotiations, Maximilian, short of money, had found French pressure too great and had signed the above truce, thus making the Anglo-Burgundian alliance stillborn.

When English ambassadors arrived in France to tell Louis of the alliance with Burgundy and to demand once again that he accept Edward's arbitration in the struggle between France and Burgundy, the French king greeted them with news of the truce he had signed with Maximilian. He made it clear to them that, if Edward continued to support Burgundy, his French pension would be cut off. To show that he meant business, he did not send the payment of the pension due at Michaelmas (September 29), 1480. To add to Edward's troubles, the Scots, stirred up by Louis, swept across the English border and burned a strong castle in Northumberland.

Under these circumstances, Edward had no choice but to soften his tone and seek a rapprochement with France. He realized that his Burgundian alliance was worthless and that he could never hope to receive the same substantial pension from Maximilian that he had been getting from Louis. In March, 1481, Edward sent an envoy to the French monarch suggesting the reestablishment of the Treaty of Picquigny. Louis suggested instead a return to the revision of 1478 whereby the treaty was prolonged until one year after the death of whichever king died first. He also promised to start paying Edward's pension again.

Apparently King Edward was quite satisfied when he received this proposal. He continued negotiating for a while with Louis rather than appear to have given in too easily. However, these negotiations seem to have been merely token. Maximilian sent desperate requests to England for help. Edward refused and

advised Maximilian to seek the longest truce possible with
France. Perhaps Louis, whose health was declining, would die
before the expiration of a long truce. To put further pressure on
both Maximilian and Edward, Louis then refused to prolong any
further the Franco-Burgundian truce of August 1480. The peace
conference scheduled for October 1480 had never been held.
Therefore, as agreed, the truce had been extended to the end of
March 1481 and then reextended until June.

Louis had now reduced Edward to terms. In June 1481 Edward
agreed to the prolongation of the truce of 1478, in which neither
the Duke of Burgundy nor the Duke of Brittany was named as an
ally of England. Nothing more would be said about English
mediation in the Franco-Burgundian war. In return, Louis
promised to renew regular payments of Edward's pension, and
the conclusion, at the proper time, of the marriage contract. He
also promised to stop aiding the Scots against England. In August,
a French envoy arrived in London with the Easter term of the
pensions. Louis signed the reconfirmation of the truce in
September 1481, and Edward ratified it a month later.[22]

The whole situation was completely changed by the sudden
death of Mary of Burgundy in March 1482, following a fall from a
horse. Louis, whose health was declining, heard the news with
joy. Once again the death of an opponent had helped him. Mary
left two children, Philip and Margaret. If Louis could arrange a
marriage between the dauphin and Margaret, with her French
fiefs as dowry, his problems would be solved. This, of course
would mean canceling the marriage plans with Elizabeth of
York. Edward IV was planning an invasion of Scotland and, like
Louis, his health was failing. Louis therefore decided to risk
offending him and try to reach a marriage agreement with
Maximilian.

The French king then struck his final blow at Maximilian: he
published the prolongation of the Anglo-French truce. The
Habsburg duke had evidently been unaware of this agreement.
He now saw that he had no hope of receiving help from England
and began negotiations with Louis XI in November.[23]

Before describing the terms of the treaty which ended the
long struggle between France and Burgundy there is one aspect
of Louis XI's anti-Burgundian policy which is worthy of mention,
as it was not used by any of his opponents against him. This was

his attempt to make use of economic warfare.

For centuries, England had maintained close commercial relations with the Low Countries, which had passed under Burgundian control, chiefly in the woollen trade. Louis XI sought to attract English and other foreign commerce to France. In April, 1464, a treaty was signed with the Hanseatic League granting them extensive trading privileges. His efforts to persuade English exporters of woolen goods to sell in France, rather than in the Low Countries, were unsuccessful. At the time of the marriage of Charles the Bold and Margaret of York, in 1468, a thirty-year trade agreement was signed between England and Burgundy.

In 1470, Louis decided to try to ruin the great fairs in Flanders, at Bruges and Antwerp, from which Charles the Bold derived considerable wealth. He began forbidding French goods from being sent to Burgundian lands. Then he summoned delegates from the most important French towns to meet at Tours, in October 1470, to ask their advice on the best place to establish a fair to rival those of Flanders. The delegates suggested either Rouen or Caen in Normandy. The king chose Caen because it was closer to the sea. The fairs of Caen were established by November. They were to be held on the same days as those of Antwerp, and extensive privileges were granted to the merchants trading there. The Low Countries, being a highly industrialized and densely populated region, was unable to produce sufficient food to feed its people. Louis was trying to reduce the prosperity and food supply of the area to make it rise against the Duke of Burgundy due to the resulting hardships.

The French king then tried to get his ally Henry VI, whom he had briefly reestablished on the throne of England in 1470–71, to take similar measures. He attempted to overcome the reluctance of English merchants with alluring offers of trading privileges in France. He sent them samples of French merchandise to try to persuade them that France could supply England just as well as the Low Countries. The return of Edward IV to the English throne spoiled these plans.

It appears that Louis XI had trouble enforcing his ban of 1470 on trade with Burgundy, because he had to keep renewing it. He was determined to continue his economic pressure. In only one of the series of truces between them, that of March 1473, was he forced to agree to the renewal of trade with Burgundy. However, he soon shut off this commerce again. Although at peace with Charles the Bold at this time, he forbade the export of grain to Flanders, and imposed a tax on goods exchanged either way between Flanders and France in 1474. In February 1475 he renewed his order forbidding his subjects to trade with Burgundy.

Louis also used financial weapons against Charles the Bold. By the 1470s, Charles had spent the fortune inherited from his father and was forced to resort to borrowing, particularly from the rich Medici firm of Florence. Louis was a good friend of the Medicis and of Florence. He was able to persuade them to stop lending money to Charles. In 1473, he was unable to borrow from the Medici bank in Bruges. By the time the Treaty of Soleuvre was signed, in 1475, Lorenzo de Medici was prepared to cut off Charles's credit completely.

Louis's economic warfare against Charles the Bold was only partially successful. The fairs of Flanders do not seem to have suffered very much from his attempts to ruin them by building up rival fairs at Caen (transferred to Rouen in May 1477). Antwerp was the least affected. It was the principal banking - center of the Low Countries and its fair the most important. It was too rich and too well established to be harmed by Louis's efforts.

The French king's embargo on trade with all Burgundian lands and his success in cutting off Charles's credit appear to have been more effective. By the end of 1475, the duke's subjects, with their trade and food supply dwindling, were becoming discontented and less willing to vote taxes. These factors undoubtedly contributed to the fact that the Estates of Burgundy, in August 1474, and those of Flanders, in July 1475, urged Charles the Bold not to undertake a campaign because of his deteriorating economic strength. As already described, Charles ignored their advice, agreed to support an English invasion of France, and besieged Neuss. After peace was made between France and England, Charles was forced to sign the Treaty of Soleuvre with Louis XI in September 1475. Among other things, it called for a renewal of trade, to the delight of the Flemish merchants.

In January 1476 Louis signed a commercial treaty with the English freeing them of virtually all restrictions and taxes on trade with Guyenne. The chief economic advantages of the treaty accrued to the English, although the revived trade did restore the prosperity of Bordeaux. Louis's purpose in making the agreement appeared in the final clause. All trade between England and France was to be in English or French ships. This would exclude Flemish or Breton carriers. In the meantime, French pirates, with Louis's secret approval, preyed upon those trading with Burgundy, notably the Venetians.

After the death of Charles the Bold, Louis continued his economic struggle against Mary and Maximilian. The blockade was continued and French troops systematically destroyed the crops in Flanders. French ships attacked the Flemish herring fishermen, whose catch was very important to the food supply of Flanders. Louis tried, unsuccessfully, to persuade the Hanseatic League to stop supplying the Low Countries with grain. In vain did Maximilian seek a truce with Louis and a renewal of commerce.

Flanders then adopted a defiant position of semirevolt against Mary and, after her death, refused to accept the rule of her husband, Maximilian, altogether. This attitude was partly a reaction against the harsh policy of Charles in restricting the liberties of the proud Flemish towns, but it was also due in part to the shortage of food and the damage to trade caused by Louis XI's economic policy. The merchants of the Flemish towns were suffering from Maximilian's attempt to carry on the war with France, and wanted peace. Pressure from the Estates of Brabant, Hainault, Zealand, Holland, and Flanders, as well as his critical military position, finally forced Maximilian to seek an end to the war. It would be a mistake to overemphasize the economic policy of Louis XI in causing Maximilian to sign the treaty with France which marked the ruin of the House of Burgundy. Still, it certainly influenced him to some extent. Incidentally, among the peace terms, Louis agreed to revoke the ordonnance forbidding his subjects to attend the fair at Antwerp and promised to stop interfering with the herring fisheries of the Low Countries.[24]

The long struggle between Louis XI and Burgundy was finally ended by the Treaty of Arras, concluded in December 1482. Negotiations were chiefly with delegates from Ghent, who held the children of Maximilian and Mary. The dauphin was to marry Marguerite of Austria, daughter of Mary and Maximilian, and receive Franche-Comté and Artois as a dowry. Marguerite was brought to France to await marriage with the dauphin when they should be of age. No mention was made of the Duchy of

Burgundy, Picardy, and the counties of Ponthieu and Boulogne.
Louis merely kept them, considering their incorporation into the
French royal domain as rightful and nonnegotiable. By March
1483 the Treaty of Arras and the promise of marriage of the
dauphin to Marguerite of Austria had been ratified by the
princes of the blood, the peers of France, the estates of the
various *bailliages* and *sénéchaussées*, and the towns

Edward IV was furious and began to prepare for war with
France but, prematurely aged by his carnal excesses, he died in
April 1483. Once again, death had removed a dangerous enemy
of Louis XI, as in the case of his brother Charles, Charles the
Bold of Burgundy, and Mary of Burgundy. The planned English
invasion was abandoned.

Edward IV was succeeded by his twelve-year-old son, Edward
V. The truce with England was due to last one more year. Louis
ordered it respected. He had no more fear of England.

In June 1483 Edward V was dethroned by his uncle, who
proclaimed himself Richard III. To assure his position, Richard
sought peaceful relations with France. The remarkably casual
letters exchanged between the English usurper and the dying
French king, in the summer of 1483, indicate that neither was
very worried about the other at the moment. The payment of the
pension, like the truce, should have continued for one more year
after the death of Edward IV. Louis made no payments to
Richard III, however. An uneasy truce now existed between the
two countries. Anglo-French relations were certainly in a much
more reassuring position, from the French viewpoint, than they
had been at Louis's accession.

As for the long, bitter struggle with Burgundy, Louis had
brought it to a successful conclusion. By the Treaty of Arras, he
gained the Duchy of Burgundy, Picardy, Ponthieu, and Boulogne
immediately, while Franche-Comté and Artois would pass into
the French royal domain on the marriage of Marguerite of
Austria and the dauphin. The partition of the Burgundian lands
was carried further as Duke René II had retaken Lorraine and
Sigismund of Austria had regained Alsace. Maximilian, however,
retained the rest of the Low Countries. This Habsburg presence
in that area was destined to constitute a new threat to the French
monarchy in the next century, but no one could have foreseen
this danger at that time.[25]

It is unfortunate that the relations between France and

Burgundy during the reign of Louis XI did not follow the colorful pattern described by Commynes. His story of the foreign policy of both powers, particularly, that of France, being motivated largely by a great personal struggle between Louis and Charles the Bold is much more dramatic than the more prosaic truth. His description of Louis XI, after the humiliation he suffered at Péronne in 1468, devoting most of the rest of his life to avenging himself by bringing about the defeat of Charles the Bold and the downfall of the House of Burgundy makes intriguing reading. The shrewd diplomacy by which he is supposed to have achieved this is fascinating.

In actual fact, as we have seen, Louis played a very minor role in the formation of the alliance that was destined to defeat Charles. While he hated and feared Charles, his primary concern in the realm of foreign affairs, until 1477, was defensive. He feared an English invasion and uprisings of the turbulent French nobility, particularly if either should be supported or encouraged by Burgundy. It was for this purpose that he sought the friendship of the Swiss and the Duke of Austria. Also, throughout much of this time, he was involved in warfare with the King of Aragon.

Commynes's account of the shrewd diplomacy by which Louis XI was supposed to have prepared the fall of Charles the Bold has been accepted by most historians as the crowning diplomatic feat of the king's career and has done much to establish Louis's reputation as a brilliant diplomat. The proof that this story is untrue certainly tarnishes this image somewhat. Nevertheless, he still showed great diplomatic skill throughout this whole series of events. His defensive alliances, first with Liège and then with the Swiss and Austria, were clearly sensible checks against possible Burgundian aggression. His policy with regard to England throughout these years truly showed masterful statesmanship. The English invasion of 1475, in alliance with Burgundy, constituted one of the gravest threats that Louis ever faced. Although he was helped by the failure of Charles the Bold to give full military support to the alliance, Louis's negotiations with Edward IV, and the treaty by which he persuaded the English to withdraw from France, showed great diplomatic ability. Then, after the death of Charles the Bold, the means by which Louis XI kept the English from interfering while he conquered Burgundian lands prove conclusively his remarkable diplomatic skill.

Louis's policy with regard to Burgundy, after the death of Charles the Bold, was largely opportunistic. The duke had been Louis's most powerful and rebellious vassal, and had prevented him from exercising any authority in Charles's French fiefs. When he was dead, the Burgundian army largely shattered after three consecutive defeats, and his daughter, Mary, in a very weak position it took no great perspicacity for Louis to recognize his opportunity. He promptly turned to military force to overrun most of the lands which the Duke of Burgundy had held in France. He did not seize the Burgundian lands outside of France, with the exception of Franche-Comté. After Mary's death, and when he had placed her husband, Maximilian, in a hopeless military position, he turned once again to diplomacy and negotiated the Treaty of Arras, which legalized his conquests.

Even while he was still struggling with Mary and Maximilian to annex the above Burgundian lands, Louis also managed to gain the entire inheritance of King René of Anjou. This consisted of Anjou and Maine in France, and Bar and Provence just east of the French frontier. Once again, a timely financial investment probably helped the Spider King reap the dividends he sought. In September 1478 he instructed a royal official to pay King René a sizable sum of money to persuade him to revoke his gift of Anjou, Provence, and Bar to his grandson René II, Duke of Lorraine. On King René's death, in 1480, Louis seized Anjou and Bar. Provence escaped both the king and the Duke of Lorraine, for the moment, and went to King René's nephew, Charles II, Count of Maine. Charles had no heirs, however, and promised his inheritance to Louis. On his death, in 1481, Louis gained Maine and Provence. Thus, he had increased significantly the size of the French royal domain.[26]

CHAPTER 6

The Last Years

B EGINNING in 1479, Louis became increasingly preoccupied
with an even more implacable foe than the Duke of
Burgundy—death. Both Commynes and the Milanese
ambassador commented on his declining health in 1479. He
became more irascible and solitary. Louis suffered his first attack
of apoplexy in 1479 or 1480. He temporarily lost his memory and
his power of speech. He began to regain both after two or three
days and had largely recovered in about two weeks. He had a
second attack in 1481. Once again he lost the power of speech,
but recovered it in a few hours. He was dangerously ill
throughout the winter of 1481–82.[1]

A false picture has emerged from the writings of some
historians and novelists of the aging monarch shut up in tight
seclusion, under heavy guard, throughout his declining years in
his castle of Plessis-les-Tours, which is described as a grim
fortress. The length of time he spent under these conditions has
been exaggerated and the nature of his castle distorted. It is true
that Plessis-les-Tours was, for some years, Louis's favorite
residence, but it was only during the last year of his life that he
retired into seclusion there. In May 1482 he went to the province
of Orleannais. He spent the summer at a house that he owned at
Cléry near the church of Nôtre-Dame, where he planned to be
buried. Late in the summer he returned to Plessis-les-Tours and
finally did shut himself up in this heavily guarded retreat.

Plessis-les-Tours was by no means a somber, melancholy
fortress. It was a large, pleasant manor house which Louis had
built just outside Tours where his father had owned a hunting
lodge. It was a well-lit, comfortable dwelling. From the upper
story the king could see the town of Tours. The entrance was by
a drawbridge between two large towers. Then there was a large
courtyard. The king's dwelling, with its handsome gallery,

looked out on the courtyard. At first Louis used Plessis chiefly as
a hunting lodge. The park was stocked with rabbits, deer, and
wild boar. As the king began to spend more time at Plessis he had
some alterations made. He had his books moved there. He even
had some cages of singing birds and a few of his favorite dogs
placed right in his bedroom.[2]

In Louis's last years, few were admitted to Plessis. Elaborate
precautions were taken to keep out intruders. The castle was
surrounded with a barrier of iron spikes. Forty crossbowmen
were placed on the walls with instructions to fire at anyone who
approached at night.

After his illnesses of 1480 and 1481, Louis became suspicious
of everyone. He refused to see anyone most of the time except
trusted junior officials who owed their position to him. He feared
that some of his enemies would attempt to put him under the
control of a regency, claiming that he was no longer capable of
ruling. He knew that he was hated by many of the great lords of
the kingdom and that he was unpopular among the lower classes
as well because of his heavy taxes. Commynes even believed that
someone might have tried to assassinate him if he had not been so
well protected. He looked pale and emaciated, and he began to
wear heavy robes of red satin to hide his thinness. By the time he
returned to Plessis in the late summer of 1482, seldom to emerge
again, he retained only a few valets close to him. Only his doctor,
Jacques Coitier, had frequent access to him.[3]

Louis realized that he had not long to live and began to give
some thought to his son and heir, Charles, whom he had not seen
for several years. He had had his son raised under strong guard at
the castle of Amboise, about seventeen miles from Tours. The
capable royal official Jean Bourré was entrusted with his
upbringing. The boy's mother, Charlotte of Savoy, also looked
after him. Charles was a delicate child, and Louis was anxious
about his health, particularly since he was his only male heir.
Bourré sent the king frequent reports about the state of his son's
health. No one could visit Charles without special permission and
no outsiders were allowed to stay there. This precaution was
partly due to Louis's fear of the plague, a loose term for various
epidemics which periodically ravaged parts of fifteenth-century
Europe. The king also had in mind his own rebellious youth, and
was anxious to keep Charles away from those who might have a
bad influence on him.

Louis had his doctor and astrologer, Pierre Choisnet, prepare the *Rozier des Guerres* (Rosebush of Wars), a book of maxims for the guidance of his son. It said that the king exists only for the welfare of the state. The king was the good gardener of the garden of his people. He should keep the laws and enlarge the royal domain. He should govern personally and know all. He should punish the evil, reward the good, and fear flatterers. The three pillars of government were justice, the respect of the governed, and mutual love between king and subjects. The king should know the art of war, but his principal duty was to try to keep his kingdom in a state of peace. He should only fight if absolutely necessary. The king should not fight personally, but should mastermind the campaign. The king's justice should be firm. Choisnet then compiled a brief history of France for the dauphin's use and included it in the *Rozier*. Most of the maxims seem to have been dictated by Louis himself. Therefore the book is of interest as a compilation of Louis's theories of kingship. Those which he did not personally dictate, he at least approved. Of course, as is true of most people who give good advice he did not necessarily always follow his own maxims.

Louis then sent the book to his son with this note:

Since, just as pleasant odors comfort those in love, so does the good and virtuous advice of wise men, and, since it is our wish that when, by the grace of God, you come to reign over and govern this noble kingdom of France, filled with good morals and virtues, you may know and have ready in your hands and in your heart that which is suitable and very necessary for the good government thereof, I send you this *Rozier* concerning the guard and defense of the state. From which *Rozier*, when you have reached the age of flourishing youth, you will smell a rose each day, and you will find there more pleasure and comfort than in all the roses in the world . . . and you will know which of your predecessors have acted the best.

Knowing the character of Louis XI, there is something rather touching in this note to his son. He was a man who was virtually incapable of feeling love for anyone. He hated his father, hardly knew his mother, disliked both of his wives, and showed no love for his daughters, one of whom he treated cruelly. Although he took great pains to see that his son Charles was well cared for and protected, he rarely saw him. Surely in this dedicatory note we can see the stern old king trying to express some trace of real and sincere affection for his son. He usually much preferred his favorite hunting dogs to people.

In September 1482 the ailing king made one of his last trips from Plessis and traveled to Amboise. There, in the presence of his chief advisors, he had instructions read to his son for the administration of the kingdom. The twelve-year-old prince stood awkwardly, shuffling from one foot to the other, listening to the orders and advice of a father whom he scarcely knew. Louis instructed him to seek the advice of the good and loyal councillors who had served him so well. He advised him, when he became king, to retain the present office holders. He admitted his own mistake in having dismissed his father's officials when he had ascended the throne. Charles solemnly promised to obey these instructions.[4]

Louis then returned to Plessis. Throughout the fall and the winter of 1482–83 his health continued to fail. He became thinner and weaker. He was surrounded by astrologers, doctors, and quacks, and he paid large sums for their various cures. His chief doctor, Jacques Coitier, became a rich man. Louis heaped lands and revenues upon him in 1482. In February 1483 he gave Coitier two seigneuries, the revenue from one salt warehouse, and a house in Dijon. Commynes says that he paid the doctor 10,000 écus per month for five months.

Among his various ailments Louis believed that he had leprosy. He sent for two things that were thought to be remedies. In November 1482 he wrote to Lorenzo de'Medici asking him to send him Saint Zenobi's ring, a relic that was supposed to cure this disease. He also had tortoise blood sent from Cape Verde. Modern authorities agree that the king did not have leprosy at all, but merely some sort of disagreeable skin condition.

By this time, Louis hoped chiefly for divine aid to keep him alive. He sought the help of various saints by heaping gifts upon their churches, and he had all the clergy of France pray for him. He had two famous holy men come to Plessis, Brother Bernardin and Francis of Paola, a hermit from Calabria in southern Italy. He hoped that their prayers and intercession with God might save his life. He counted particularly on the saintly Calabrian hermit. He wrote to the town council of Lyons in February 1483, asking them to welcome Francis of Paola and to make a litter for him to carry him the rest of the way. He wrote them again in March, repeating his instructions to welcome the holy man when he arrived. When Francis finally reached Plessis Louis built him a hermitage in the court of the castle and begged him humbly to pray continuously for the prolongation of his life.[5]

During the last five or six months of his life, Louis was suspicious of everyone, even his own daughter, Anne, and his son-in-law, Pierre de Beaujeu. In June 1483 Beaujeu and Dunois returned from Amboise, where they had been arranging for the engagement of the Dauphin Charles and Margaret of Burgundy, the three-year-old daughter of Mary and Maximilian. Before allowing them to report to him, Louis sent a captain of the guard to make sure that their men were not wearing coats of mail under their robes.

To show that he was still able to act and still in control of his kingdom, Louis appointed and fired office holders and gave and removed pensions with unaccustomed frequency. He handed out severe punishments in order to be feared and for fear of losing authority. He wanted to make sure that everyone in the country knew that he was still alive and active. Chiefly to show his activity, he had animals purchased for him all over Europe for his zoo.

In fact, Louis knew that he was dying. He still had not lost all hope, however, as he believed that divine intervention might save his life. He secured papal permission to have the Holy Vial sent from Rheims. It contained the holy oil with which French kings were anointed at the time of their coronation. Its removal from Rheims was an unprecedented action. In July he wrote separate letters to the cathedral chapter of Rheims and to the abbot and the monks of the monastery of Saint-Rémy in Rheims instructing them to deliver the Vial to three of his councillors and informing them that he had papal approval. When the Vial arrived at Plessis he had one drop of the holy oil it contained placed upon him. He then had the vessel put on a sideboard in his room between the Staff of Moses and the Cross of Victory.

These frantic efforts by Louis XI to cling to life warrant some comment. They probably were not due to an exaggerated fear of death. Louis was no coward. Also he believed that, with the intercession of various saints to whose churches he had made generous donations and with the help of his particular protector, the Virgin Mary, the joys of heaven and life eternal awaited him. A more likely explanation is that he realized that he had achieved a very powerful position in both France and Europe. He had many ambitious projects in mind and he wanted time to carry them out.

It is no wonder that Louis XI was frustrated by the cruel irony of the situation. Never had his power been as great as during the last year of his life. He was feared and obeyed throughout France and respected throughout Europe. After the Treaty of Arras in December 1482, with Maximilian, France was clearly the most powerful nation in all Christendom. Commynes only exaggerated slightly when he said that the Flemish did Louis's bidding, Brittany stood in fear of him, the King and Queen of Spain and the Italian states sought his friendship, the Swiss obeyed him "like his subjects," and the Kings of Scotland and Portugal were his allies. His subjects trembled before him. Whatever he commanded was carried out immediately without excuses. "He was so obeyed that it seemed that all Europe was made only to obey him." Louis had struggled throughout his entire reign to achieve such a position of power. Now he lay dying and would have no chance to reap the fruits of his triumph. He was a bitter man and fought desperately against the inevitable.

The king made his last public appearance in June 1483 before delegates of the towns that he had summoned to Plessis. He was dressed in a long robe of crimson velvet with marten's fur and wore two scarlet bonnets on his head. He removed the bonnets and appeared almost bald, with a few gray hairs cut short. The townsmen had respectfully removed their hats. Louis instructed them to put them back on, but remained bare-headed himself. He then addressed them, saying that he desired three things for the benefit of France: that merchants be able to come and go freely, that justice be swifter and surer, and that there be one law and one standard of weights and measures for the entire kingdom. These were doubtless some of the policies that Louis would have attempted to carry out, had he lived.[6]

On August 25, 1483, Louis was forced to take to his bed with what proved to be his last illness. Three days later, Louis suffered a cerebral congestion of some sort. He had difficulty breathing, was unable to speak, and was partially paralyzed. He soon regained the power of speech but was very weak and thin. His chief doctor, Jacques Coitier, told him with brutal abruptness that he was finished ("il est faict de vous"). Although he had struggled so bitterly against death, Louis accepted his fate now bravely and without complaint.

Knowing that his end was near, Louis sent for the dauphin and summoned his son-in-law, Pierre de Beaujeu. He entrusted Beaujeu with complete charge of the dauphin's person and appointed him as regent to govern the kingdom until young Charles should come of age. He told Beaujeu that the country needed at least five or six years of peace. He warned him to stay on good terms with England and to leave Brittany alone, at least until Charles was old enough to rule.

Louis then sent the royal seals to Charles at Amboise, referring already to his son as "the king." He also sent his guard, his archers, his hunting dogs, and his birds.

Louis remained lucid to the end. He continued issuing instructions for the government of the kingdom and, according to Commynes, "constantly said something of sense." As the end approached, Francis of Paola and several churchmen stood at the foot of his bed, reciting prayers for the dying. Louis himself prayed aloud from time to time. He died between seven and eight o'clock on the evening of August 30, 1483. In keeping with his scorn for tradition and pomp, he had left instructions that he should not be buried with great ceremony at Saint-Denis in Paris, as was traditional for French kings. Instead, as he had wished, he was buried quite simply at the church that he had had built at Cléry. He had even had the tomb and funeral monument prepared in advance.[7]

There were probably very few who grieved over the passing of this unusual man who seemed incapable of feeling or inspiring affection. Still, Frenchmen ever since owe him a debt of gratitude. He ascended the throne of a country just beginning to struggle back from the devastation of the Hundred Years' War and weakened by the power of several great nobles to defy the authority of the government. More than any other man, he was responsible for transforming France into a strong nation state destined to play a major role in world history for the next four and a half centuries.

Notes and References

In order to save space several citations have been combined into a single reference and placed at the end of each appropriate section.

Chapter One

1. Charles Petit-Dutaillis, *Charles VII, Louis XI et les premières années de Charles VIII (1422-1492)*, Vol. IV, part 2, of *Histoire de France depuis les origines jusqu'à la Révolution*, ed. E. Lavisse (Paris, 1902), pp. 17-29.
2. Pierre Champion, *Louis XI*, 2nd ed. (Paris, 1928), I, 91-92.
3. *Ibid.*, pp. 94-95.
4. *Ibid.*, pp. 96-97.
5. *Ibid.*, pp. 99-104; J. Huizinga, *The Waning of the Middle Ages*, trans. F. Hopman (Garden City, N.Y., 1954), pp. 250-53.
6. Champion, I, 105.
7. *Ibid.*, pp. 107-11; *Lettres de Louis XI, Roi de France*, ed. Joseph Vaesen and Étienne Charavay (Paris, 1883-1909), I, 164-66; J. Russell Major, *Representative Institutions in Renaissance France* (Madison, 1960), p. 39; F. Lot and R. Fawtier, *Histoire des institutions françaises au moyen âge* (Paris, 1958), II, 163.
8. Champion, I, 111-13.
9. *Ibid.*, pp. 115-19; Enguerrand de Monstrelet, *La Chronique d'Enguerran de Monstrelet*, ed. L. Douët-d'Arcq (Paris, 1857-62), V, 301-306.
10. France was divided, for administrative purposes, into districts called *bailliages* and *sénéchaussées*. The two terms were virtually synonymous, with *sénéchaussée* being more common in the south.
11. Champion, I, 121-26.
12. *Ordonnances des Rois de France de la Troisième race*, XIII, 306-13, cited by Champion, I, 126.
13. Mathieu d'Escouchy, *Chronique*, ed. G. du Fresne de Beaucourt (Paris, 1863-64), III, 4-29; Jean Chartier, *Chronique de Charles VII, roi de France*, ed. M. Vallet de Viriville (Paris, 1858), I, 253-57; Thomas Basin, *Histoire de Charles VII*, ed. and trans. Charles Samaran (Paris, 1933), I, 256-58; Monstrelet, V, 411-12; Champion, I, 127-34.
14. Monstrelet, V, 413-16; Champion, I, 134-36.
15. Champion, I, 137-38.

16. *Ibid.*, pp. 138-40; Monstrelet, V, 468-69.
17. Champion, I, 140-41.
18. *Ibid.*, pp. 141-42; *Lettres de Louis XI*, I, 187.
19. Monstrelet, VI, 60, 77-80; Champion, I, 143-47; Basin, I, 284-88; Chartier, II, 36-42.
20. Champion, I, 147-48; Monstrelet, VI, 81-82.
21. Champion, I, 149. The terms of the truce are published in Monstrelet, VI, 97-107.
22. Champion, I, 155-59; Basin, II, 46-50; Escouchy, III, 92-94. For a Swiss account of the campaign, see *Dictionnaire historique et biographique de la Suisse* (Neuchâtel, 1920-33), I, 407; *Ibid.*, V, 676; *Ibid.*, VII, 502-503. It adds much useful information, but differs in interpretation from the French accounts.
23. Champion, I, 161-65; *Lettres de Louis XI*, I, 191-95; Escouchy, I, 22-23; *Dictionnaire historique de la Suisse*, I, 407; B. de Mandrot, "Les Relations de Charles VII et de Louis XI avec les cantons suisses, 1444-83," *Jahrbuch für schweizerische Geschichte* (Zurich, 1880) V, 61-62.
24. Champion, I, 166-68; Escouchy, I, 40-42.
25. *Lettres de Louis XI*, 199-201; Champion, I, 169-73; Escouchy, I, 43-50.
26. *Lettres de Louis XI*, I, 201; Champion, I, 175.
27. Champion, I, 137, 175-79.
28. *Ibid.*, pp. 181-82.
29. *Ibid.*, pp. 183-88; *Lettres de Louis XI*, I, 196.

Chapter Two

1. Emmanuel Pilot de Thorey, ed., *Catalogue des actes du Dauphin Louis II, devenu le roi de France Louis XI, relatifs a l'administration du Dauphiné* (Grenoble, 1899), I, 2-4, 61-63; Champion, I, 189-91.
2. Pilot de Thorey, I, x, xiv, 158-59, 167-69, 276-77, 283-84, 287-88, 291-93; Champion, I, 193-96.
3. Pilot de Thorey, I, 178, 215, 278, 426; *Ibid.*, III, 45-46. For a detailed description of the nature of *feux* in Dauphiné in the fifteenth century see *Ibid.*, p. 34, note 1, and p. 38, note 2; Champion, I, 195-96.
4. Pilot de Thorey, I, 34, 41, 250, 368-69, 376; Champion, I, 196-97.
5. Pilot de Thorey, I, 360-61; *Ibid.*, II, 98-99, 122-25; Champion, I, 197-98.
6. Champion, I, 199-201.
7. *Ibid.*, 201-205; Pilot de Thorey, I, 256, 307, 315-17, 321-23, 325, 337; *Lettres de Louis XI*, I, 68-69, 227-28, 230-31, 242-52; *Dispatches with Related Documents of Milanese Ambassadors in France and Burgundy, 1450-83*, ed. Paul Kendall and Vincent Ilardi

(Athens, Ohio, 1970), I, 166-72; Paul Kendall, *Louis XI* (New York, 1971), p. 99.

8. Georges Chastellain, *Oeuvres*, ed. Kervyn de Lettenhove (Brussels, 1863-66), III, 177-92; *Lettres de Louis XI*, I, 77-78; Champion, I, 199-212.

9. Chastellain, III, 209-12; Champion, I, 212-14; *Dispatches*, ed. Kendall and Ilardi, I, 218-21, 250.

10. *Lettres de Louis XI*, I, 80-82, 104-109, 116-17, 133-34, 136-37; Chastellain, III, 215-25, 235-39, 289-93, 297, 301-306, 309-10, 327, 407-11; Champion, I, 214-18, 219-21, 229-30; Olivier de la Marche, *Mémoires*, ed. Henri Beaune and J. D'Arbaument (Paris, 1883-88), II, 410-21; *Dispatches*, ed. Kendall and Ilardi, I, 218-21.

11. *Lettres de Louis XI*, I, 140n, 331-32; *Dispatches*, ed. Kendall and Ilardi, I, xxxix-xl, 266-69, 314-19; *Ibid.*, II, xiii-xiv, 2-25, 42-52, 432, 437, 440, 444, 455-61, 462-66, 467-69, 470-74; Kendall, 99-100, 102-104.

12. *Lettres de Louis XI*, I, 127-28; Chastellain, IV, 30-37, 54-62; Champion, I, 230-36; *Ibid.*, II, 1-9; Petit-Dutaillis in Lavisse, IV, part 2, 322. I am indebted to Professor Richard Jackson of the University of Houston for the information on the coronation of Louis XI. It is based on a contemporary eye-witness description found in a manuscript in the Bibliothèque Nationale in Paris which corrects the somewhat inaccurate account by the Burgundian chronicler Chastellain which has been used by all previous biographers of Louis XI. Professor Jackson will include it in a forthcoming book on the coronation ceremonies of French Kings.

Chapter Three

1. Jean de Roye, *Journal de Jean de Roye, connu sous le nom de Chronique Scandaleuse, 1460-1483*, ed. B. de Mandrot (Paris, 1894-96), I, 23-30; Champion, II, 11-15, 18; Thomas Basin, *Histoire de Louis XI*, ed. and trans. Charles Samaran (Paris, 1963), I, 32; Petit-Dutaillis in Lavisse, IV, part 2, 324.

2. René Gandilhon, *Politique économique de Louis XI* (Paris, 1941), pp. 137-40; Petit-Dutaillis in Lavisse, IV, part 2, 115-30, 156-58, 177-80; John Fortescue, *Governance of England*, ed. Plummer (Oxford, 1885), p. 114, cited by Petit-Dutaillis in Lavisse, IV, part 2, 130; François Villon, *I Laugh Through Tears*, trans. G. P. Cuttino (New York, 1955), p. 26; Henri Denifle, *La Désolation des églises, monastères, et hôpitaux en France pendant la Guerre de Cent Ans*, 2 vols. (Paris, 1897-99), rpt. Brussels: Culture et Civilisation, 1965. Volume I of Denifle consists of documents describing the destruction of chuch property.

3. Petit-Dutaillis, in Lavisse, IV, part 2, 116, 130-32, 139, 149-51;

259; 277-78, 318-19; Major, pp. 25-45, *passim*.
   4. *Dépêches des ambassadeurs milanais en France sous Louis XI et François Sforza*, ed. B. de Mandrot, (Paris, 1916-23), I, 21, 99-102, 137, 197, 341; *ibid.*, II, 88; *ibid.*, IV, 149-50, 194, 215-16, 233. The reports of the Milanese ambassadors constitute a very important source of information about the reign of Louis XI. The Italian states were the first to develop permanent embassies. Milan maintained a series of fully accredited resident ambassadors at the court of Louis XI from 1463 to 1475. This was the first embassy of its kind at the French court and, during most of the 1460s, the only resident embassy established by any Italian state north of the Alps. Philippe de Commynes, *Mémoires*, ed. Joseph Calmette and G. Durville (Paris, 1924-25), I, 65, 67, 130; *ibid.*, II, 74-75, 325; *Lettres de Louis XI*, V, 152; *ibid.*, VI, 158; *ibid.*, X, 349-50; Champion, II, 181-214; Gaston Dodu, "Louis XI," *Revue Historique*, CLXVIII (1931), 55-57; Petit-Dutaillis, in Lavisse, IV, part 2, 324-31.
   5. *Lettres de Louis XI*, II, 34-35; *Ibid.*, X, 175-77; Champion, II, 24-25, 57-59; Petit-Dutaillis, in Lavisse, IV, part 2, 330-37; *Dépêches des ambassadeurs milanais*, III, 29-30; Major, p. 50.
   6. *Lettres de Louis XI*, II, 119-20, 145-46, 155-56, 210-18; Champion, II, 33-38, 47-55; Petit-Dutaillis in Lavisse, IV, part 2, 325, 337-40; *Dépêches des ambassadeurs milanais*, I, 197; *ibid.*, II, 181, 376-77.
   7. J. Calmette and G. Périnelle, *Louis XI et l'Angleterre, 1461-1483* (Paris, 1930), pp. iii-21.
   8. *Ibid.*, pp. 22-45; *Dépêches des ambassadeurs milanais*, II, 97.
   9. Calmette and Périnelle, pp. 51-54, 59-63.
   10. Richard Vaughan, *Philip the Good* (London, 1970), pp. 357-58, 369-72; Petit-Dutaillis in Lavisse, IV, part 2, 340-41; *Dépêches des ambassadeurs milanais*, II, 236-37, 269-70.
   11. Petit-Dutaillis in Lavisse, IV, part 2, 341-42; Commynes, I, 189; *Dépêches des ambassadeurs milanais*, I, 361-62.

Chapter Four

   1. Champion, II, 61-67; Petit-Dutaillis in Lavisse, IV, part 2, 343-47; *Lettres de Louis XI*, II, 288-92; *Dépêches des ambassadeurs milanais*, II, xxxi-xxxii; Henri Stein, *Charles de France, frère de Louis XI* (Paris, 1921), pp. 52-53, 112.
   2. Vaughan, pp. 374-80.
   3. A *lance* consisted of six men.
   4. Jean de Roye, I, 51, 67; Commynes, I, 33; *Dépêches des ambassadeurs milanais*, III, 90, 108, 130, 168-69, 223, 237-50, 254-64, 408-11, 417-21; Champion, II, 61-74; Petit-Dutaillis in Lavisse, IV, part 2, 347-49; *Lettres de Louis XI*, II, 230-37, 244-46, 248-53,

Notes and References

259-66, 271-72, 288-92, 329-42; Stein, pp. 94-96; Vaughan, pp. 381-88.

5. Commynes, I, 39-40, 80, 82; Jean de Roye, I, 68, 76-77; Basin, *Histoire de Louis XI*, I, 204-12; *Dépêches des ambassadeurs milanais*, III, 311-13, 327, 373-75, 379; Stein, 100-104; *Lettres de Louis XI*, II, 332-34; Petit-Dutaillis in Lavisse, IV, part 2, 349-50.

6. Champion, II, 77-82; Petit-Dutaillis in Lavisse, IV, part 2, 350-51; Vaughan, p. 390.

7. Commynes, I, 88-91; Basin, *Histoire de Louis XI*, I, 230-34; *Dépêches des ambassadeurs milanais*, IV, 101-102, 141-44, 285-86; Petit-Dutaillis in Lavisse, IV, part 2, 351-52; *Lettres de Louis XI*, II, 321-22; *ibid.*, III, 13-14; Calmette and Périnelle, pp. 67-77.

8. Richard Vaughan, *Charles the Bold* (New York, 1974), pp. 41-43.

9. *Ibid.*, pp. 11-15, 23-28.

10. Calmette and Périnelle, pp. 78-91; *Lettres de Louis XI*, III, 143-45, 154-59; Basin, *Histoire de Louis XI*, I, 286-88; Petit-Dutaillis in Lavisse, IV, part 2, 355.

11. Petit-Dutaillis in Lavisse, IV, part 2, 355-57; *Lettres de Louis XI*, III, 183-88, 198-201, 240-41, 252-55, 258-61, 277-78; Stein, pp. 252-53; Calmette and Périnelle, pp. 91-99; Vaughan, *Charles the Bold*, pp. 44-48, 53-54.

12. The only accuate, detailed, and critical account of the meeting at Péronne is in Karl Bittmann, *Ludwig XI und Karl der Kühne. Die Memoiren des Philippe de Commynes als historische Quelle* (Göttingen, 1964), I, part 1, 193-367. The direct quotation on my p. 93 is from Bittmann, I, part 1, 356. For Commynes's famous account, see Commynes, I, 125-34, 142-45. For the events at Liège in September and October 1468, see Vaughan, *Charles the Bold*, pp. 28-35. For further information on events at Péronne and Liège, see *ibid.*, pp. 55-57; La Marche, III, 86; *Lettres de Louis XI*, III, 295-96; Kendall, pp. 209-10, 212. Unfortunately Kendall does not cite any of his sources in his footnotes. Therefore, when he quotes an original source, one can only cite the page number in Kendall without knowing where he obtained the quotation.

13. Bittmann, I, part 2, 400-409; Vaughan, *Charles the Bold*, p. 58.

14. Bittmann, I, part 2, 409-19; Commynes, I, 169-71; Champion, II, 106; *Lettres de Louis XI*, IV, 31-33, 45-46; Petit-Dutaillis in Lavisse, IV, part 2, 361-62.

15. Calmette and Périnelle, pp. 107-108; Kendall, p. 228.

16. Bittmann, I, part 2, 419-20; Vaughan, *Charles the Bold*, p. 59.

17. Calmette and Périnelle, pp. 99-121; *Lettres de Louis XI*, IV, 110-14, 123-25, 130-31; Cora Scofield, *The Life and Reign of Edward the Fourth, King of England and France and Lord of Ireland* (New York, 1967), I, 524-25; Kendall, pp. 228-37; Petit-Dutaillis in Lavisse, IV, part 2, 363-64; Vaughan, *Charles the Bold*, 64-65.

Chapter Five

1. Petit-Dutaillis in Lavisse, IV, part 2, 364-66; *Lettres de Louis XI,*
IV, 190-93, 211-13; Commynes, I, 186-87, 212-17; Calmette and
Périnelle,pp. 136, 138, 143; Kendall, pp. 237-40; Vaughan, *Charles the
Bold,* pp. 66-72.
2. *Lettres de Louis XI,* IV, 256-58, 277-79, 285-89, 291-92,
352-58, 363-65; Commynes, I, 186-89, 217-18; Petit-Dutaillis in
Lavisse, IV, part 2, 364, 366; Calmette and Périnelle, pp. 143, 146-48;
Vaughan, *Charles the Bold,* pp. 72-73, 76.
3. *Lettres de Louis XI,* IV, 305-07, 324-28; Petit-Dutaillis in
Lavisse, IV, part 2, 366-67; Vaughan, *Charles the Bold,* p.73; Bittman, I,
part 2, 623-27.
4. Commynes, I, 227-28, 233-39; *Lettres de Louis XI,* IV, 331-33;
ibid., V, 4, 25-26, 32-35, 107n.1, 117n.1, 130n.1, 132; Petit-Dutaillis in
Lavisse, IV, part 2, 367-68; Champion, II, 126-28; Kendall, pp.
248-53; Vaughan, *Charles the Bold,* 73, 76-77, 79, 82. As for the value
of Commynes's work as an historical source, although Bittmann has
proven it inaccurate in many of its major interpretations, he admits that
it still has considerable merit. When used with caution, the *Mémoires* of
Commynes still provide some valuable information about the reign of
Louis XI.
5. Bittmann, II, part 1, 62-68, 77, 80; Petit-Dutaillis in Lavisse, IV,
part 2, 368.
6. Petit-Dutaillis in Lavisse, IV, part 2, 370-74; Kendall, pp.
263-71; Vaughan, *Charles the Bold,* pp. 84-88, 92-97, 100, 103-107,
112-54; Bittmann, II, part 1, 84-89, 99.
7. Vaughan, *Charles the Bold,* pp. 261-68, 272-79.
8. Bittmann, II, part 1, 592-609; Vaughan, *Charles the Bold,* p. 274;
Commynes, II, 16, 100-101, 115-16, 144.
9. Vaughan, *Charles the Bold,* pp. 279-91; Kendall, p. 270;
Bittmann, II, part 1, 226.
10. Vaughan, *Charles the Bold,* pp. 291-98; Bittman, II, part 1,
595-96.
11. Vaughan, *Charles the Bold,* pp. 299-306.
12. *Ibid.,* pp. 306-11.
13. *Ibid.,* pp. 312-20, 328, 332-35, 341-45.
14. Calmette and Périnelle, pp. 156, 160, 164-73, 175-77, 180-217;
Commynes, II, 27, 43-48, 54-56, 59-67, 75, 80; Thomas Rymer,
Foedera, conventiones, litterae, et cujuscunque generis acta publica
(The Hague, 1741), V, part 3, 66 ff.; Jean de Roye, II, 344; Petit-
Dutaillis in Lavisse, IV, part 2, 377-79; Vaughan, *Charles the Bold,* pp.
340, 344-52; Kendall, pp. 271-81, 284-87, 291; *Lettres de Louis XI,* V,
363-64.
15. Vaughan, *Charles the Bold,* pp. 353-58.

16. Petit-Dutaillis in Lavisse, IV, part 2, 377-81; Kendall, pp. 294-95, 303-304.
17. Vaughan, *Charles the Bold*, pp. 359-97.
18. *Ibid.*, pp. 399-415.
19. *Ibid.*, pp. 416-32.
20. Commynes, II, 168-69; *Lettres de Louis XI*, VI, 111-13, 194-95; *ibid.*, VII, 53-57, 306-307; Petit-Dutaillis in Lavisse, IV, part 2, 384-87, 389; Kendall, pp. 315-22; Champion, II, 179. For legal arguments justifying Louis XI's annexation of the French lands of Charles the Bold, see Paul Saenger, "Burgundy and the Inalienability of Appanages in the Reign of Louis XI," *French Historical Studies*, 10 (Spring 1977), 1-26.
21. Calmette and Périnelle, pp. 219-32; Commynes, II, 241-44, 246-49; Kendall, pp. 322-24.
22. Calmette and Périnelle, pp. 232-50; Kendall, pp. 324-31; *Lettres de Louis XI*, VIII, 199-201, 349-57.
23. Kendall, pp. 359-60; Petit-Dutaillis in Lavisse, IV, part 2, 389; Calmette and Périnelle, pp. 251-56; Commynes, II, 277-79; Champion, II, 323.
24. Gandilhon, pp. 230-33, 365-93; Kendall, pp. 295-97; *Lettres de Louis XI*, II, 229-30.
25. Lavisse, IV, part 2, 389-90; Commynes, II, 299-304; *Lettres de Louis XI*, X, 27-31, 37-38, 40-41, 85-87; Paul M. Kendall, *Richard the Third* (New York, 1965) pp. 282-83.
26. Petit-Dutaillis in Lavisse, IV, part 2, 408; *Lettres de Louis XI*, VII, 157-59.

Chapter Six

1. Commynes, II, 280-82, 284, 285; Petit-Dutaillis in Lavisse, IV, part 2, 417-18.
2. Champion, II, 351-55.
3. *Ibid.*, 356-57; Petit-Dutaillis in Lavisse, IV, part 2, 417-18; Commynes, II, 288-92, 296-97.
4. Champion, II, 335-45.
5. *Ibid.*, 368; Petit-Dutaillis in Lavisse, IV, part 2, 418-19; Commynes, II, 292, 296; *Lettres de Louis XI*, IX, 190-91, 218-19, 228-29; *Ibid.*, X, 16-17, 76-79, 90-91.
6. Champion, II, 364-67, 370-71; Commynes, II, 297-99, 307-308, 313-14, 318-22; *Lettres de Louis XI*, X, 126-31.
7. Commynes, II, 311-17; Champion, II, 371-74; Petit-Dutaillis in Lavisse, IV, part 2, 419.

Selected Bibliography

PRIMARY SOURCES

BASIN, THOMAS. *Histoire de Charles VII*. Ed. and trans. C. Samaran. Paris: Société d'Édition "Les Belles Lettres," 1933. Vols. I and II.

————. *Histoire de Louis XI*. Ed. and trans. C. Samaran. Paris: Société d'Édition "Les Belles Lettres," 1963. Vol. I. By a contemporary writer clearly hostile to Louis XI. Useful as an opposite view to Commynes's laudatory account.

CHARTIER, JEAN. *Chronique de Charles VII, roi de France*. Ed. Vallet de Viriville. 3 vols. Paris: Jannet, 1858. Of some use for the youth of Louis XI.

CHASTELLAIN, GEORGES. *Oeuvres*. Ed. Kervyn de Lettenhove. Brussels: Heussner, 1863 - 66. Vols. II and III. Vol. III contains a valuable account by an eyewitness to part of the period when the Dauphin Louis was at the court of Burgundy.

COMMYNES, PHILLIPPE DE. *Mémoires*. Ed. J. Calmette and G. Durville. Paris: Champion, 1924 - 25. Vols. I and II. Written by one of Louis XI's closest advisors. Long the chief source of information about Louis and his reign. Although much of his account has recently been proven inaccurate by Karl Bittmann, it is still of value, if used with caution.

Dépêches des ambassadeurs milanais en France sous Louis XI et François Sforza. Ed. B. de Mandrot. 4 vols. Paris: Renouard, H. Laurens successeur, 1916 - 23. A very valuable source. Reasoned opinions by skilled observers about conditions in France, and the policies and character of Louis XI.

Dispatches with Related Documents of the Milanese Ambassadors in France and Burgundy, 1450 - 1483. Ed. P. Kendall and V. Ilardi. 2 vols. Athens, Ohio: Ohio University Press, 1970. Only two volumes of an intended multi-volume work have appeared. They cover the period 1450 - 1461 and contain some useful information on Louis before he became king.

ESCOUCHY, MATHIEU DE. *Chronique de Mathieu d'Escouchy*. Ed. G. du Fresne de Beaucourt. 3 vols. Paris: Renouard, 1863 - 64. Of some value for the youth of Louis XI, particularly for the events of the *Praguerie*.

LA MARCHE, OLIVIER DE. *Mémoires*. Ed. H. Beaune and J. d'Arbaumont. 4 vols. Paris: Renouard, 1883 - 1888. A useful account written by a high official at the court of Charles the Bold.

Lettres de Louis XI Roi de France. Ed. J. Vaesen and E. Charavay. 11 vols.

Paris: n.p., 1883 - 1909. Perhaps the most valuable single primary source of information.

MONSTRELET, ENGUERRAND DE. *La Chronique d'Enguerran de Monstrelet.* Ed. L. Douët-d'Arcq. 6 vols. Paris: Renouard, 1857 - 62. Useful for the youth of Louis XI. The chronicle ends in 1445.

ROYE, JEAN DE. *Journal de Jean de Roye connu sous le nom de "Chronique Scandaleuse,"* 1460 - 1483. Ed. B. de Mandrot. 2 vols. Paris: Renouard, 1894 - 96.

RYMER, THOMAS. *Foedera, conventiones, litterae, et cujuscunque generis acta publica.* The Hague: Joannem Neaulme, 1741. Vol. V, part 3. Contains the terms of the Treaty of Picquigny.

THOREY, E. PILOT DE, ed. *Catalogue des actes du Dauphin Louis II, devenu le roi de France Louis XI, relatifs à l'administration du Dauphiné.* 2 vols. Grenoble: Imprimerie de Maisonville, Victor Truc Successeur, 1899. Vol . III, supplt., ed. G. Vellein. Grenoble: Grands Établissements de L'Imprimerie Générale, 1911. The chief source of information on Louis's administration of Dauphiné, 1447 - 1456.

VILLON, FRANÇOIS. *I Laugh through Tears.* Trans. G. P. Cuttino. New York: Philosophical Library, 1955. One of the best English translations of the greatest French poet of the fifteenth century.

SECONDARY SOURCES

1. Books

BITTMANN, KARL. *Ludwig XI und Karl der Kühne. Die Memoiren des Philippe de Commynes als historische Quelle.* Veroffent-lichungen des Max-Planck-Instituts für Geschichte, No. 9, Vol. I, Parts 1 and 2; Vol. II, Part 1. Göttingen: Vandenhoek and Ruprecht, 1964 - 70. In course of publication. Indispensable for a proper understanding of the policies of Louis XI. Proves, to the satisfaction of most specialists, by massive research in contemporary documents, that the *Mémoires* of Commynes are unreliable in many places. Commynes had previously been considered the most reliable source of information for much of Louis's plans, motives, and diplomacy.

BRIDGE, JOHN S. C. *A History of France From the Death of Louis XI.* Oxford: At the Clarendon Press, 1921. Vol. I.

CALMETTE, JOSEPH, and G. PÉRINELLE. *Louis XI et l'Angleterre.* Paris: Éditions Auguste Picard, 1930. The most valuable work on Louis XI's relations with England.

CHAMPION, PIERRE. *Louis XI.* 2nd. ed. 2 vols. Paris: Librairie Ancienne Honoré Champion, 1928. For many years, the best biography of Louis XI. As it relies on the *Mémoires* of Commynes, much of which has recently been proven to be unreliable by Karl Bittmann, its value has been greatly diminished. No better biography of Louis has yet been written, however.

CLEUGH, JAMES. *Chant Royal: The Life of King Louis XI of France (1423 -*

1483). Garden City, New York: Doubleday and Co., 1970. A popular biography of little value. Contains some interesting information.

DENIFLE, HENRI. *La Désolution des églises, monastères, et hôpitaux en France pendant la Guerre de Cent Ans.* 2 vols. Paris, 1897 - 99; rpt. Brussels: Culture et Civilisation, 1965. Vol. I contains many documents describing the devastation. Vol. II is a detailed account of the earlier period, down to about 1380.

Dictionnaire historique et biographique de la Suisse. 7 vols. Neuchâtel: Administration du dictionnaire historique et biographique de la Suisse, 1920 - 33.

FERGUSON, WALLACE K. *Europe In Transition, 1300 - 1520.* Boston: Houghton Mifflin, 1962.

GANDILHON, RENÉ. *Politique économique de Louis XI.* Paris: Presses Universitaires de France, 1941. The best and most detailed treatment of Louis's economic policy.

HUIZINGA, J. *The Waning of the Middle Ages.* Trans. F. Hopman. Garden City, New York: Doubleday Anchor Books, 1954. A brilliant study of the forms of life, thought and art in France and the Low Countries in the fourteenth and fifteenth centuries.

KENDALL, PAUL M. *Louis XI: The Universal Spider.* New York: W. W. Norton, 1971. The most recent biography of Louis XI. Very well written. Uses some previously unpublished Milanese documents. Probably the best biography of Louis in English. As he relied heavily on the *Mémoires* of Commynes, the value of his book has been greatly diminished by the recent research of Karl Bittmann.

————. *Richard the Third.* New York: Anchor Books, 1965.

LEWIS, D. B. WYNDHAM. *King Spider; Some Aspects of Louis XI of France and his Companions.* New York: Coward-McCann; Hartford: E. V. Mitchell, 1929. Interesting and original.

LEWIS, P. S. *Later Medieval France: The Polity.* London: Macmillan, 1968.

LOT, FERDINAND, and ROBERT FAWTIER. *Institutions royales.* Vol. 2 of *Histoire des institutions françaises au Moyen Âge.* Paris: Presses Universitaires de France, 1958.

MAJOR, J. RUSSELL. *Representative Institutions in Renaissance France, 1421 - 1559.* Madison: The University of Wisconsin Press, 1960. The best book on French representative institutions of the period.

PETIT-DUTAILLIS, C. *Charles VII, Louis XI et les premières années de Charles VIII (1422 - 1492).* Vol. IV, part 2 of *Histoire de France depuis les origines jusqu'à la Révolution.* Ed. E. Lavisse. Paris: Librairie Hachette, 1902. Though dated, still contains probably the most detailed account of the reign of Louis XI.

————. "France: Louis XI: In *The Cambridge Medieval History.* Ed. C. W. Previté-Orton and Z. N. Brooke. 1936; rpt. New York: Macmillan, Cambridge: At the University Press, 1964. Vol. VIII.

SCOFIELD, CORA L. *The Life and Reign of Edward the Fourth, King of*

England and France and Lord of Ireland. 2 vols. London, 1923; rpt. New York: Octagon Books, 1967.

SÉE HENRI. *Louis XI et les villes.* Paris: Librairie Hachette, 1891. Still the standard work on the subject.

STEIN, HENRI. *Charles de France, frère de Louis XI.* Paris: Auguste Picard, 1921. In addition to providing information on Louis's brother, and the relations between them, publishes many useful documents.

VAUGHAN, RICHARD. *Charles the Bold.* New York: Barnes and Noble, 1974. Uses Bittmann's new research extensively. The most up-to-date and the best documented history of the rule of Charles the Bold and his relations with Louis XI.

_____. *Philip the Good.* London: Longmans, Green, 1970. The best study of the rule of this powerful Duke of Burgundy.

2. Articles

BONNAFOUS, M. "Toulouse et Louis XI." *Annales du Midi,* 34 (1927), 1 - 54.

DODU, GASTON. "Louis XI." *Revue Historique,* 168 (1931), 43 - 86.

DOUCET, ROGER. "Le Gouvernement de Louis XI." *Revue des Cours et Conférences,* 24 (1923).

MAJOR, J. RUSSELL. "The Renaissance Monarchy: A Contribution to the Periodization of History." *Emory University Quarterly,* 13, No. 2 (1957), 112 - 24.

MANDROT, B. DE. "Les Relations de Charles VII et de Louis XI avec les cantons suisses, 1444 - 83." *Jahrbuch für schweizerishe Geschichte,* 5 (1880), 60 - 182.

PERRET, P. M. "Boffille de Juge, comte de Castres, et la république de Venise." *Annales du Midi,* 3 (1891), 159 - 231.

POCQUET DU HAUT-JUSSÉ, B.A. "Une Ideé politique de Louis XI: la sujétion éclipse la vassalité." *Revue Historique,* 226 (1961), 383 - 98.

ROBINSON, W. C. "Money, Population and Economic Change in Late Medieval Europe." *Economic History Review,* ser. 2, 12 (1959 - 60), 63 - 76.

SAENGER, PAUL. "Burgundy and the Inalienability of Appanages in the Reign of Louis XI." *French Historical Studies,* 10 (Spring 1977), 1 - 26.

TAUZIN, J. C. "Louis XI et la Gascogne." *Revue des Questions Historiques,* 59 (1896), 403 - 41.

Index

198